Gurdjieff Reconsidered

Arriving in New York Harbor, 15 January 1924: Gurdjieff salutes America.
Source: The Gurdjieff Foundation of New York

GURDJIEFF
RECONSIDERED

The Life, the Teachings, the Legacy

ROGER LIPSEY

FOREWORD BY
Cynthia Bourgeault

Shambhala

BOULDER · 2019

Shambhala Publications, Inc.
4720 Walnut Street
Boulder, Colorado 80301
www.shambhala.com

9 8 7 6 5 4 3 2 1

First Edition
Printed in Canada

♾ This edition is printed on acid-free paper that meets the American National Standards Institute Z39.48 Standard.
♻ This book is printed on 100% postconsumer recycled paper. For more information please visit www.shambhala.com.

Shambhala Publications is distributed worldwide by Penguin Random House, Inc., and its subsidiaries.

Designed by Lora Zorian

LIBRARY OF CONGRESS CATALOGING-IN-PUBLICATION DATA
Names: Lipsey, Roger, 1942– author.
Title: Gurdjieff reconsidered: the life, the teachings, the legacy / Roger Lipsey.
Description: First edition. | Boulder: Shambhala, 2019. | Includes bibliographical references and index.
Identifiers: LCCN 2018021357 | ISBN 9781611804515 (pbk.: alk. paper)
Subjects: LCSH: Gurdjieff, Georges Ivanovitch, 1872–1949.
Classification: LCC B4249.G84 L56 2019 | DDC 197—dc23
LC record available at https://lccn.loc.gov/2018021357

For my daughter Jeanne

Contents

List of Illustrations

Frontispiece: Arriving in New York Harbor, 15 January 1924:
Gurdjieff salutes America
Source: The Gurdjieff Foundation of New York

1. The enneagram
Source: Jim Kendrick

2. The Prieuré des Basses Loges at Fontainebleau-Avon
Source: The Gurdjieff Foundation of New York

3. A. R. Orage in the late 1920s
Source: Martha Welch de Llosa

4. Emblem of the Institute for the Harmonious Development of Man
Source: The Gurdjieff Foundation of New York

5. Interior of the Study House at the Prieuré
Source: The Gurdjieff Foundation of New York

6. Aphorism written in the Prieuré script
Source: Jim Kendrick

7. Prieuré children in winter
Source: The Gurdjieff Foundation of New York

8. Return to the Prieuré from Paris
Source: The Gurdjieff Foundation of New York

9. Julia Osipovna, the Prieuré, ca. 1924
Source: Institut G. I. Gurdjieff, Paris

10. Solita Solano, ca. 1928, portrait by Berenice Abbott
Source: Berenice Abbott Archive, Ryerson Image Centre. Published with permission.

Foreword by Cynthia Bourgeault

The name G. I. Gurdjieff first showed up on my radar screen in the spring of 1982. I was doing a year's sabbatical fellowship at the Collegeville Institute for Ecumenical and Cultural Research in Minnesota when a colleague casually flipped onto my desk a copy of P. D. Ouspensky's *In Search of the Miraculous*, the classic gateway into the Gurdjieffian universe. "I saw the word 'miraculous' in the title and immediately thought of you," she said coyly. She has yet to this day to own up to any ulterior motives.

Like many who find themselves drawn to this teaching, I devoured the book in great gulps, finding my own heretofore stable Christian universe gently rocking on its foundations. As Gurdjieff himself makes clear, the wormhole into receptivity often opens through deep disappointment—"Blessed are the troubled, for they have seized hold of life," in the words of the Gospel of Thomas. In my case, this disappointment constellated around a growing frustration as to why a religion that boasted at its epicenter one of the most compassionate and inclusive masters to have ever walked the planet should habitually express itself in ways that are rigid, judgmental, and exclusive. In the teaching being laid out before me, I could see exactly why, and the seeing kept right on opening. It opened outwardly, allowing me to understand why the whole institutional process kept running off the track. (As Jacob Needleman, an astute contemporary Gurdjieffian commentator, dryly observes, "To ask Christians in their usual state of consciousness to follow the teachings of Christ is like asking stones to sprout wings and fly to the sea.") But it opened inwardly as well. Or perhaps I should say it closed inwardly—drawing the noose more and more tightly around those same qualities of inconsistency and lack of conscious presence in myself. I found myself resonating with the experience of a participant in one of those early Gurdjieff meetings (quoted by Roger Lipsey later in this book); I was "aware that I had been brought to the very brink of a conscious possibility in which there was a strange combination of both suffering and rejoicing."

In due course I found my way to the Work—the name familiarly given to the formal network of groups, spread across several continents, who devote themselves to the practical study of Gurdjieff's teaching. It took some doing, for even more so then than now, the Work preferred to keep itself slightly below the radar and followed the protocol of traditional esoteric groups in making the entry gate a bit of a test of mettle. But after a couple of false starts, I eventually found myself sitting in an apartment in upper Manhattan, face-to-face with the formidable Dr. William Welch, one of the towering patriarchs of the earliest era of the Work. You will make his fuller acquaintance toward the end of the present book. He listened to my story with grave, measured attention, as if weighing me in the balance, then assigned me to a Canadian hub working closely under his supervision. To my teachers and fellow seekers there I owe an enduring debt of gratitude for opening the eyes and heart of this formerly charmingly oblivious "talking head" to the wider world of presence and conscious attention. I came back from those seven years of active participation with my Christianity totally reinfused and transformed, set to a far vaster scale and transposed to a road map that finally pulled the whole picture together.

I had been discreetly warned, of course—another venerable tradition of esoteric schools—to be circumspect in how I shared these ideas. Not secretive, exactly, but since the core premise of all inner work is that the capacity to receive a teaching is directly linked to one's state of being, it could be counted a virtual certainty that these ideas would be misheard and subtly distorted on both ends of the transmission chain. Even so, as I found my own life horizons being blown wide open by some of the real, unique, and demonstrably practical ideas and frames accessible through the Work, it seemed that they merited wider circulation. It seemed that their true home was directly within the greater intellectual and spiritual lineage of the West, where in our own increasingly troubled planetary times they were more urgently needed than ever.

Of course, if one believes in the kind of providential causality that attends such transmissions, this would be obviously the case, for if Gurdjieff is indeed who he claimed to be—whom he was also recognized to be by some of the most acute and sensitive minds of our time—he was no free agent but "one under authority," clearly on a cosmic assignment. Born in Armenia in 1866, raised in a spiritual and cultural melting pot where Orthodox Christian, Sufi, Yezidi, and shamanic influences actively intermingled, he early on became convinced that there had once been a level of being and an understanding of cosmic accountability—"What are we here for?"—now lost to contemporary humans. His prophetic mission, so it seems, was to gather those ancient shards of knowledge and assemble them, painstakingly, into thought categories and practices applicable to the modern West. And that is exactly what he did. After a twenty-year search conducted principally in the Near East, Central Asia, and Tibet, he arrived in St. Petersburg on the eve of World War I and set up storefront as a teacher, not least of sacred dancing. He soon collected a circle of highly accomplished disciples, P. D. Ouspensky numbered among them. Again as if on providential cue, the group was displaced steadily westward by the political upheavals of the early twentieth century and finally came to rest in the environs of Paris, where Gurdjieff experimented for over three decades with a variety of teaching formats including his celebrated "Institute for the Harmonious Development of Man." From this Parisian command post the teaching was transmitted worldwide by streams of faithful students.

For those unfamiliar with this teaching, I might describe it as an early run-up on what we would now call "mindfulness training," combined with an intricate cosmology and an even more intricate metaphysics that has continued to intrigue the more nerdishly inclined. Many people who know the teaching only through its ideas find it overly intellectual and off-putting. But the Work also has extraordinary heart, carried largely in the aforementioned sacred dances (or "Movements," as they're more widely known), which provide not only a powerful integrative counterbalance to the intellectual content but also a de facto liturgical expression of searing emotional intensity. Over the roughly hundred years now that the teaching has been in existence, it has attracted an impressive array of artists and intellectuals, including Frank Lloyd Wright (through his wife, Olgivanna), Jean Toomer, Katherine Mansfield, A. R. Orage, Jane Heap, Kathryn Hulme, René Daumal, P. L. Travers, and in our own time, Peter Brook, Andrei Serban, and Jacob Needleman. In a quiet and indirect way, it has been in active dialogue with some of the most acute and discerning minds of our century and has cast its subtle influence over the Western intellectual tradition in ways still largely unappreciated.

But it is just here that the irony enters, upon which Lipsey is about to call the question so forcefully. For while these Gurdjieffian ideas have clearly attracted more than their fair share of the intellectual cream of the crop, the ideas themselves have yet to be assimilated—or even seriously considered—by the greater intellectual tradition itself. Not as philosophy, not as metaphysics, not as literature or the arts, not as spiritual practice. In all these quadrants, the shorthand appraisal is and remains that Gurdjieff was a "crank" and his legacy a "cult." Once these stereotypes first began to circulate in the 1920s, the branding stuck, and it has yet to be disarmed.

In part, of course, this is due to the Work's own aforementioned preference to stay slightly below the radar. But this reticence is more than met from the other side by recycled prejudice and no doubt an overly gerrymandered intellectual terrain that allows this teaching to fall between the cracks. The old clichés are simply passed on, keeping the Gurdjieff material effectively cordoned off from the greater Western tradition with which it stands in such powerful and potentially game-changing dialogue.

Gurdjieff himself had his doubts about what he contemptuously dubbed "the bon-ton literary establishment." He did not make it easy on those who were unable to examine their own prejudices or discern a more subtle level of teaching at work behind a presenting surface that could be deliberately provocative or even outrageous. What has long been needed is a good translator, someone who can bridge these gaps with more patience than Gurdjieff himself and more subtlety than those who meet his teaching only from the usual intellectual and cultural reference points.

In both of these respects Roger Lipsey is supremely the man for the job. With all the forbearance and subtlety so clearly visible in his earlier masterpiece on Thomas Merton, *Make Peace Before the Sun Goes Down*, he demonstrates his remarkable capacity to re-open clogged channels of communication. Tremendously literate, with a sweeping breadth of knowledge of the Western intellectual tradition, he is also a longtime student of the Work—now one of its respected elders—and his long years of laboring in this vineyard will be immediately apparent, to those who know the Work, through the signature fragrance of his presentation.

A reconsideration can be two things, he writes in his opening chapter: either a refinement of an existing reputation or a radical break from received opinion. In *Gurdjieff Reconsidered* he sets out to do both—"because two unlike views of Gurdjieff and his teaching have never mingled; they have glared at each other." While these two tasks may initially appear contradictory, in Lipsey's hands they become complementary and form the seamlessly interwoven tapestry of his investigation.

The first two-thirds of the book consists of a careful reconstruction of the whole Gurdjieffian teaching, decade by decade, through its various iterations. With a deeply nuanced comprehension, he lets the whole evolution unfold before our eyes, appreciated at its own depth, in its own light. Drawing on his panoramic knowledge of the Western cultural tradition, he notes surprising similarities with thinkers as diverse as Rabelais, Pythagoras, and Diogenes, and skillfully contextualizes the teaching squarely within the venerable philosophic lineage of skeptical inquiry.

Even more moving is the "refinement" of our portrait of Gurdjieff that emerges from these pages—substantially in Gurdjieff's own words, and in those of his closest and most perceptive students. It is an insider's portrait, to be sure: the account given here is intimate and honest, both light and shadow unflinchingly revealed. Moving beyond the images that have figured so large in the media—Gurdjieff as the crank, the charlatan, and the cultist—Lipsey allows us to see this titan of a man and teacher as he slowly emerges through three decades of conscious labor and intentional suffering. We watch at close range as "The Tiger of Turkestan" who took the world by storm in the 1920s slowly gives way to the "lion in winter" of the 1930s, followed in the wartime years by the emergence of a sublime quality of love in this by-now old man who stood his ground in Paris during the depths of the Nazi occupation, feeding the hungry not only in soul but in body as well, and transmitting into the world a beam of radiant energy that can be felt to this day by those so attuned.

In the reappraisal mode, Lipsey traces the gradual and then rapid demonization of the Work, beginning first in the sensationalist journalism of the 1920s and then erupting more aggressively, in attacks by the literary intelligentsia, after Gurdjieff's death in 1949. These were spearheaded by the disenchanted former Gurdjieffian Louis Pauwels and then continued by the Traditionalists in a frontal assault launched by Whitall Perry on behalf of his circle. Lipsey analyzes the Pauwels controversy in some detail, and with good reason, for it is here that you will find the origins of the continuing stigmatization of the Work. He looks just as closely at Perry; absent Perry's rather frantic accusations, many who align themselves with the tradition of Sophia Perennis (perennial wisdom) would recognize a natural congruity with the Gurdjieff teaching. It is a thoughtful and much needed chapter, not only for clearing away some of the roadblocks to a better assimilation of the Gurdjieffian tradition but also in helping us to understand why those roadblocks came to be there in the first place.

As I said before, Roger Lipsey is subtle. To me, at least, his long years of dedication in the Work shine through in the way he constructs this book, particularly in the short afterword, which is in all respects a masterpiece. No diatribes, rhetorical fireworks, or sweeping grand finales, just an allusive invitation, carried in a few carefully placed words. Contextualizing this teaching within its rightful spiritual lineage one final time, Lipsey draws at last upon the great prophets of our own era—Martin Luther King Jr., Andrei Sakharov, Nelson Mandela, Václav Havel, Dag Hammarskjöld, Mahatma Gandhi—to distill the essence of the Gurdjieff teaching in its simplest and most universal import: "However great their personal sacrifice, each understood the need to call men and women back to themselves, to simple decency, mutual respect, and at least the minimum of policies and attitudes needed for survival as a species among other species on a generous planet."

Yes, oh yes! And here perhaps you will hear the real heart of the matter as to why this rapprochement is so long overdue. Not just for the repatriation of an unjustly marginalized spiritual master, but because the vision Gurdjieff illuminated is more urgently needed than ever. In this body of teaching resides angles of approach and practical tools to be found nowhere else. To name just a few: the Law of Three and Law of Seven, the enneagram, universal materiality, reciprocal feeding, the Five Being-Strivings, non-identification, "conscious labor and intentional suffering." These are all key concepts residing in the Work that, when applied as a single integrated vision, have the strength to break the deadly gridlock that Neoplatonic, binary metaphysics still imposes on perennial wisdom. They have the power to catapult us into a new era that Gurdjieff heralds with gusto and tough love.

I have watched this teaching come alive in people's hearts. As it now moves in spite of itself more into the mainstream, carried forward by popular initiatives such as the Enneagram of Personality, "Movements intensives," and perhaps my own Wisdom Schools, I watch it growing, re-energizing, re-imaging not only the cultural institutions it touches, but the Work itself: "new wineskins" and "seed fallen into the ground" rolled into one. And so in the end, I am enormously hopeful that the rapprochement is already underway, and that what this book will do will be to bring ownership, legitimacy, and a firmer sense of connection to the Western cultural heritage, with which the Work stands so necessarily and so fruitfully in dialogue. It is time for that voice to be heard, and for Gurdjieff's still astonishing vision to enter fully into conversation with a postmodern intellectual tradition grown nearly moribund for lack of real presence and real hope.

Let the grand dialogue begin!

Acknowledgments

The first debt of gratitude is to Dave O'Neal, senior editor at Shambhala Publications with whom I have published three books in the past. We had wished this to be the fourth, but that was not to be. Dave suffered a serious stroke in December 2017 and must dedicate his energies to recovery. A salute to this courageous friend and man of letters.

A salute also to the president of Shambhala Publications, Nikko Odiseos, and to Matt Zepelin, the editor who stepped in at his request. Matt's clarity of mind and warmth of understanding have been evident throughout our new association. Matt's associate editor, Audra Figgins, kept me on the rails, as did Jill Rogers, copy editor, and Emily Wichland, proofreader. On the design side, Lora Zorian, Shambhala's overall design director, is responsible for the lucidly presented page and chapter design, and Hazel Bercholz designed the lastingly intriguing cover. Peter Schumacher, in marketing and publicity, taught me more lessons than he knows. Thanks to you all in Boulder.

I am grateful to Cynthia Bourgeault for welcoming our invitation to write the foreword. She is the very author I had hoped would accept to share her knowledge and perspective.

Alexandre de Salzmann, Stephen and Anne-Marie Grant, Pierre and Marga Zuber, Kent Kramer, Thomas Daly, Jr., Patty Welch de Llosa, and Joseph Azize have been so helpful. Thanks to you all.

The archives of the Gurdjieff Foundation of New York and the Institut G. I. Gurdjieff, Paris, preserve unique material. Archives are where the historian and biographer belong. I am most grateful to have been given access to this material. I must especially thank my friends and colleagues, Kathy Minnerop and Alexandre Musat, for their guidance through the files in their care.

Galina Natenzon educated me about topics in later nineteenth-century Russian literature. This is not the first time I have relied on her, again most gratefully. Another of my educators, Jim Kendrick, generously agreed to re-create a key Gurdjieff aphorism in the Prieuré script (fig. 6).

Early readers of this book in typescript—Anne and Charles White, Basarab Nicolescu, Paul Beekman Taylor, Rebecca Herbert, Robert Curran, Kenneth Krushel, Jon Thompson, and Gerri Kimber for the Katherine Mansfield material—have been a source of encouragement, factual correction, and wise critique. Warmest thanks to you all and to several others in France.

Tracy Cochran, friend and literary agent, and her husband, Jeff Zaleski, have been close during these two years of research and writing. As early readers they have offered advice and encouragement much needed, always welcome.

Dianne Edwards has once again managed the process of securing publishers' permission where needed, and Anne Ricci has once again perseveringly created the database of citations and notes underlying this book. Thanks to you both; no book without you. Heather Ecker set the endnotes and bibliography in order and pursued certain illustrations and publications rights—large tasks willingly undertaken.

My wife, Susan, partnered closely with me throughout the preparation and writing of this book. She knows the historical material and, beyond that, knows the life of the Gurdjieff teaching in our generation. Thanks without measure.

Errors of fact and interpretation that may remain cling only to me.

—Roger Lipsey

Gurdjieff Reconsidered

There were several . . . who, with a sincerity proceeding from their separate spiritualized parts, strove for High Knowledge only with the aim of self-perfection. . . . One . . . was named Pythagoras.

—G. I. Gurdjieff,
Beelzebub's Tales to His Grandson, 1950

Every century, and ours above all, needs a Diogenes; but the difficulty is to find men who have the courage to be him, and men who have the courage to bear him.

—Jean le Rond d'Alembert,
Essai sur la société des gens de lettres, 1753

CHAPTER 1

Disparu! Éteint!

I MAKE A POINT of visiting her bookstore, the ideal Parisian bookstore if you care for old editions, rarities, surprises. Widow of a well-respected poet, she presides with touching goodwill over history and taste in the form of books, thousands of books, shelves and stacks of books and journals. A relaxing, joyful place—a place of memory. One day I asked how she would respond were I to say just one word: Gurdjieff. "Disparu! Éteint!" she replied, as if tamping down a lid. "Vanished! Extinguished!" She hadn't heard anything about him in years. The last sign of life she could recall was in the late 1970s when the director Peter Brook's film version of Gurdjieff's autobiography, *Meetings with Remarkable Men*, had attracted interest among thoughtful people. It was an essential outing to see the much-discussed film. But that died away, she said, and the rest was silence. She was surprised when I told her that there is a flourishing though largely unpublicized Institut G. I. Gurdjieff in Paris, linked to similar foundations and societies nearly worldwide. Surprised but not interested. Gurdjieff and the teaching that bears his name are now all but sealed off from both mainstream history and current concern. There are too many things to care about in our immensely troubled world. Why would one care about Gurdjieff?

This book reconsiders that question as fully as possible, no stone unturned, no grain of sand unexamined for whatever small message may be inscribed on it. But what is a reconsideration? The word generally promises either the refinement of an existing reputation or a radical break from received opinion. The reconsideration in these pages has features of both types because two unlike views of Gurdjieff and his teaching have never mingled; they have glared at each other. We must look at them both. With meticulous respect for sources, I hope to redraw in part the portrait of Gurdjieff from decade to decade of his life in the West. If all goes well, that will be a refinement. I wish also to display, question, and break the received opinions on Gurdjieff, opinions that have revolved for many years around a small number of stereotypes and that find their way casually, as if there were nothing more to say, into review articles, biographies of other figures, and cultural commentaries. It is long past time for Gurdjieff and his teaching to be better understood. We trail him behind us rather than carry him forward.

Apart from Gurdjieff's own writings, music, and choreography, which we will explore, there is an informed, attractive literature written by two generations of his students. Among many authors, I think at once of P. D. Ouspensky and of Thomas and Olga de Hartmann for the earlier years in Russia and the hard emigration to Western Europe; of Fritz Peters and Tcheslaw Tchekhovitch for the 1920s, when Gurdjieff was director of his institute near Fontainebleau; of Solita Solano, Kathryn Hulme, and Margaret Anderson for the 1930s, when Gurdjieff was living modestly in Paris and teaching only a few students; of René Zuber, Kenneth Walker, and J. G. and Elizabeth Bennett for the postwar 1940s, when American and British followers of Gurdjieff could at last rejoin the French whom Gurdjieff had regularly seen throughout the war and Nazi occupation. To those who found their way to him in those late years—he died in 1949—he offered unique experiences virtually on a daily basis. Whether they recognized it or not, they must have offered him the solace of knowing that his efforts since he had begun teaching in Russia, in 1912, might just flower in future generations. I should add that Paris was not the only locus of Gurdjieff's activity; he made numerous trips to New York City and on occasion other American places, engaging the interest of Americans from the mid-

1920s forward. They, in turn, wrote books when the time came to look back. There are, as well, several considerable biographies, and even a metabiography that seeks to correct perspectives and detail in prior biographies. Overall, there is a surprisingly large published literature in which Gurdjieff is central and revered, in addition to archival resources only now in part coming to light.

In this mass of material there are countless anecdotes recording what Gurdjieff said or did at one moment or another. That will matter to us. As for Diogenes, the ancient Greek Cynic who was unmistakably one of Gurdjieff's predecessors in attitude and teaching style, brief tales of things said or done have weight. Of Diogenes nothing but anecdotes survive, but we can know the man and still experience the pressure of his teaching through that alone. It is the same with Gurdjieff, and because at this time there are still living, direct students of Gurdjieff, and students of direct students, the informal library of anecdotes continues to grow. The meaning of some of these anecdotes or teaching tales is transparent—for example, Gurdjieff's learned discussion of "onion soup without onions," to which we'll come in due course. Others are koan-like provocations that linger in one's memory. Georgette Leblanc, the multitalented singer, actress, and companion of the playwright Maurice Maeterlinck, who came later in life to Gurdjieff's circle, once said to him, "I am almost frightened. Life rises in me like the ocean." And he to her, "It is only a very small beginning."[1]

Many of those who worked with Gurdjieff have said that he was unknowable, an enigma. In case we were to miss the point, a surprising number of book titles start there—René Zuber's *Who Are You, Mr. Gurdjieff?*, Margaret Anderson's *The Unknowable Gurdjieff*, J. G. Bennett's *Gurdjieff: A Very Great Enigma*. The most recently published account from a participant in Gurdjieff's late years says as much: "I agreed with many others . . . in admitting that no one truly knew Mr. Gurdjieff. One can describe . . . events, anecdotes lived in his company, but the wholeness of his person remains impossible to grasp."[2] Yet the author of these words, François Grunwald, a psychiatrist with unimaginably keen skill in characterization, did offer something of a portrait based on his first encounter with Gurdjieff in the later 1940s: "His great black eyes, extraordinary in expression, questioned me. . . . I'll try to depict those indescribable eyes: they revealed a serenity from which radiated intense affliction, a sort of sacred sadness, and at the same time ironic malice. One might perceive something altogether different in his eyes, although the deep suffering which so many sensed never waned."[3] In the course of these pages, others who knew Gurdjieff will have the same opportunity to evoke him. At some level he may remain unknowable, but like a mosaic of small photographs of a distant planet, their composite impressions cannot help but sum to a portrait.

What of the other view and literature, the one that rejects Gurdjieff and his teaching with mockery, violent righteousness, or disdain? I was struck again by its longevity, its apparent eternity, when not long ago I was innocently reading a tribute in the *Financial Times*, written by a highly respected British scholar of late classical and early Christian history, who happens to have a second expertise and love of fine gardening and landscape design. The article concerned a palatial garden in Turin, designed by the late Russell Page, a Briton who was a dominant influence on garden style in Great Britain, on the continent and, toward the end of his career, in the United States. Page's book, *The Education of a Gardener*, is universally admired. Imagine my surprise to find, in the midst of the professor's pastoral tribute, a bilious swerve toward Gurdjieff and his teaching.

> Few of his fans now realize that Page's landscaping related to an underlying faith. After moving to Paris he became a keen follower of the cuckoo teachings and mystic baloney of that Greek-Armenian exile from Russia, George Gurdjieff, and his assistant P. D. Ouspensky. He even married Gurdjieff's daugh-

ter at the maestro's request. Gurdjieff's teachings on harmonious dancing, on healing by physical adversity and cosmic rays were stupendous nonsense, but were powerfully presented by his seductive gaze. Their stress on a hidden harmony in the universe appealed especially to Page the landscape gardener.[4]

The assault concludes by calling Page's views "wondrous nonsense." The professor's language is vastly disproportionate, nearly punitive, as if Russell Page had violated an inviolable code. The professor's comments are wrath with no basis in knowledge. What he writes of Gurdjieff's teaching is designed to ridicule; I scarcely recognize the teaching as he dismissively describes it—some combination of stardust, sweat, and suggestibility. What he writes of Gurdjieff himself is caricature based on a decades-old tradition of caricature passed from author to author, reviewer to reviewer, without a glance at Gurdjieff himself. Misrepresentations of this kind became something of a parlor sport, a free zone where critics could outdo one another's scorn and condescension without fear of correction. Who was on duty, so to speak, to make the correction? The Gurdjieff teaching had long since largely abandoned public space and debate; it had its own concerns. Yet questions remain: Why is the reception of Gurdjieff and his teaching, particularly among some intellectuals—and in this instance one of earned fame—so lastingly sour? And why is Gurdjieff by and large forgotten? The questions are thoroughly explored in later pages and touched on here.

I know of Russell Page in an altogether different light. There is a striking photograph of him with Gurdjieff during a late "car trip"—Gurdjieff often assembled small caravans of students and family to visit places of interest in France. An immensely tall man, Page stands near Gurdjieff during a break in travel; obviously at ease, they clearly know each other well. Page seems to have known how to engage Gurdjieff playfully. For example, at table in the late

1940s, "Gurdjieff said he must finish the arrangements because he wanted to go in a day or two to Tibet. 'Tibet, Monsieur?' said Page. 'Or Dieppe?' Mr. G. gave him a perfectly wicked and sly smile and said, 'Either very expensive,' as though apart from that the destination did not matter much."[5] There is another photograph: Russell Page as a pall bearer at Gurdjieff's funeral, early November 1949.

Severe or casual dismissiveness among some intellectuals then and now has a number of roots, the earliest dating to the years 1923–1924. At that time, newly established in France, Gurdjieff invited public attention by receiving visitors, including journalists, at his Institute for the Harmonious Development of Man in Fontainebleau-Avon, roughly an hour from Paris by train or car. I'll often refer to it as the Prieuré. The Institute's new home was a spacious manor house, the Prieuré des Basses Loges, once a convent, later the home of a royal mistress, still later owned by the principal lawyer defending Captain Alfred Dreyfus in the years around 1900. Visitors to the Prieuré were hospitably received, some spoke with the founder (through a translator at that time), others prowled the extensive grounds and learned what they could, and many witnessed Saturday evening performances of the sacred dances, for which Gurdjieff became known when he brought the dances and his hardworking troupe to the public through theatrical performances in late 1923 (Paris) and the first months of 1924 (New York City and elsewhere in the United States).

Both journalists and distinguished visitors could not miss an unassailable truth: a visit to the Institute was a visit *elsewhere*. Its values were different, its intentions and way of life differed, and Gurdjieff himself was *other*; he matched no norm. Indecipherable to the majority of casual visitors, he may well have been the first authentic guru in the modern West—but what was that? The word itself was scarcely known, let alone the function of that sort of teacher. Sacred dances? Many acknowledged that they were beautiful and the performers capable of intricate movement—but why didn't they smile? Dancers are supposed to smile. And the Institute itself, with its novel and challenging printed statement of purpose—really?[6] Is such a school needed? Apart from obvious exceptions, aren't adults adult, with completed identities, no fundamental reworking necessary? It was too much for most observers and, though there were exceptions, newspaper reports for the most part lurched toward entertaining distortion and condescension.[7] Gurdjieff abandoned publicizing the Institute and his work in choreography. In later years he was typically abrupt with journalists; he wanted no part of them. Despite the mixed public reception in those early years, there were visitors who stayed, audience members who recognized in the dances and the dancers a new way of being.

The literature of rejection and disdain has another root in those years: the passage through one another's lives of Katherine Mansfield, the now classic author, and Gurdjieff at the newly founded Institute. Chapter 4 looks more closely at this enduringly vivid and touching encounter, but something should be noted now. New Zealand-born, reaching out to and reaching London in 1908 to found her literary career, Mansfield quickly became "one of us"—friend (and sometime rival) of many in the literary elite, discovered and first published by Alfred R. Orage, editor of the leading literary journal of its time. Driven by superb powers of observation and sharp wit, her short stories became part of the canon of twentieth-century literature. And she sickened. When she was diagnosed with tuberculosis in 1917, her life became a pilgrimage or flight from place to place, from healthy mountain air to doctors who offered some hope of a cure to quiet times in England and on the continent when she believed that all could again be well. Through her notebook for 1919 we can visit a key moment in these increasingly difficult years to hear something of her private sensibility, not yet fully revealed in her stories. Her words there will help us grasp why she found her way to Gurdjieff and the Institute in the last few months of her life: "Honesty . . . is the only thing one seems to prize beyond life, love, death, everything," she wrote. "It alone remaineth. O those that come after me—will you believe it? At the end truth is the one thing worth having—it's more thrilling than love, more joyful, & more passionate. It simply cannot fail. All else fails. I, at any rate, give the remainder of my life to it & it alone."[8]

She was drawn to the Institute because, there too, she was "one of us"—a participant by virtue of her longing for another quality of truth and experience, which she had glimpsed from time to time, and by virtue of her willingness to take herself in hand, to question herself. In the teaching cycle Gurdjieff had offered in Russia before the Revolution, he had introduced the idea of "magnetic center," an innate capacity in some people to detect and move toward liberating truth, to look past the familiar. It is a raw, untutored capacity. Naturally it speaks the language of a given time and place, but it belongs to itself, finds its own way, answers to no one until satisfied that it has come home—however it understands "home." Katherine Mansfield possessed such an inner compass.

Guided by Orage, who also became a resident at the Institute in its very first weeks of existence, October 1922, Mansfield left behind physical therapies that had done her no good and wished to rework her life in some new way that she understood the Institute to offer. "I am going to Fontainebleau next week to see Gurdjieff," she wrote that month from Paris to her husband, John Middleton Murry. "Why am I going? From all I hear he is the only man who understands there is no division between the body and the spirit, who believes how they are related. You remember how I have always said doctors only treat half. And you have replied, 'It's up to you to do the rest'? It is. That's true. But first I must learn how. I believe Gurdjieff can teach me."[9]

Mansfield came to the Prieuré on a two-week trial basis after being examined in Paris by a British doctor, one of the early residents, who confirmed to Gurdjieff that she was mortally ill with little time left. Gurdjieff understood the possible consequences of lengthening her stay, but Mansfield already had friends, among whom were the women Gurdjieff had assigned to make her life comfortable. The best account is from Tcheslaw Tchekhovitch, a mighty young man with a big heart—once a professional wrestler and circus strongman—who had accompanied Gurdjieff since meeting him in Constantinople. Tchekhovitch noticed one day that Katya (as he called her) was sad and, asking why, learned that Gurdjieff had suggested she would be better off in a sanatorium. Tchekhovitch took matters in hand: "A strange determination came over me on her behalf: not to give up, not to lose hope. I could not believe Gyorgi Ivanovich would refuse to let her stay at the Prieuré if she expressed her wish sincerely, from the depths of her being. Gently, I spoke my mind. 'You know as well as I that Gyorgi Ivanovich is a good man. He won't refuse, if you speak to him frankly.' Then, wanting to provide her with a request he could not turn down, I added, 'Don't just ask to stay. Tell him it's the only way for you to find true happiness.'"[10] No doubt she put her question effectively and found allies in three women who were "not easily put off." Tchekhovitch continued, "'Gyorgi Ivanovich, people have already said plenty of scandalous things about you, so one more isn't going to make much difference! We'll share that burden with you.' 'All right, then,' he said, looking at them intently. 'So be it. We'll all bear it together!'"

As Gurdjieff must have known, it was not a burden that could be shared. He alone would face opprobrium, were their Katya to die at the Prieuré. Out of sheer kindness he permitted her to stay. Letters to her husband and a conversation with Orage, later recorded by him, as well as a conversation with P. D. Ouspensky, bear witness to the joyous weeks of discovery and self-discovery, of comfort and fellowship, she experienced. No witness of the life of the Prieuré has left a more sensitive and vivid record—to be explored in chapter 4. She died suddenly on January 9, 1923; her grave in the local Avon cemetery is a few yards from the Gurdjieff family plot.

And because she was "one of us" in England, and soon enthusi-astically read in French translation, anger and blame descended—as virtually everyone who cared for Gurdjieff and the Institute had anticipated. It was as if Gurdjieff had irresponsibly deprived English letters of a treasured person. Rejection and disdain had charac-terized much of British opinion even in advance of Mansfield's death—newspaper reports and word-of-mouth were marching on, and the inexplicable departure to the Prieuré of A. R. Orage, such a central figure in English letters, was alarming. James Moore, author of *Gurdjieff and Mansfield*, makes the relevant inventory. Wyndham Lewis described Mansfield as "in the grip of the Levantine psychic shark." D. H. Lawrence qualified the Institute as a "rotten place." During Mansfield's few months at the Prieuré, Vivian Eliot, the poet's wife, reported of an acquaintance that "she is now in that asylum for the insane called La [*sic*] Prieuré where she does religious dances naked with Katherine Mansfield."[11] François Mauriac, a notable Catholic author and eventually a member of the Académie française and Nobel laureate, wrote many years after Mansfield's death that "in the end it was to Gurdjieff, the mage, that she gave her faith, at the phalanstery of Fontainebleau, where she went to die in misery."[12] He was reviewing in 1959 the newly published French translation of the first comprehensive biography of Mansfield.[13]

Particularly in France, the stain of Mansfield's death on Gurd-jieff's reputation prevailed for decades. Conversation with the English scholar Gerri Kimber, author of a marvelous history of Mansfield's reputation in France, led to the oddest of findings: there were two stacks of received opinion from which French intellectuals drew for decades after Mansfield's death.[14] In the first stack, Mans-field was depicted as an angel, a supremely refined, loving intelli-gence briefly cast into our world and sadly snatched away. In the second stack, Gurdjieff was depicted as a devil, an untrustworthy exploiter. Neither received opinion required further thought. The Mansfield myth survived until a series of thorough biographies, from 1953 forward, offered a much more nuanced truth: she too had her struggles and lapses, not only where health was concerned. The Gurdjieff myth should have long since been put to rest: after 1950, anyone who cared to have unprejudiced knowledge of him could easily find a growing number of accurate sources.

Enough for now about reputation. Later chapters will return to the topic: another generation of French authors did what they could, with some success, to eliminate Gurdjieff as a figure worth serious consideration, and several authors in the English-speaking world, approaching with sharpened axes, did what they could to exclude both him and his teaching from the known world. For now, no matter—they'll have their say later when we look at the years just after Gurdjieff's passing. We should begin thinking about what Gurdjieff and his teaching represented. He may be unknowable but, all the same, are there no mirrors we can hold up to catch light?

THE LAST PYTHAGORAS

Reading the words just above, Gurdjieff students who practice the sacred dances, or Movements as they are more typically known, may recall a dance named just that way: "The Last Pythagoras." One of a suite of dances dedicated to Pythagoras, it is a marvel of music and movement—ordered, joyful, and energetic. The dance comes to mind because Gurdjieff himself can in part be understood as "the last Pythagoras"—or in any case the Pythagoras of our era.

In his major book, *Beelzebub's Tales to His Grandson* (which developed across multiple languages from the mid-1920s through to its English-language publication in 1950), Gurdjieff was ferociously satirical where ancient Greek culture was concerned—though he was born to Greek parents and spoke Greek from his earliest days (as well as Armenian, and soon Russian and Turkish).[15] He attributes to "bored fishermen" in early Greece a game with nasty millennial consequences: inventing pseudosciences with complex names as an entertainment to ease them through long days of inactivity when they took shelter from storms at sea. The account is a droll oblique criticism of scientific culture in Gurdjieff's day and ours and likely of the way our minds work. But Pythagoras was the exception. In the *Tales*, where he is one of few named figures from history or legend, he is depicted as a person of depth and compassion who helped to devise a novel means of passing down essential, endangered knowledge from generation to generation. Gurdjieff was recurrently concerned with the preservation and transmission of knowledge. The narrator of the *Tales*, the reformed and wise Beelzebub, knew Pythagoras personally, admired him, and must have walked the streets of ancient Babylon with him as they came and went from meetings.

Who was Pythagoras? A sixth-century philosopher, mathematician and geometer, cosmologist, music theorist, school master, political counselor, dancer, healer, dietitian, and more: a comprehensive culture hero at the outset of recognizably Western tradition. We know of him through ancient biographies, two of book length, others more like essays and fragments. His biographers in the third and fourth centuries of our era lived so long after him that their material can only be a compilation of sources in which some fragments of history and much legend mix. I have never resented texts of this kind because it is the text itself that exercises influence, changing and inspiring minds over great lengths of time. Absent Pythagoras himself, texts will do, and these are what Gurdjieff read as a young man, like many other young men and women before and since.

But we haven't yet captured the mystique of Pythagoras; there was one. There was something about him so lofty, so completely other, that his pupils were known to say that there are men and women and a "third thing"—by which they respectfully alluded to their teacher. Some were persuaded that he had a golden thigh, that he was a child of the gods. Some believed that he heard the music of the spheres, directly. He had traveled widely through his youth and middle years to centers of knowledge across the ancient world and received instruction from priests and magi. His teachings were a summary of what was known and a vast addition to the known. And then, he formulated his teachings in words difficult or riddling enough that the uninitiated couldn't make sense of them. His aphorisms, compact expressions of insights and values, were collected numerous times over and passed down through the centuries. The school he created, rigorously disciplined, hard on its pupils but ultimately offering a reward of very special knowledge, was the first to define itself—or to be defined by legend—as esoteric, ordered by a pattern of successive initiations.

For him the cosmos was numbers, perhaps an infinity of numbers but still ordered by numbers and understandable through numbers. For him music was medicine—he could cure undue passions and stimulate intellects through his music. And who can forget that he was the first to measure the mathematics of the musical octave—and to torment high school students ever after with the square of the hypotenuse? For his own purposes he sometimes danced to reinforce his health, but his pupils must have seen him dance and tried it out for themselves. What was his ancient tai chi? In sum, the legend of Pythagoras, the inspired scientist, educator, and heaven-turned man of spirit, is nearly endless and endlessly attractive.

If it became explicit later through Gurdjieff's dances and book that he revered and in certain respects followed the example of Pythagoras, it was already evident to some from the early days of the Institute for the Harmonious Development of Man that Pythagoras was nearby. The name of the Institute is Pythagorean, its promise Pythagorean. But that wasn't the only sign. It may well have been Orage who first noticed; later accounts seem to stem from him. Denis Saurat, a French academic teaching in England who visited the Prieuré in February 1923, reported that the Institute was "'something in the nature of the Pythagorean societies,' as Orage vaguely announces, 'but much more severe.'"[16] The closing comment is a teasing exaggeration comparing apples with long since petrified oranges—one can almost see Orage adopting a theatrically grim expression—but it is true that the way of life in early years at the Prieuré was demanding.

Clifford Sharp, an English journalist with a connection to Orage, had much the same impression that winter.

> As far as the writer's knowledge goes, the only recorded institution with which Mr. Gurdjieff's school can at all be plausibly compared is the school which was established in southern Italy by Pythagoras about 550 B.C. The Pythagoreans lived in a colony and were subjected to all kinds of abstinences and physical exercises as a preparation for the extraordinary intellectual work which they accomplished. They were deeply concerned with rhythm, with movement, with the analysis of the octave, and with other . . . subjects which are studied at Fontainebleau. In some respects the parallel is indeed almost absurdly exact. . . . It is not suggested here that Gurdjieff is another Pythagoras, but if parallels are to be sought this particular parallel is certainly irresistible— and no others are adequate, save perhaps some which might be discovered in the origins of Gothic architecture. So far at any rate as the modern world is concerned, the Gurdjieff Institute is a unique phenomenon. Its possibilities are either nothing or else almost infinite.[17]

The modern world was of two minds about Gurdjieff and his teaching. In New York, where Orage became Gurdjieff's representative from 1924 through 1930, the Pythagorean parallel continued to come to mind. Looking back in 1937 to Gurdjieff's New York visit in the winter of 1924, Gorham Munson—editor and author and a familiar participant in avant-garde circles—wrote that "if it cannot be said that the visit of Gurdjieff took America by storm, it can be said that it raised a conversational storm in the circles of the intelligentsia. . . . The Gurdjieff visit . . . was not nearly the sensation in the press that it was in conversation, where it stirred up quite as much rejection as it did curiosity. All that spring and into the summer months the question of Gurdjieff—a new Pythagoras or a charlatan?—was the most controversial topic at intelligentsia gatherings."[18] Gorham Munson was among those not of two minds: he was drawn to the teaching, warmly related to Orage, and attuned to what Gurdjieff offered. What Gurdjieff offered was so new—a new view of human possibility and obligation, a new means of self-development, a new residential school to explore it all—that he couldn't realistically expect a mass response. "Shun public roads and walk in unfrequented paths"—an aphorism attributed to Pythagoras. What a difficult choice. Some made the choice without difficulty, as if reaching a home they hadn't known was home.

When we explore life at the Prieuré in chapter 4, the Pythagorean heritage will be evident again. But there was something more in the way Gurdjieff approached his fellow human beings, in appearance the very opposite of Pythagorean purity and fastidious remoteness. When François Grunwald first looked into Gurdjieff's eyes and saw serenity and sacred sadness—classic values of Western spirituality—he also saw ironic malice.

"I Am a Cynic": Diogenes Again

Luc Dietrich was a writer in his late twenties whom Gurdjieff called "Petit"—he was extremely tall and thin—and also "*mon collègue*" to acknowledge, I think sincerely, that like Gurdjieff he was indeed a writer. During the late 1930s and the Occupation, Dietrich had the unique custom of giving notebooks to his most trusted friends in the circle around Gurdjieff with a question written out at the top of each page—questions he so wished his friends to answer that they actually did so. Some of those notebooks or transcriptions have survived, among them one to Henri Tracol, a slightly older man of the same generation who in later years became a remarkable teacher. "How to define," Dietrich queried Tracol, "the right attitude toward Mr. Gurdjieff? What should the pupil's attitude be?" Tracol gave the question good thought before responding.

> Never forget what one is seeking from him.
> Never lose sight of the fact that he is the master, but also that he is a man. And keep a tight rein on any subjective reaction with regard to him.
> Be always on the alert. Do not let yourself be caught in the traps he sets.
> Know how to be open to him without abandoning yourself.
> Know how to exact from him the Word.[19]

A miniature tapestry, Tracol's words offer a first insight into the dynamics—hope, discipline, danger, clarity of mind—at Gurdjieff's apartment and table in the last decade of his life, 1939–1949. To keep in mind one's aim in seeking his teaching and company; that seems straightforward, doesn't it? But there was so much color and change and surprise from day to day in Gurdjieff's company that one could easily believe that the experience was about color, change, and surprise. Those were conditions and atmosphere—"skillful means," to borrow a perfect phrase from the Buddhist lexicon—but not the fundamental point. And then, Tracol insists on an easily admitted point: the teacher was also a human being. If one thigh was golden, so to speak, the other was flesh like one's own. Gurdjieff's students needed to keep both perspectives in mind, but what follows from that, in Tracol's reasoning, is more difficult: to set aside all subjective reactions to him. Gurdjieff was deliberately and often provocative; this was both a principle of his approach to those who worked with him and a daily practice. We'll soon see what Gurdjieff thought about that, why it mattered to him fundamentally. Tracol's injunction was for most people impossible to carry out perfectly, but the point was to survive one's own reactions when they occurred, to take up one's station inside them, so to speak, and see what they were. Self-knowledge lay that way.

He set traps? It was an integral part of his method, a means of revealing pupils to themselves in a new, strictly honest light, which they themselves could recognize. All or nearly all could be forgiven later, but not before the threads were pulled tight. An incident recalled by François Grunwald offers a pure example from the late 1940s.

To go to his apartment was to accept to be put on trial, constantly; to accept that certain of one's tendencies hitherto unnoticed would be revealed. One evening when there were so many people in the dining room that I had taken my plate to the adjoining room, he had me summoned to announce that someone had coughed in the room where I was having dinner and that I must launch an inquiry as to just who it was. A cunning actor, he gave me a severe look. I was there, standing, beside myself, blushing, embarrassed, ill at ease. In a few moments Madame de Salzmann out of compassion rescued me: "Tell him it was you; it's of no importance, and in any case no one coughed." And Gurdjieff added: "Stupid thing, always wanting to defend yourself. Have you seen now?" And indeed, later I often noticed this feature about which I had had no idea.[20]

It was a trap well set, causing no harm; on the contrary. Jeanne de Salzmann was Gurdjieff's closest pupil, perhaps the only person of whom he could say, as he did once, that she had never let him down. We'll see in later pages that as his heir she inspired and shaped the Gurdjieff teaching for nearly forty years after his death. Her thought in those decades is recorded in *The Reality of Being: The Fourth Way of Gurdjieff*.[21]

"Know how to be open to him without abandoning yourself." This was likely more difficult than it sounds. Any reader who has encountered a genuinely eminent man or woman, a person who has mastered realms of experience or knowledge for which one particularly cares, may be familiar with a certain draining of identity: What am I worth—not much—in light of this massively accomplished person? Gurdjieff was acutely aware of this trap and did not in the least wish to capture his students in it; as we'll soon see, he gave it explicit thought, and some of his provocations and offensive behavior were intended to free his circle, as needed, from enslaving admiration. And yet that particular trap cannot help but make itself known in the relation between serious student and accomplished teacher, and it is a measure of the student's resourcefulness, once the trap is recognized, to free oneself without losing an ounce of regard for the teacher.

There is one final point in the miniature tapestry that we should think through before looking at Gurdjieff's renewal of the Cynic critique—really, assault—on illusory, unearned self-satisfaction: "Know how to exact from him the Word." This was the point, always the point, no matter how challenging it surely was to work with a teacher across such a broad spectrum, from utter purity to traps. And "the Word" in those years was not only a word, it was a state of being that flowed from Gurdjieff and taught more about human possibility than words. Words could clothe that state and elucidate it, but no more than that.

Traps, challenges, provocations, rough waves around stillness— we are surely ready now to consider Gurdjieff's fidelity to another ancient Greek teacher whom Plato with little love called "a mad Socrates": Diogenes of Sinope, the foremost Cynic. Diogenes would not have occurred to me as a predecessor had Gurdjieff himself not mentioned it—things can be like each other without being genuinely linked. The accepted explanation for Gurdjieff's provocations probably originated with J. G. Bennett, who knew the Middle East and Turkish language well and wrote extensively about Gurdjieff and his teaching. Bennett made the link to the Sufi "way of blame," or *malamati*, a self-abnegating practice by which deliberate offenses against conventional behavior free the practitioner from congenial social support and establish a psychologically sheltered zone for religious practice. I have no basis in research for questioning this interpretation, although as far as I know Gurdjieff never mentioned it. What Gurdjieff did mention was the Cynic path, which is much the same. I wouldn't be surprised if the way of blame has a root in Cynic tradition—much passed from later Greek culture into the Islamic world. No one can doubt Gurdjieff's long exposure during his years of travel and search to Sufi schools and practices, and the Movements are rich in examples of dervish ritual dances. Gurdjieff had few evident nostalgias, but one was for "*mon pays*, Turkestan" and for the customs, quality of people, and even scents of Persia as he knew it, ca. 1890–1900.[22] What follows concerning the Cynic way of life and teaching style sheds light without canceling other views.

In the hearing of Kathryn Hulme, later the best-selling author of *The Nun's Story*, Gurdjieff was speaking at some point in the 1930s with a young man, Donald Whitcomb. Hulme later recorded in her journal that Gurdjieff had turned to Whitcomb, "with a serious, gentle look on his face." The language that follows is Gurdjieff's Russo-English, similar to his Russo-French: effective, expressive, unconstrained by grammar, all his own. Noticeably, in this expression of regard for the Cynic approach, Gurdjieff begins by defining what he calls "objective *bon ton*," consideration for others based on caring attention—not a traditionally Cynic theme but a Gurdjieffian theme too little recognized.

Truth, Donald, one fault you have. Though you are known as kind man, good nature, and though everyone hope you not wish give offense, you do this unconsciously sometimes. That spoils all life for you. You not have considerateness for state of surroundings. Necessary always know what is around you—state of man around you. With cow, you can merde on face and he not take offense. He lick, he smile, he shake head; not understand, not offense take. But man around you is already more high—he have states. You must know what is state of every man around you in room. Man of course is most of time asleep but this make even more important that you be sensitive. . . because when he awake, even if only for one moment, he is already in state—for this one moment is delicate, sensitive. . . perhaps is only moment in his life when he can be enlightened. So you must consciously try to understand, to be sensitive for him. I know what is state each man around me because I am educate man, I have knowledge. You must always try have considerateness for state of surroundings. This if you wish be objective bon ton. Never can you offend one thing on earth. Even if you offend one worm—one day . . . one day . . . he you will repay. . .

You notice . . . never anyone take offense anything I say? Even you know what words I use. But never you see man angry with me when I tell. You know why? Because I am cynic. (Discussion about cynic, skeptic, iconoclast, etc.) Excuse—not skeptic. Skeptic means: you believe, I not believe; you hope, I not hope. . . Cynic is the word. Cynic means a man who is not afraid to tell truth, exact how is, yet never he offend people when he tell because he is so right, he tell so exact. Never can they be offended, because the truth he tells.[23]

Diogenes, whom we again know largely through Late Antique sources, was a master of edgy philosophical theater. A contemporary of Plato's who had studied with a leading pupil of Socrates, he had a perfectly remarkable, and perfectly wicked, sense of humor. He tended to teach, or at least to offer his acerbic commentaries, to whomever might heed him, through spontaneous improvisations in which words were only part of the message. We might call him today a performance artist. Someone once came upon him imploring a statue for alms. "What are you doing?" was the natural question. "I'm practicing," he said, "so that when people refuse me I won't mind." He was fearless, funny, bitter, wholly in earnest. Society had no more clear-sighted critic: any pretention whatever was evident to him and mocked when the time came with a unique blend of moral lucidity, spiky humor, and mercilessness. That speaks to what he was: a moralist, animated by something quite like sacred sadness and ironic malice. He set himself spiritually and literally at a distance from society by living in a large clay urn, dressing shoddily in just one cloak, allowing his beard to grow as it pleased, owning nothing more than a walking staff and a wallet for bits of food or stray things of interest. A familiar figure in whatever city he chose to live, he was valued despite himself: when some mischievous children in Athens smashed up his urn, the city fathers promptly ordered its replacement. "Chose to live"? Not quite. Once he found himself captive in the Cretan slave market, noticed a man of merit, and grandly announced, "Sell me to this man—he needs a master." That is what Diogenes became until granted his freedom: the householder confided his children's education to him. For once Diogenes abandoned theater and offered a sober, modest education; well-motivated children were not to be mocked, they were to be worked with. "A good spirit (*agathos daimon*) has entered my house"—such was the father's comment. It is touching to read about this change of mood and method in the best biography, a work from the third century of our era that Gurdjieff would have read as a young man.[24]

Some episodes of Diogenes' wise theater of the absurd are familiar to many readers—for example, walking in the street in broad daylight with a lantern, saying, "I am looking for a man." Taking a leisurely sunbath when Alexander the Great approached with his retinue and loomed over the famous, eccentric philosopher: "What can I do for you?" asked Alexander. Diogenes's answer: "Move out of my light." Alexander's men laughed as they walked off, but Alexander silenced them: "Understand," he said, "that if I weren't Alexander, I would want to be Diogenes." These are familiar anecdotes; there are many others. A favorite: once Plato came upon Diogenes washing lettuce in a stream. Everyone knew that Plato had traveled to the court of the Sicilian tyrant Dionysius and sought favors from him. "If you spent time at the court of Dionysius," Plato said, "you wouldn't have to wash lettuce." Diogenes in reply: "And if you had washed lettuce, you wouldn't have paid court to Dionysius."

There is much play on the word *cynic* itself, which means "doglike." Someone asked Diogenes why he was called a hound. In response: "I fawn on those who give me anything, I yelp at those who refuse, and I set my teeth in rascals." About bodily functions he was shameless—there too, philosophical theater. For example, it defied custom to eat in public, but he didn't mind: subverting both custom and the glory of formal logic, he once argued, "If to breakfast be not absurd, then neither is it absurd to breakfast in the marketplace; but to breakfast is not absurd, therefore it is not absurd to breakfast in the market place."

Around Diogenes there must always have been people shaking their heads—what will he do or say next? Yet he was loved; he was and remains an ineffaceable model of intelligent dissent, fearless critique, unsparing engagement, of a flamboyant but utterly serious theater of ideas and values. One last story: The ideal hinge between Diogenes of Sinope on the Black Sea and Gurdjieff of the Caucasus. Diogenes was entering a theater as everyone else was coming out, and someone asked why. "This," he said, "is what I have practiced all my life."

So, too, Gurdjieff. He was Diogenes-like, though not only that;

alongside the example of Pythagoras, the Cynic heritage offers a second basis in long culture to think freshly about him. Gurdjieff's major book, *Beelzebub's Tales to His Grandson*, written from the summer of 1924 through the early 1930s and revised until publication in 1950, carries a telling subtitle: *An Objectively Impartial Criticism of the Life of Man*. Recalling the Cynic project, this is an impersonal and unyielding promise to the reader. In the first pages a statement of purpose enlarges on the promise in a way that, like Diogenes, cuts closer to the bone: "To destroy, mercilessly, without any compromises whatsoever, in the mentation and feelings of the reader, the beliefs and views, by centuries rooted in him, about everything existing in the world."

Confronting unquestioned or comfortable illusion was only the beginning of the new vision Gurdjieff wished to share; there was much more ahead. But readers of the *Tales* sometimes underestimate the extent to which the book is not only intricately symbolic in many passages, not only esoteric in the Pythagorean sense that close reading can uncover coded illuminations. It is also, as stated, a critique of the contemporary human condition; it is about America and France and Russia, to choose three topics among endless others, and about Americans, French, and Russians. It is about our unbelievably hopeful endowment as human beings made in the image of God—so Gurdjieff faithfully acknowledges more than once—and our equally unbelievable irresponsibility toward that endowment. This is not an esoteric message; it is plain statement sustained throughout the *Tales*.

I don't think it makes sense to tie Gurdjieff too closely to any prior model, be it Diogenes, Pythagoras, or other. Some authors warmly disposed toward him have linked him to one or another tradition or lineage, as if he were *that*, but lightly disguised for the sake of freedom of movement in the more secular, science-minded West. I think it preferable to minimize speculation in this regard and take Gurdjieff at his word. He made unmistakably clear that he thought it necessary to start again, to rethink everything, to cultivate values rooted in wise tradition but "renewed"—this was a key word and thought in his lexicon. When he first began teaching in Moscow and St. Petersburg in 1912, and when the revolutionary collapse of Russian society forced his emigration westward, ultimately to France, I believe that he could legitimately have presented himself as a representative of any one of three traditions—Orthodox Christianity, Sufism, and Tibetan Buddhism—had he sought the appropriate ordination or authoritative assent. He had learned from all three in depth during his years of travel in search of decisive knowledge. But he chose otherwise: he came to the West as an independent teacher—in a sense, as no one, as one of us. In *Meetings with Remarkable Men*, he tells only so much and no more about his origins. If he was to make his way in the West, it would not be by any category of external prestige or authority but by the strength of his ideas and the persuasive uniqueness of his person. An elderly friend of mine who studied with Gurdjieff in the 1940s told me that once when she was in his apartment he opened a special cabinet to fetch something, and she was sure that if she could only look over his shoulder, she would see an image or photograph of his root guru, to use a dignified Tibetan term—the teacher to whom he owed the most. But she never told me what she saw, and perhaps she didn't maneuver adroitly enough to see anything.

All of this said to recall his firm independence, there remains a little more to notice about the link to Cynic tradition. Memoirs about Gurdjieff almost invariably dwell on two seemingly opposite features: on one hand his radiant presence, experienced by others as a felt energy but also a stillness, and on the other hand the intense theater he often created by word, facial expression, gesture, improvised scene setting—occasioning every possible emotion and response from shared laughter and delight to fear and trembling, revolt, alarm, interpretive alertness in front of a puzzling unknown. He seemed by nature to be a hugely skilled actor, and he was fearless. I should add at once that the Gurdjieff teaching can be conveyed in many different styles and tones, no gift for drama required. But the founder had that gift and, as noted earlier, it generated a vast collection of anecdotes and striking turns of phrase, best categorized now as compact teachings, much like the vivid tales of the Hasidim collected by Martin Buber from eighteenth- and nineteenth-century records of conversations and events among certain rabbis and their disciples. Such things are originally no more than moments in a flow, but recorded later by concerned disciples they become talismans of the larger world where they appeared.

Gurdjieff could be memorably severe with his pupils or memorably gentle, in keeping with a long-deliberated view of his obligations as a teacher. He could express that view in complex language, as we'll see in a moment, but also in the language of everyday life. An example of the latter was recorded by his pupil Margaret Anderson, the pioneering editor who, with her equally brave colleague Jane Heap, first published—and stood trial in the United States for publishing—excerpts from James Joyce's *Ulysses*, at the time considered obscene. "One night," Anderson recalled, "when we were dining with Gurdjieff in Paris, someone said, 'Such a nice man, Mr. Gurdjieff, who came to lunch today.' 'Yes,' Gurdjieff said, 'nice man—because here at table was asleep. Everyone nice when asleep. But you press on one of his corns and then you see what kind of man he is.'"[25] The nice man was likely a guest at his table—Gurdjieff was hospitably courteous to guests, although not above playing harmless tricks on pretentious guests as little demonstrations for his pupils, generally undetected by their victims. On the other hand, toward his pupils and their weaknesses and illusions, he could be fierce. Annie Lou Staveley, an American pupil of Jane Heap's who found her way to Gurdjieff's table and Movements classes in the late 1940s, makes this ever so clear.

"'For what you could be,' he said more than once, 'I have nothing

but benevolence. But as you are I hate you—back to your grandmother!' Mercilessly he showed us that 'as we are.' He held the
mirror up and one was helplessly exposed in the flimsy combination of notions, prejudices, fragments of conditioning by parents
and teachers . . . as well as hypocrisy, pretentions, featherweight
thoughts, and so on and on. If he said to one or another, as he did
sometimes, 'You have very good façade!' it was certainly not at all
reassuring."[26] His imprecation "back to your grandmother" is not
offhand, though it may seem so. During the Prieuré years he had
more than once said that the quality of human beings deteriorates
from generation to generation—if "grandfather forgets, grandmother forgets"—implying that there are key elements of culture,
of sheer humanness, that must without fail be remembered and
passed on. On occasion he would add that it is an honor and a service to one's ancestors to put an end, through one's efforts toward
self-understanding, to whatever unfortunate consequences their
forgetting may have caused.

Gurdjieff had decided long ago that he would need to be unsettling, at times severe, even unreasonably difficult or offensive when
he thought that approach would best serve his students. On the
other side, he would give his all to help people when the person and
moment called for that. He rarely revealed his motives for acting in
one way or another; those around him simply had to assess what was
going on and decide if it was somebody else's concern or their very
own. But in the first book he published, the only one he saw in his
lifetime, he clearly stated the motives behind his behavior. *The Herald
of Coming Good* was written and hastily published in 1932–1933. This
was a time when the Institute for the Harmonious Development of
Man was on the verge of closing, and ultimately closed, for lack of
funds: the global Depression had taken its toll on Gurdjieff's own
resources and his pupils' generosity. Gurdjieff's editor of genius,
A. R. Orage, had no hand in the English translation, which was
awkward, and the book—almost certainly intended to rescue the

Prieuré as the home of the teaching—must have struck Gurdjieff after some months as not just ineffective but harmful. He withdrew whatever copies he could from circulation, and in years to come original copies were scarce. Yet there is much of value in the book; it is a rough read, but an essential one if we are to better understand Gurdjieff's renewal of the Cynic attitude and teaching style.

He wrote there that at the time he began teaching in Russia he took a vow to live what he called an "unnatural life" for twenty-one years—unnatural in the sense that he would thereafter act toward the people around him on the basis of several compelling insights about human nature, which did not figure among his early convictions and moral principles; they imposed themselves later. Two of those insights concern us here. The first was to prevent people, insofar as possible, from succumbing to idolatry, to an excess of admiration. He was determined to "counteract . . . the manifestation in people with whom I came in contact of that inherent trait which, embedded as it is in the psyche of people and acting as an impediment to the realization of my aims, evokes from them, when confronted with other more or less prominent people, the functioning of the feeling of enslavement, paralyzing . . . their capacity for displaying the personal initiative of which I then stood in particular need."[27] If he was to have able pupils and helpful associates as time went on, they would have to find their way to the attitude evoked by Henri Tracol in his response to Luc Dietrich: open to Gurdjieff but psychologically free and self-possessed.

To this end, Gurdjieff sometimes created his own theater of the absurd, Diogenes-like to the last painful detail. Louise March, well known in the Gurdjieff community, particularly in the United States, and the first translator of his writings into German, joined Gurdjieff at the Prieuré in 1929. In her memoirs she offers several tales of deliberate misdeeds she witnessed while with Gurdjieff in New York during one of his visits in the 1930s: "When the *Bremen* docked in New York, Gurdjieff stepped off the boat with an

Armagnac bottle half-visible in his coat pocket. This was during Prohibition. I said to him, 'Put it deeper. It shouldn't be seen.' He didn't. It was like the time when, at a gathering of people newly interested in his ideas, he started scratching himself. Embarrassed, I leaned toward him and asked, 'Why are you doing that?' He replied shortly, 'Fleas,' and scratched again."[28]

Those vignettes are like another, recalled by C. S. Nott, an English pupil who in later years wrote two valuable accounts of life and teachings at the Prieuré and decades following. Nott's connection to Gurdjieff dated to New York, 1924, when Gurdjieff brought the Movements there and, with Orage's help, began in small gatherings to lay out the main lines of the teaching.

> The meeting was timed for nine, but it was almost ten before we saw Gurdjieff. He came in from another room, wearing a grey suit and an old pair of carpet slippers and holding a large baked potato. Everybody became frigidly silent. He sat on the edge of the low platform facing us and began to eat. He seemed to be playing a part—that of a benevolent, middle-aged gentleman at a party. He made a joke, and the rather tense atmosphere disappeared in a peal of laughter. After a few remarks his expression changed, and he said, "Perhaps someone have question?"[29]

This was play—of course it was play—but play of a certain kind, harmlessly shocking, deliberately putting at risk his reputation as a proper sage. Abrupt changes of mood and substance—"Perhaps someone have question?"—were well within Gurdjieff's repertory; for willing souls they taught a certain emotional flexibility. In the Movements there are also such changes: from total vigor to contemplative inwardness, and back again. A training for life, I'm sure, though in a Movements class there isn't time or need for reflections of that kind.

On occasion Gurdjieff gives the impression of playing as if he were a child, playing to shake off solemnity and entertain his pupils for the sheer joy of doing so. If there was unmistakable sacred sadness in the man, there was also joy. Kathryn Hulme tells a story of New York 1949, when Gurdjieff was on the point of returning to Paris: "G shows us all the 5 and 10 cent gifts he has bought for presents. Of one item he is especially proud. He has bought dozens. 'Small thing is,' he says, 'but for them in Paris is new and wonderful.' He illustrates how he will, with a bow, present this rare gift from America, how they will receive it, awestruck. He hands Leighton the gift. It is a ten-cent folding bunion knife."[30]

There was a second compelling insight governing the "unnatural life" Gurdjieff had adopted at the beginning of his years as a teacher. His study of human nature had led to the conviction that vanity and what he called in *The Herald* "self-conceit"—later restated as "egoistic self-love"—were dominant psychic factors in most people. He put it as follows, in the detailed language he adopted in some of his writings:

> The fundamental cause of almost all the misunderstandings arising in the inner world of man, as well as in the process of the communal life of people, is chiefly this psychic factor, which is formed in man's being during the period of preparatory age exclusively on account of a wrong education, and in the period of responsible age each stimulation of which gives birth in him to the impulses of "Vanity" and "Self-Conceit."
>
> I categorically affirm that the happiness and self-consciousness, which should be in a real man, as well as in a peaceful communal existence between people . . . depend in most cases . . . on the absence in us of the feeling of "Vanity."[31]

It was an insight with consequences. "I never considered," he wrote further, "and under no circumstances encouraged, in the people I met the impulse[s] . . . of 'Vanity' and 'Self-Conceit,' but on the contrary considered myself obliged to adopt a critical attitude towards them, and risked all prosperity."[32] On one hand, Gurdjieff vowed "to 'cultivate' inwardly and manifest towards everyone I met the feelings of love, pity, benevolence, etc. . . . and maintained almost always," he continued, "in relation to everyone I met without distinction the aforesaid benevolent impulse; helping them, for instance, with useful advice, money, and things essential for life, such as food, letters of recommendation, etc."[33] On the other hand, he vowed to be merciless toward vanity and egoistic self-love, including his own, including all of the consequences of illusion, cruelty, artificiality, and so on nearly without end, which flow from those traits of character. "I still further intensified, in relation to all people coming in contact with me, my inner benevolence, but accompanied it by . . . remembering and, in conversations, deliberately manifesting, under a mask of serious irritation, the device I have practiced since the beginning of my aforesaid twenty-one year period of artificial life, and which I have summed up in the phrase: 'To quarrel ruthlessly with all manifestations dictated in people by the evil factor of vanity present in their being.'"[34]

To what end? Gurdjieff's response to this question is, at last, expressed nearly in the unelaborated language of everyday life: "the manifestation in human intercourse of a 'naked' relationship based on love, pity, trust, sympathy, etc., free from all kinds of evil conventions outwardly established in our life."[35]

Several months after Gurdjieff's death, Jeanne de Salzmann had occasion in London with a circle of his pupils to reflect on the very topics we have been exploring.

I would like to say a few words about Mr. Gurdjieff's way of teaching. Most of the misunderstandings and disagreements about Gurdjieff's methods and behavior come from the fact that he worked at the same time on our two natures.

On the one hand, Gurdjieff worked on our essence. He listened to our inner need with tireless patience and kindness, which hurt because we always felt unworthy. He took an interest in our difficulties. He gave practical help to take the next step. With unbelievable exactness he indicated the definite inner act that each had to carry out at the given moment to free himself further from his automatism. Here there was on Gurdjieff's part never any acting, and no pressure. This was truly a gift from above, which left the impression of love and compassion for the human condition. He made us feel our possibilities, our potential and, with the means he gave, he brought the hope of seeing them grow.

On the other hand, Gurdjieff worked on our functions in a relentless way—continual pressure, greater and greater demands, putting us in horrible situations, shocks of all kinds. Not only did he not attract us but, in pushing us to extreme limits, he forced us to resist him, to react against him. And he did this without mercy.

Here was the grandeur of Gurdjieff. The first way, work on our essence, was outside life, wholly concentrated on inner action. The second, work on our functions, was in life itself and through life. With one hand he called us; with the other he beat us, showing us our slavery to our functions. Very few people had the chance to experience both sides. Yet it is impossible to understand Gurdjieff's methods or behavior without having received . . . both . . . aspects of his work.[36]

The Decades of a Teacher

A FEW YEARS AGO I had occasion to interview some of the sisters and brothers at the Monastero di Bose, located more than picturesquely in the foothills of the Italian Alps, for an article exploring their shared life and values and something of the personal histories that had brought them to the monastery.[1] One of the sisters spoke of visiting Bose when she was a university student of philosophy in a nearby city. She had had no intention of returning, but she returned and unexpectedly felt addressed to the core. In time, as she put it, she "joined the history" of that community, that intention toward a Christian mind and heart now two thousand years old. She had become certain that it was still new and at work there. Her words "joining the history" stayed with me. I can't imagine a better way to describe what occurs in the encounter with a teaching, its people and history, if the encounter is in some sense destined. One knows nothing or little from prior experience, yet a spark jumps the gap from one's privacy to that history, which gradually becomes one's own—nearly the history of one's extended family, through an instinctive process of adoption. One assumes its potential and risks, its blessings and burdens, and in years to come may carry a share of responsibility for its future. A further observation: one joins at a specific moment when much that has already occurred is like a fresco on the wall: colorful, full of instruction, fixed. But there are also living people all around one, teaching, sharing, stumbling, starting again, making demands, offering friendship, providing invitations to enter and find one's place. There are pots and pans and customs. For younger participants, the older men and women may be all that matters, the living reality. But in time they may raise their eyes to the fresco; what it conveys becomes important. When I was young, someone from whom I was learning hand over fist looked at me with interesting compassion and said, "You have no sense of relation with Gurdjieff at all, do you?" It was true, I didn't. I had no reason to look past my questioner and his generation.

Exploring Gurdjieff and his teaching from decade to decade, chapters two through six do not offer a comprehensive biography. The next round of significant biography may be written by scholar-authors equipped to work fluently with sources in Russia, Armenia, Georgia, Turkey, perhaps even Tibet; I hope so. For the three earliest periods—the decades of travel and search followed by years of teaching in Russia and slow migration to the West—I ask and respond to a very few key questions. For the Prieuré years, about which much has already been well and thoroughly written, there remain topics to explore anew: Gurdjieff's talks setting the tone and adjusting course; the life of direct practice of the teaching, music, and dance; the texture of incidents; the idea of school that outlasted the Prieuré and remains an adaptable model. In retrospect, the Prieuré is the paradigmatic place and time, only sometimes an Eden but a garden all the same, in which the development of Gurdjieff's teaching in the West has its roots.

Gurdjieff in the 1930s has not, I think, been fully understood. It was a period of loss with no promise of better to come, but it was not only that. The Prieuré was gone, most of Gurdjieff's formerly close associates were out of touch, he had few though strikingly gifted pupils in Paris, his visits to America were unsettling, and he himself could often seem, and be, irritable. On the other hand he shared life with those few gifted pupils, and they in turn recorded on a daily basis their experience with him. Was he aware of the undeclared enterprise of multiple Boswells who shuttled from meetings and meals to set down what sometimes seems his every word and gesture? A small circle of women whom Gurdjieff called "the Rope," as if they were scaling a mountain and tied to one another, were so attuned to him that they spoke his language when with him—his Russo-English—and recorded his language with unfailing fidelity. Those years were their *kairos*, their time of irretrievable insight and beauty, and they knew it. The records they created were an instinctive combat with the passage of time. Once Gurdjieff described the remarkable Solita Solano as an "*antiquaire* for the future"—a dealer in antiques for the future; it was perhaps a sign that he knew, after all, what they were up to.[2] The result of their efforts was a vivid record of a teacher sometimes in anguish but always giving. From what we know of those years, hard as they were, much of Gurdjieff's teaching can be regenerated as almost brutally incarnate: to be lived without compromise.

Where the 1940s are concerned, we will pay close attention. The themes there are the consolidation of a French group capable of inspiring others for decades to come; the postwar arrival of pupils from Great Britain and America; and for Gurdjieff himself, now aged, a detectable sense of fulfillment and ease after many ordeals. In the classic pattern of some older artists graced with lasting energy, he created a series of thirty-nine new Movements for the French pupils closest to him in these years, a mirror in dance of everything he cared for, all of the values and states of being he wished to convey.

Is there a mnemonic? No reduced formula can capture so much experience. But if there were a mnemonic, it would be something like: Russia, theory; Prieuré, practice; 1930s, loss; 1940s, fulfillment.

CHAPTER 2

Tibetan Tea Very Wise Creation

GURDJIEFF'S PREFERRED MEANS of travel was strictly organic. "Once in Russia I lived like a gypsy," he recalled. "I had horse, donkey, tent, friends. I make 20 or 30 kilometers one day, then stop rest two days. Only such travel is real. Then you know how is—you know if each place has two or three stones. Go this way from Paris to Turkestan and will complete education have." While on the topic, he took time to praise goats and donkeys: "I once go 300 kilometers on goat—special goat, special training; over the Pamirs to Kashmir. Donkey also good for difficult places. Donkey special psyche has. If not wish go, he will die first. You can beat, you can kill, if he not wish, not will do. But if you understand psyche and are friend with, then he will take from you all heaviness and go until he dies. Oh, many friends have I among donkeys."[1]

This preference goes some way—perhaps not very far—toward explaining why in later years he was unanimously considered by his pupils to be alarmingly dangerous behind the wheel. The transition from horses, goats, and donkeys to Citroëns was never quite completed. Adapting to the circumstances of European life in later years, Gurdjieff maintained his principles—as one of his pupils, George Adie, later the founder of an Australian group, makes clear: "Once, when I had to travel to Germany," Adie recalled, "I told Mr. Gurdjieff that I was planning to go by air. . . . He asked: 'Why fly? Why fly?' I was about to reply that it was faster and would save having to travel overnight, but . . . he came from a different direction altogether. He said: 'Go by train. You take your seat, there is the countryside, you look out, and you work.'"[2]

For Gurdjieff students and for readers well disposed toward his writings, there is no nagging question about the extent of Gurdjieff's decades of travel with his companions, the Seekers of Truth, in the Middle East, Central Asia, and North Africa. *Meetings with Remarkable Men* reflects experience across a vast geography, and *Beelzebub's Tales* and other texts obliquely enlarge that geography. The sacred dances or Movements presented to the public in 1923–1924 offer a parallel geography, with dances attributed to specific monasteries, temples, and brotherhoods primarily across Central Asia but also in the multiple worlds of Orthodox Christianity. To map the dances, insofar as possible, would be nearly to map the man, or at least his itinerary through a now lost landscape of religious practice and histories.

But *Meetings* is not a Michelin Guide to lost worlds. A young man wrote to me not long ago, asking how to visit the monasteries through which Gurdjieff had passed. There is no route. Fact and symbol blend in *Meetings* and other writings; travel in search is itself the dominant symbol of the book, and we all have unknown landscapes inside. Gurdjieff would sometimes wrap fine meanings in tall tales or run a line of hidden teaching through apparently straightforward story without bothering to signal where fact ends and symbol begins. It is also likely that he disguised the identities of some or all of his companions, and it is indisputably true that he refrained from revealing much that one senses behind what is revealed. With mixed results, authors have tried to track him through the years of search, but he didn't wish to be tracked, I believe because he was resolutely committed to starting again, to letting whatever he could offer as a teacher stand or fall on its merits. He did provide detail where he chose to do so—for example, river travel on the Amu Darya, which has its headwaters near the border of Afghanistan and Tajikistan, evoked with flair in quasi-cinematic detail as if he were a self-assured nineteenth-century Russian author of travel adventure. But the Sarmoung monastery in a remote part of Central Asia, where he writes that he spent crucial years: Does it or did it exist? Is it a composite of several centers of knowledge and practice? Is it marked on some map somewhere? All such questions have led critics to ask if he actually traveled where he said he did, and to cast doubt.

Some of his pupils have also asked, though with love. In conversation with members of the Rope in the 1930s, the topic somehow turned toward the story in *Meetings* about painting lowly sparrows to resemble canaries and selling them in the street market to earn money for expensive books. "Sparrow I know like myself," Gurdjieff said with surprising tenderness. Alice Rohrer, one of that circle, responded: "Yes, you used to paint them to resemble canaries. I always wondered if that were true or a fable like the ladder in the desert. Stilts in sand and ladder." She was referring to a memorable symbolic episode in *Meetings*. Gurdjieff resumed, "No, those stories true, only ten percent is fantasy. That reminds me how I suffer when Soloviev died. For three months I was not myself. Such friend was—more than brother. I love him more than a mistress."[3] Soloviev's story in *Meetings* is one of the most touching, though a reader might legitimately wonder what is fiction and what fact in the tale, ultimately tragic, of a man who rose from degradation to become more than a brother. But here, in privacy among just a few people, Gurdjieff speaks unmistakably of a man he knew and cared for. On another occasion with members of the Rope, he had much the same thing in mind: "If two people have lived a common aim together," he said, "they will always have a feeling of brotherly love, whether they love or hate each other, and nothing in family love can equal this feeling."[4]

One of the modest, cottage joys of people interested in Gurdjieff is to come across confirmations that he knew whom he knew, that he had been where he said he had been. Such windfalls are rare and not needed, but from time to time the wind blows. I cannot write "for example," as there are so few examples. One of the most distinguished figures in *Meetings* is Dean Borsh, senior priest in the cathedral town of Kars (today in eastern Turkey), who took young Gurdjieff under his wing to provide formal education at the cathedral school. Dean Borsh was a great friend of Gurdjieff's father, with whom he often held long conversations at day's end in the hearing, not accidentally, of the boy. If there is an antecedent for the conversations in *Beelzebub's Tales* between grandfather and grandson, it is this. But was there a Dean Borsh? Or someone otherwise named who played the crucial role of early mentor? Not long ago the death certificate, dated 1899, of archpriest Damian Yambrosievich Borshch, of the Kars military fortress cathedral, was discovered in an unlikely archive created by members of the Mormon Church with an interest in genealogy.[5] Such a find places a stabilizing pin, so to speak, on the map of Gurdjieff's early life and travel. The map won't blow away.

There is another pin to be placed gently. In character it is inconceivably serendipitous. Some years ago my wife and I joined a dear friend, throughout his career a librarian in Kathmandu and now a Buddhist monk, in his family village in the mountains rimming Kathmandu Valley. Our friend knew of our interest in music and organized a *pancha baja*, a five-piece traditional band, to play for us in a clearing just below his house. We had such a good time. It was lively dance music and in a little while some adolescent girls jumped in front of the band and danced. Apart from a few details, their dance was one that my wife and I had been learning in a Movements class in New York two weeks earlier. When we recovered, we reasoned that Gurdjieff must have traveled in Nepal, taken note of that dance with grand precision, and years later reconstituted it as part of the dance repertory at the Prieuré. There was a further implication: we were just seventy miles overland from the Tibetan border. If Gurdjieff had come this far—a point that looked to us inarguable—then surely he toiled on, into Tibet, or exited Tibet by way of Nepal and India.

We should look a little further into Gurdjieff's experience of Tibet as a proxy for all of his travel during the years of search. Tibet was the most distant and probably least accessible destination throughout those years, though Gurdjieff made it clear that travel in remote tribal regions of Central Asia was dangerous and called for a most knowing kind of personal diplomacy and cultural understanding. There are legends and hearsay about Gurdjieff in Tibet, unverifiable short of new archival discoveries; there is also sheer nonsense. But there are signs in his books and recorded conversation of direct experience and intimacy with Tibetan daily life.

In the later nineteenth century and into the twentieth, Tibet possessed unique prestige. Geopolitically, it was a focus of the "Great Game," the competition for influence in Central Asia between Czarist Russia and the British Raj. Among people interested in spirituality, it was often viewed as the homeland of sacred, initiatory knowledge. Both for political agents and for spiritual seekers, it was all but inaccessible: the world's highest mountains, a harsh environment through much of the year, and a protective government that barred the way—all this without even considering the language barrier. To reach Tibet and become the disciple of spiritually advanced lamas was the dream. Few could lay claim to doing so; some who laid claim were deceptive.

Helena Petrovna Blavatsky, the genuinely formidable Russian cofounder in 1875 of the Theosophical Society, said that she had reached Tibet; reliable biographers think it unlikely. Whether factually true or not, Madame Blavatsky (1831–1891) had set the agenda in certain respects for subsequent "seekers of truth," seekers of a valid and transformative understanding of, let's dare to say, all things under the sun. Gurdjieff seems to have been of two minds about her. I was walking once with Louise Goepfert March at the Rochester Folk Art Guild, which she had founded on a farm in the Finger Lakes region of New York State on the model of the Prieuré, with the added, more muted scent of the early craft-focused Bauhaus. We were speaking of Madame Blavatsky. "Mr. Gurdjieff said that she was almost right," Mrs. March offered. As it happened, we were passing the Guild's sheepfold filled with ewes and lambs. "Mr. Gurdjieff's favorite animal," she mused, "all sacrifice." To be almost right is quite an achievement. On the other hand, Gurdjieff told Orage at some point in the 1920s that "when he was twenty-one years old, he read the works of Madame Blavatsky and took her indications seriously. He traveled to every place she mentioned in *The Secret Doctrine*, but he found that nine out of ten of her references were false. This cost him years of effort and suffering."[6]

What then of Gurdjieff in Tibet? So far, we have one fragment of evidence: the dance in backcountry Nepal. There is another fragment, on which nothing definitive can be based, and yet . . . At the Prieuré in 1929, Gurdjieff asked Alexandre de Salzmann to repaint the Monks' Corridor at the top of the house. It was a long hall giving access to small living quarters right and left occupied by residents, including Katherine Mansfield in her time. Jeanne de Salzmann's husband, Alexandre, was a well-known artist and theater designer associated for years with the German magazine *Jugend*, an arbiter of taste before World War I, and with Émile Jaques-Dalcroze, founder of the Dalcroze school of music, which is still well represented in Western cities.[7] The colors Gurdjieff chose for the hallway were the crimson and saffron yellow of Tibetan monks' robes. "These are the most beautiful colors," he commented to Salzmann.[8]

Some years ago when the Prieuré was uninhabited and abandoned (it is now renovated as residential apartments), my wife and I with two friends broke into it as gracefully as possible and toured what remained. We are not housebreakers; this was a must. The Monks' Corridor was a strange sight: curled tongues of heavy white paint, dating I suppose to years when the Prieuré had become a home for the elderly, transformed the space from one end to the other into something better suited to an amusement park, a little house of horrors. Curious, we snapped off curls of paint for a better view of whatever lay underneath. At the wainscot level we uncovered two colors side by side: crimson and saffron yellow. Salzmann had used a fresco technique; integrated with the plaster walls, his colors had survived. This is indirect evidence, I know, hardly evidence at all—but it's an odd thing, isn't it?

"Tibetan tea very wise creation," Gurdjieff said to members of the Rope as he served them. "From centrum come and little by little through the ages man learn about this. Two days boil bones of yak, put in grains of wheat and butter. All is here what man needs."[9] The signs are that he served a modified version—few yak bones in Paris—but everyone enjoyed the tea. From the centrum? Occasionally Gurdjieff used this expression, indicating that whatever it was (food, customs, values) originated long ago and far away, in the beginning, before humanity lost its way. Though the word *centrum* seems Latinate, the source is as likely to be Armenian *kentron*—center. However that may be, the expression breathes Gurdjieff's nostalgia for a remote world and era of wiser men and women. As well, it conveys the tacit message that there is something central in human experience that must not be betrayed. Mircea Eliade, the outstanding historian of religions, often used the expression *in illo tempore*—at that time, in that primordial era when sound knowledge of how to be and what to do prevailed. It means the same.

Cooking interested Gurdjieff throughout his life. He prepared meals for his pupils many thousands of times, always on the basis of Caucasian, Russian, and Asian cuisines. Shopping for ingredients and food preparation were grounded physical activities, surely welcome for that reason alone. They were also preface to a ceremony: sharing food at Gurdjieff's table.

At some point in the 1920s in Paris there was a cook-off, a friendly competition between Gurdjieff and the Romanian sculptor

Constantin Brancusi—famous among his friends as a host and cook—with the poet Ezra Pound serving on an improvised panel of ravenous judges. It seems unimaginable, doesn't it, but the event is well documented; Brancusi probably visited the Prieuré, enjoyed a meal there, and one thing led to another. Pound later wrote to a friend that Gurdjieff would have fared better in Paris, or at least with him, had he stuck to cooking.[10]

"There is such custom about food," Gurdjieff once said of Tibet. "Each day of year is for one special dish. Only next year can you repeat, not next month, if you are . . . educate man who can compose something different."[11] He had also experienced physical challenges that only a person thoroughly determined to be at length in the region could report. Again speaking with members of the Rope:

> He tells how he used to have to butter his whole body, then cover with rubber underdrawers (made in Germany) then over all about 6 inches thickness of fur garments—and even then he was cold in Tibet—only part of body have satisfaction was face under hood, warmed by breath. Such cold you never can imagine. Also such smell . . . after many week! One other very cold place he stayed for whole winter—was in the Pamirs. There live under snow—have houses under snow and even tunnel connecting each house like streets—and so cold was that when you lit fire, the solid snow ceiling melted just an instant then froze over immediately.[12]

Such memories one doesn't invent. Nor, I suppose, Gurdjieff's brief remark that he was wounded by a "stray bullet" in Tibet in 1902, his life saved by three European and two Tibetan doctors who must have been immediately at hand.[13] In Paris once, in the hammam, or steam bath, where Gurdjieff periodically liked to convene with some of his pupils, he and the war veteran François Grunwald inventoried their scars; they were not imaginary.[14]

Though there is more table conversation touching on Tibet, as well as references dating as far back as 1918 to Tibetan dishes Gurdjieff prepared, there is no need to rehearse it all. There are just two further points worth considering here. Gurdjieff in the *Tales* distinguishes Tibetan religion from Buddhism elsewhere and describes it as a renewal of Buddhism realized by "Saint Lama"— in reference to Padmasambhava, the eighth-century teacher who brought Buddhism to Tibet. This must be a sign of unreserved respect. Gurdjieff's Beelzebub reports that he happened to be in Tibet at the time of what he calls the "charming 'military expedition,'" the Younghusband expedition of 1903–1904, which reached Lhasa from India at the cost of many Tibetan lives.[15] What Beelzebub recounts about the deliberations of Tibetan leaders—to resist, to kill, or for religious reasons to allow unhindered passage to the intruders—strikes me as eyewitness, though of course I don't know if that is actually so. Further, Beelzebub recounts the death by gunfire, accidental or intended, of the foremost lama of the era, with dreadful consequences for the transmission of unique knowledge to the next generation. It is among the darkest passages in the *Tales*.

Gurdjieff's years as a seeker of truth in remote parts of the world had very considerable scale, very considerable danger, and led to results still unfolding in generations of participants in the teaching who joined its history too late to know him directly. Something of that scale is allusively reflected in a memory he shared with the Rope "about great bird migrations. . . . Tonight he was describing an oasis . . . which was part in sand and part 'on continent,' . . . somewhere between Tibet and China. Birds passing south—'from summer house'—must stop and rest in this oasis because after it there is no resting place for a long time. Here one can see every kind of bird—a most beautiful place. If you shoot in air 'bird flow down.'"[16] I have that impression of his travels: without shots being fired, bird flow down.

CHAPTER 3

The First Exposition:
Russia 1912–1917

THERE HADN'T REALLY BEEN a Gurdjieff literature until the publication in 1949 of P. D. Ouspensky's In Search of the Miraculous: Fragments of an Unknown Teaching, followed within months by Gurdjieff's own Beelzebub's Tales to His Grandson. Both had been read privately for years. Late in life Gurdjieff had heard chapters from Ouspensky's book and welcomed it—"I hear myself speaking"—while Ouspensky had resisted Gurdjieff's Tales in typescript, as he had resisted and distanced the man himself since the mid-1920s. Their relations were complex; several authors have done everything possible to clarify.[1] But our topic here is Ouspensky's Fragments, a genuinely brilliant exposition of the Gurdjieff teaching as first offered in Russia, in the context of the gathering confusion and eventual violence of Russian life just before and during World War I.

The Gurdjieff teaching is an integrated pattern of ideas, practices, purposes, dances, music, literature, and sustained inquiry. But this is a list, and a teaching is not a list. Try again. The Gurdjieff teaching lives only when there is fresh experience, insight, and (when needed) statement from day to day. It is constantly being lost, and with good fortune found again, by men and women through several generations who have lived it as fully as proved possible for them. Whatever light they possess in their own lives and offer to others owes much to the teaching and ultimately to Gurdjieff himself, whether or not they studied with him in his lifetime. As a reader, you won't have missed the fact that thus far I have not much concerned myself with "expounding" the teaching and, apart from certain pages, that will remain so. I take the risk, I think safe, that the teaching is evident in every reported exchange, every incident in these pages and needs no restatement—for the most part story can remain story, the flash of insight can remain a flash. There are many sustained expositions of the Gurdjieff teaching, Ouspensky's the noblest and most deeply intelligent among them—although his term *fragments* is accurate: not all of the teaching is in his pages. What is there has proved enough to kindle lives—and many other books. From another perspective it has been a quarry, and every stone raised it and placed elsewhere remains recognizable.

Gurdjieff in the Russian years is a systematic lecturer. How surprising, because we already know something of his temperament, of the coexistence in him of Pythagoras and Diogenes, high knowledge but also disruption "for the sake of Heaven," as Martin Buber's nineteenth-century rabbis might have said. Yet in the small private circles with which he met in Moscow and St. Petersburg, he is all but professorial, the expositor of a complex and largely unknown vision of the human condition, of our unexplored resources and possible path, of our place in the cosmic scheme. Ouspensky himself, already a seasoned author and cultural journalist at the time he met Gurdjieff in the winter of 1915, had a professorial cast: he practiced a closely reasoned, clean art of writing, not a word in excess. Because *Fragments* is Ouspensky's account, noted down later, of Gurdjieff's exposition over a period of several years, the question can be asked: Was Ouspensky's professorial decorum transferred in his pages to Gurdjieff, who had some other way, perhaps more dramatic, of presenting material? That doesn't seem to be so. Ouspensky said of Gurdjieff that he "liked his manner of speaking, which was careful and precise"; the care and precision of the exposition in *Fragments* must be the result of two caring and precise thinkers, Gurdjieff as teacher, Ouspensky as inquirer.[2] What is attractive and memorable, among other traits of this first exposition, is Gurdjieff's ease and timing. His characteristic intensity is there, of course, but he takes evident delight in the harmony and depth of ideas, their mutual fit, the light they shed across from one to the other—and the receptivity of his small audiences on the eve of revolution. Ouspensky proved able to duplicate Gurdjieff's timing by opening a topic, carrying it some distance, then letting it go until pages later, often at some distance, where the topic reappears. In later years Gurdjieff thought it best to leave the table a little hungry, not replete—leave the last bite, he advised, and to a particularly insistent pupil he advised leaving the next to last bite. Ouspensky's version of the first exposition has something of that character.

The book is theory, by and large. Its emphasis is a sequence of ideas, though Ouspensky and others meeting with Gurdjieff in Moscow and St. Petersburg undertook practices proposed in the course of those meetings; their reports on their experiences are part of the fabric of the book. Some readers encounter the book as nothing short of an epiphany; it reveals them to themselves in an entirely new light, clarifies the underlying causes of their sufferings, and shows a way forward. Other readers, naturally, look elsewhere for inspiration—this isn't a history they will join. And still others over the years have exploited certain elements in the book, while disregarding much else, to ridicule the teaching. We might look more closely at the first and third types of readers; the second has already gone elsewhere.

For readers who feel thoroughly addressed, *Fragments* is a feast of new ideas and self-recognitions. Who are such readers? Of many kinds, but Gurdjieff did point to a shared characteristic:

There is one general rule for everybody. In order to approach this system seriously, people must be *disappointed*, first of all in themselves, that is to say, in their powers, and secondly in all the old ways. . . . If he is a scientist he should be disappointed in science. If he is a religious man he should be disappointed in his religion. If he is a politician he should be disappointed in politics. . . . But you must understand what this means. I say for instance that a religious man should be disappointed in religion. This does not mean that he should lose his faith. On the contrary, it means . . . realizing that the religious teaching he knows is not enough for him, can lead him nowhere. . . . A man must be sufficiently disappointed in ordinary ways and he must at the same time think or be able to accept the idea that there may be something—somewhere.[3]

It calls for a degree of moral daring to recognize that disappointment; to do so is a step forward—but toward what? In response the Gurdjieff teaching offers not reassurances but life-giving challenges among fellow seekers—for one has taken a step, however instinctively, toward becoming a deliberate seeker. All that is active and inquiring, that longs to live more fully, can flow into that identity. It isn't a new boundary, a new ego style or doctrine, a new assertion replacing broken assertions—although it can be any or all of those things if one isn't careful. It is a birth of purpose that concerns "one's whole mass," to use a good Gurdjieffian term in *Fragments*.[4] This is one of Gurdjieff's most compelling offers to thoughtful men and women: to become a seeker, increasingly experienced, deeper year by year, and—why not?—more knowingly sensitive to others year by year, and this for a lifetime.

In later writings and conversation, Gurdjieff would endow this quality of disappointment, or disillusion as he would also say, with unshakable dignity. Important at the beginning, it remains important to the end. In *Beelzebub's Tales*, he refers more than once to "old and honorable beings who had had a great deal of experience and in consequence had become disillusioned about everything that ordinary planetary existence could in general give them. And owing to this, they had fewer properties such as 'egoism,' 'vanity,' and so on."[5] Elsewhere in the *Tales*, he speaks of certain people who "had not yet acquired enough experience to be convinced that their dreams—ensuing from that abnormal education of theirs—could never be realized, and they were therefore not disillusioned enough to be fully impartial and just."[6] Initial disappointment with oneself and with what life has so far offered can transmute over time into good judgment, centrally useful to oneself and others.

I am temporarily at sea about how further to speak of *Fragments*. To inventory its ideas, even in short versions, is wearisome—there are too many—and shallow. Many I's, mechanicality, sleep and awakening, three centers, the need for self-observation from moment to moment, the struggle between yes and no, the distinction between personality and essence—all of this and much more is extraordinary when thoughtfully assimilated, but as a superficially annotated list it has no power. Better to read *Fragments* than a list. But there is a promising middle position: to think through just one major idea in the first exposition and in that way hear Gurdjieff's voice in those years.

The notion of "being" in mainstream Western culture is vague and incidental. It hasn't much weight of its own, while the notion of knowledge is clear and vast: knowledge is every sound thought in our minds, it is the object of scientific and humanistic research, it is preserved in libraries and now in media of new kinds, it is shared through words and images. When we speak of R & D, research and development, we are not speaking of the research and development of being—which is a reasonable though mischievous way to state the purpose of the Gurdjieff teaching. What an immense disproportion between the term *being*, to which scant specific meaning attaches, and the term that dominates our civilization.

In *Fragments* (and later writings of his own) Gurdjieff gives new meaning to *being* and relates it to knowledge in a way that remains deeply interesting. His first reflections on being appear early in *Fragments*: "Our starting point is that man does not know himself, that he *is not* . . ., that is, he is not what he can and what he should be."[7] In the emphasis on "is not," the force of thoughts in later pages is foreshadowed. In his own voice, restated by Ouspensky, what follows is the core of his thinking and by far the longest quotation in this book—for which apologies if necessary.

There are two lines along which man's development proceeds, the line of *knowledge* and the line of *being*. In right evolution the line of knowledge and the line of being develop simultaneously, parallel to, and helping one another. But if the line of knowledge gets too far ahead of the line of being, or if the line of being gets ahead of the line of knowledge, man's development goes wrong, and sooner or later it must come to a standstill.

People understand what "knowledge" means. And they understand the possibility of different levels of knowledge. They understand that knowledge may be lesser or greater, that is to say, of one quality or of another quality. But they do not understand this in relation to "being." "Being," for them, means simply "existence" to which is opposed just "nonexistence." They do not understand that being or existence may be of very different levels and categories. Take for instance the being of a mineral and of a plant. It is a different being. The being of a plant and of an animal is again a different being. . . . But the being of two people can differ from one another more than the being of a mineral and of an animal. This is exactly what people do not understand. And they do not understand that *knowledge* depends on *being*. Not only do they not understand this latter but they definitely do not wish to understand it. And especially in Western culture it is considered that a man may possess great knowledge, for example he may be an able scientist, make discoveries, advance science, and at the same time he may be, and has the right to be, a petty, egoistic, caviling, mean, envious, vain, naive, and absentminded man. . . .

And yet it is his being. And people think that his knowledge does not depend on his being. People of Western culture put great value on the level of a man's knowledge but they do not value the level of a man's being and are not ashamed of the low level of their own being. They do not even understand what it means. And they do not understand that a man's knowledge depends on the level of his being.

If knowledge gets far ahead of being, it becomes theoretical and abstract and inapplicable to life, or actually harmful, because instead of serving life and helping people the better to struggle with the difficulties they meet, it begins to complicate man's life, brings new difficulties into it, new troubles and calamities which were not there before.

The reason for this is that knowledge which is not in accordance with being cannot be large enough for, or sufficiently suited to, man's real needs. It will always be a knowledge of *one thing* together with ignorance of *another thing*; a knowledge of the *detail* without a knowledge of the *whole*; a knowledge of the *form* without a knowledge of the *essence*.

Such preponderance of knowledge over being is observed in present-day culture. The idea of the value and importance of the level of being is completely forgotten. And it is forgotten that the level of knowledge is determined by the level of being. Actually at a given level of being the possibilities of knowledge are limited and finite. Within the limits of a given being the *quality* of knowledge cannot be changed, and the accumulation of information of one and the same nature, within already known limits, alone is possible. A change in the nature of knowledge is possible only with a change in the nature of being.

Taken in itself, a man's being has many different sides. The most characteristic feature of a modern man is the *absence of unity in him* and, further, the absence in him of even traces of those properties which he most likes to ascribe to himself, that is, "lucid consciousness," "free will," a "permanent ego or I," and the "ability to do." It may surprise you if I say that the chief feature of a modern man's being which explains *everything else that is lacking in him* is *sleep*.

A modern man lives in sleep, in sleep he is born and in sleep he dies. About sleep, its significance and its role in life, we will speak later. But at present just think of one thing, what *knowledge* can a sleeping man have? And if you think about it and at the same time remember that sleep is the chief feature of our being, it will at once become clear to you that if a man really wants knowledge, he must first of all think about how to wake, that is, about how to change his *being*. . . .

Generally speaking, the *balance* between knowledge and being is even more important than a separate development of either one or the other. And a separate development of knowledge or of being is not desirable in any way. . . .

The development of the line of knowledge without the line of being gives a *weak yogi*, . . . that is to say, a man who knows a great deal but can do nothing, a man who *does not understand* . . . what he knows, a man without *appreciation*, that is, a man for whom there is no difference between one kind of knowledge and another. And the development of the line of being without knowledge gives a *stupid saint*, that is, a man who can do a great deal but who does not know what to do or with what object; and if he does anything he acts in obedience to his subjective feelings which may lead him greatly astray and cause him to commit grave mistakes, that is, actually to do the opposite of what he wants. In either case both the weak yogi and the stupid saint are brought to a standstill. Neither the one nor the other can develop further. . . .

Knowledge by itself does not give understanding. Nor is understanding increased by an increase of knowledge alone. Understanding depends upon the relation of knowledge to being. Understanding is the resultant of knowledge and being. And knowledge and being must not diverge too far, otherwise understanding will prove to be far removed from either. At the same time the relation of knowledge to being does not change with a mere growth of knowledge. It changes only when being grows simultaneously with knowledge. In other words, understanding grows only with the growth of being.

In ordinary thinking, people do not distinguish understanding from knowledge. They think that greater understanding depends on greater knowledge. Therefore they accumulate knowledge, or that which they call knowledge, but they do not know how to accumulate understanding and do not bother about it.[8]

It is a classic exposition that would be at home in any and every serious assessment of the human condition and our larger possibilities. Without mentioning the word, it is in part a discourse on conscience. That Gurdjieff—the man from the Caucasus, the man from nowhere—expresses it should not be permitted to prejudice or deafen one's hearing. There is an interesting question: To whom does this apply? I remember once saying with passion to an outstanding teacher of the Gurdjieff material that I willingly apply it to myself but draw the line at my father: he was exempt, so to speak. He lived by whatever light he had gained in long years, in time he would die, and as far as I was concerned he would go directly to heaven or a closely comparable destination without having wrestled with the issues raised by teachings that look beneath the surface of human experience. In other words, this fundamental teaching about knowledge and being applies to oneself.

There is a similar question. Gurdjieff sets a high standard here through a rigorous central teaching extended by haunting nuances. What, for example, is a man "without appreciation"? One may feel addressed by those words with something of the force of Baudelaire's lacerating call from his person to ours: "*Hypocrite lecteur,— mon semblable,—mon frère!*"—hypocritical reader, so like me, my brother. But still, aren't we all grateful to hear of new, worthwhile knowledge even if we happen to learn that its discoverer is unpleasant or odd? Knowledge breaks free from its origin. It has its own defenses.

The conclusion from both of these brief discussions is that the ideas of the Gurdjieff teaching, and of any valid teaching, are not weapons to be leveled at others, not new and more potent means of dismissing or judging others. They are for one's own use, and one of their most valuable results can be greater compassion and understanding of the dilemmas we all share. The Ladder of Divine Ascent, a vivid Christian icon based on the early medieval writings of St. John Climacus, is a ladder from earth to heaven crowded with monks, some of whom—even toward the top of the ladder when heaven is in sight—fall off into the waiting hands of devils. That teachings can undo a person has been clear for a very long time. That they can give new birth to a person has also been clear.

The other topic of the first exposition recorded by Ouspensky concerns universal law and cosmology. In the Russian years and later, Gurdjieff offered a vision of humanity immersed in a vast pattern of mutual dependency—an ecology reaching across all things and creatures on earth and upward through many levels to an ultimate which he chose in the Russian years to name, abstractly, the Absolute. In later years *Beelzebub's Tales* restates the cosmology in terms again of a universe of many levels, presided over by an infinitely powerful God who is nonetheless burdened with sorrow owing largely to the abuses of certain of his creatures. Remaining intact from the Russian exposition into the later writings are what

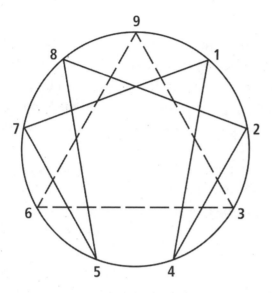

Fig. 1: The enneagram. *Source*: Jim Kendrick

Gurdjieff calls the Law of Three and the Law of Seven and key ideas such as the three foods—physical nourishment, air, impressions, and their digestion. A further idea important from start to finish was Neoplatonic and Gnostic in origin and recurrent in some later schools of thought: man the microcosm, endowed with the order and energies of the macrocosm, from which follows the familiar formula "As above, so below" and Gurdjieff's admonition, recorded in *Fragments*, that the study of the universe begins with the study of oneself.

In the Russian period there was a wealth of diagrams and numerical calculation. The geometry of what we are and where we live, the numerical values of what we are and where we live, offered fascinating material to Gurdjieff's circle, many of whom were acquainted with somewhat similar material in Theosophy. From this wealth of diagrams and calculations, in later years Gurdjieff retained just one "object," the enneagram, a linear pattern inscribed in a circle with nine points of contact on the circumference (see fig. 1), to which corresponds a so-called cyclic number, 142857, plus the circumferential points 3, 6, and 9. Multiply the cyclic number by 2 through 6, and you'll see that the integers shift position—for example, multiplication by 2 yields 285714—while multiplication by 7 ends the cycle by generating 999999. Though Gurdjieff made no claim to have originated the enneagram—he encountered it somewhere in Central Asia—it became the enduring emblem of the teaching. Both the geometric pattern inscribed on the dance floor and the cyclic number itself are the basis for dynamic and often very beautiful dances, challenging for "one's whole mass"—body, feeling, and mind.

This intellectual material—the diagrams and the concepts to which they give pattern, the numerical, Pythagorean approach to what we are and where we live—has remained an engaging study for participants in the Gurdjieff teaching equipped with scientific or mathematical training or an inclination toward that mode of inquiry.[9] Key elements of the psychological teaching are mapped into certain diagrams—for example, in the diagram of the "three-story factory" showing the role of consciousness in the digestion of the food of impressions received and the refinement of emotional perception. Gurdjieff himself in later years, as noted earlier, recast much of this material in certain chapters of *Beelzebub's Tales*: no diagrams any longer, but all the conceptual complexity you could possibly wish.

I am well aware that by now I have lost many readers. What is all this material, what is or was its necessity? Is it a Pythagorean dream? Is it a visionary science that intersects with standard science not at all, or only a little? This much is clear: it is infinitely irritating to critics who come upon the material without some knowledge of its long history in the West and therefore without tolerance for a mode of inquiry that may be "other" but is endowed nonetheless with internal consistency and the dignity of asking great, perhaps insoluble questions. On occasion this current in Western thought has produced marvels, for example the diagrams of Robert Fludd (1574–1637), which are Gurdjieffian through and through—or rather, vice versa. We are drawing near to an important point. The psychology of man's possible evolution[10] has its basis in acute observation. Gurdjieff's account of the human condition as we are and might become is "inspired common sense"— so one of his American pupils, Dr. William Welch, was apt to say. In many of its dimensions, though not all, it isn't occult or esoteric (choose your least favorite word) unless one adopts the point of view that the esoteric begins abruptly where one's own understanding ends. The psychology proposed by Gurdjieff is progressively subject to observation in oneself and through pooling observations with others; it is a matter for sustained inquiry and self-inquiry. Yet there is an issue all the same. The Gurdjieff teaching, and I believe any valid and comprehensive teaching, leads in two directions: toward experience of what we are from surface to depth and toward lucidity and service in relation to other human beings and the world at large.

What are the limits of the inner life? For the anonymous fourteenth-century author of *The Cloud of Unknowing*, a perfectly stunning guide to progressive exploration of the inner life, the diligent and fortunate seeker comes upon zones of experience that can only be described metaphorically, by wise allusions that kindle recognitions and inspire further search. Gurdjieff's choice in the first Russian exposition was to approach those zones of possible experience in part through what may seem brittle, intellectual means: diagrams, number sequences. But the topic is precisely the same. Hence the lasting interest of the materials and concepts. Further, they do not represent a closed system: among the five "obligatory being-strivings" formulated in *Beelzebub's Tales*, the third is "to strive to know ever more and more about the laws of world-creation and world-maintenance."[11] There is identical, open-ended counsel in one of the aphorisms decoratively painted on the walls and ceiling of the Study House at the Prieuré: "Take the understanding of the East and the knowledge of the West—and then seek."[12]

There is one further point to consider. I mentioned earlier that Gurdjieff's Russian circle would have been familiar with Theosophy, the leading alternative perspective in those years and, further, that Madame Blavatsky's travels, real and alleged, and her introduction in the West of Hindu and Buddhist ideas, set some part of the agenda for seekers of truth in her era. Johanna Petsche, an Australian scholar-author, has admirably initiated the first thorough study of the parallels between Gurdjieff in Russia and Theosophy.[13] From one point of view, Gurdjieff in those years was opportunistic: Theosophy was his listeners' point of departure; he could weave some of his own thinking around that. From another point of view, Theosophy was the *lingua franca* of alternative thinking in that era: however much Gurdjieff modified and radically added to Theosophical thinking and above all insisted on direct practice as the sole means of personal evolution, he did demonstrably value some ideas and atmospheres found earlier in the writings of Madame Blavatsky and her associates. He was not a Theosophist; nonetheless he owed Theosophy a debt. Years later as he conceived *Beelzebub's Tales*, Madame Blavatsky was not entirely absent. It is as if he were saying to her, though no one heard except her, "More like this, Madame."

CHAPTER 4

Sonnez Fort: The Prieuré 1922–1932

"VEGETABLES—TWO KINDS THERE ARE," Gurdjieff reminisced a decade and more after the Prieuré had closed. "One kind slowly grow, others like cress and mustard . . . can grow in one night or two, three days, such very green ones. For feast days we used to plant in dishes of black clay the night before and next day put on table before guests to eat while growing. You remember at Prieuré, Miss Gordon? Ah, such feasts we had Easter! You must remember all your life. Who was not there miss too much." To which Miss Gordon replied in proper Russo-English: "There was also other end of stick." And Gurdjieff in response: "Of course—all great things must have two such end of stick."[1] The master of the Prieuré missed it, though he wasn't one often to look back. The residents, his students, also had warm memories but couldn't disregard the hardships. And Gurdjieff himself didn't hesitate to acknowledge the other end of the stick, which fell as much and more on him than on any of the pupils. "Every stick has two ends" was one of his most familiar proverbs; it explains nearly everything.

The journey from Russia, collapsing in on itself, to safe haven in France took nearly five years. There were many stops along the way, at some of which gifted new pupils joined the circle around Gurdjieff, who was accompanied throughout by his wife, Julia Osipovna Ostrovsky. Most significantly for the future, Gurdjieff left Russia with Thomas and Olga de Hartmann: he an exquisitely trained and already well-known composer, she a young woman of aristocratic background and connections who spoke several Western European languages. She served for years as Gurdjieff's trusted secretary and, in effect, executive director; he collaborated with Gurdjieff to produce a large and deeply impressive body of music for Movements and for piano solo. P. D. Ouspensky and his wife, Sophie Grigorievna, joined Gurdjieff at several points along the way, most notably at Essentuki (a Caucasian town known for its mineral baths), later in what was then still called Constantinople (now Istanbul), and intermittently at the Prieuré. A year-long stopping point, the multicultural city of Tiflis, brought Gurdjieff into contact with Alexandre and Jeanne de Salzmann, whom we have already encountered. Alexandre's father had been one of the leading architects of Tiflis the city was a natural place for them to see through World War I and its aftermath, when the Dalcroze Institute near Dresden was no longer able to keep its doors open. One further person in Tiflis joined the circle around Gurdjieff and became a lead dancer in the troupe he brought to America: Olgivanna Hinzenberg, a Montenegrin national, later the wife of the American architect Frank Lloyd Wright.[2] One year on, in Constantinople, others joined the history then so new and at risk, among them J. G. Bennett, an English intelligence officer and born seeker of truth, as well as Tcheslaw Tchekhovitch, the professional wrestler and circus strongman who in very late years wrote a touching account of his decades with Gurdjieff. Around each of the people mentioned there proved to be a powerful destiny, a garland sometimes heavy sometimes light, and nearly all had a notable impact on the Gurdjieff teaching as it found its bearings and developed in the West.

Were there not an impressive literature about these years of forced migration—Essentuki, Tiflis, Constantinople, Berlin, Dresden, and at last Paris and its region—we would need to look more closely.[3] In light of that literature, only one point strikes me as essential here: the transition to direct practice of the teaching at Essentuki. There Gurdjieff established a communal home and over a six-week period taught and modeled new means of individual developmental work and an unfamiliar way of life in common. It was the future Prieuré in miniature. With his keen-minded appreciation of theory, Ouspensky was acutely aware of the change. He and his fellow pupils were learning complex exercises for attention and self-awareness, some calling for considerable physical mastery; work on Movements had begun, though that term for the sacred dances and exercises would only come into use a few years later in Paris; and everyone had house duties—Olga, who had perhaps never swept a floor or sewn a button, like them all quickly learned to be self-sufficient and of service to the community. North American participants in the Gurdjieff teaching knew her well in her older years. A treasure from days long past, she was a fine-boned, small woman with the quickness of a bird and the firm views that nearly a century of life conferred. "From the first day," Olga wrote of Essentuki, "everyone had his work and his responsibilities to assume. In the evening we always had dinner at seven and Mr. Gurdjieff had the habit of walking around the table and telling us about his life when he was young and his travels through many strange countries. Afterwards we all went to our rooms and tried to write down our impressions. Mr. de Hartmann always tried to write down his impression in music."[4]

Essentuki is where the music began. It may be that de Hartmann was already working with Gurdjieff on music for the dance-drama *The Struggle of the Magicians*, which Gurdjieff had hoped to produce in Moscow; there are hauntingly beautiful musical fragments under that title.[5] But it's not stretching fact too far to say that the music began at Essentuki with the Essentuki Prayer, which became the hymn of the Institute and remains a statement of emotional truth known to virtually all participants in the Gurdjieff teaching. Its simple, melancholy melody can be hummed without difficulty. One hears in it a sense of loss—nearly everything material had been lost in the revolution—and an invitation to inwardness, to a place where the fullness of human experience can be known without words.

It is a remarkable composition, a lento providing all the time one may need to experience true feelings in a pure, uncluttered way. There is a Movement set to a more rhythmic version of the music, offering an experience of prayer in motion, prayer concentrated not sentimental. At the time you read these lines there are likely to be performances of both the music and the Movement on the Internet. It's never possible to vouch for the quality of offerings of that kind; in any case, they give some impression. It is a Movement that one wishes would never end, and its slow tempo suggests something approaching timelessness. But it does end and, as in many things Gurdjieffian, the taste one retains from participating is what most matters. It becomes part of what one knows life might be. This provides, I think, a more realistic understanding of "esotericism" than anything suggested by long robes, initiatory ceremonies, and such—all things that are the awkward baggage of that poor word, which makes so many thoughtful people stand back with the hope that the train will soon go by and leave us in peace. In the Gurdjieff teaching, and I'm sure in any valid teaching, the "esoteric" emerges as experience purifies and intensifies; it is paid for through efforts of attention and caring. As Gurdjieff would sometimes say in other connections, its appearance is "mathematic"—resulting naturally from appropriate approaches and efforts in favorable conditions. For that reason it is not strange; it is brighter and more felt, a zone of experience where for a time the clouds of unknowing part and one sees what it is to be more fully human. All of this Gurdjieff began to show in Essentuki, where theory passed into practice.

THE TAPESTRY OF LIFE AT THE PRIEURÉ

I can't help but see the Prieuré as an animated tapestry in which everything notable that happened continues on a miniature scale with undiminished conviction. Toward the center of the tapestry, the Study House with Gurdjieff's dance troupe still working through new Movements while Thomas de Hartmann at the upright piano listens as Gurdjieff picks out a melody and beats a rhythm to be elaborated then and there into a creatively harmonized composition. Such music . . . Once de Hartmann was so fed up with the process that he slammed down the keyboard lid and stormed off. But he came back. In the animated tapestry all of that is still under way. Elsewhere on the property the mighty Tchekhovitch is trying in vain with a team of men to fracture a huge boulder, Alexandre de Salzmann is secretly training the Institute's pigs to obey commands when politely expressed, Katherine Mansfield sits in a corner of the kitchen watching, and moved by, the relaxed intensity of life there, and at the far edge of the tapestry a boy sent on mission by Gurdjieff waits in a horse-drawn wagon under a tree for a temperamental man who had taken refuge in its branches from the community's insults. The project is to persuade him to return to the Prieuré and resume his role as a constant unintentional irritant around whom almost no one could remain calm and spiritual—oh no.

Gurdjieff and his companions reached Paris from Berlin on Bastille Day, 1922—the fourteenth of July—and through a providential encounter with an old friend found themselves invited that summer to make use of the Dalcroze studio on the Left Bank for rehearsals and costume construction. Gurdjieff must already have had in mind public performances of the Movements or at least performances for invited guests. Dispatched to find a suitable home for the Institute, Madame de Hartmann visited the Prieuré des Basses Loges in Fontainebleau-Avon and thought it just right. The manor house with outbuildings, formal landscaping, deep forested acreage, and overall a quality of modest nobility, had been neglected for some years; there would be work to do. But the house was furnished, life could begin at once. Gurdjieff accepted Madame de Hartmann's judgment sight unseen, arranged a lease and later a mortgage-based purchase, and moved in with his small circle, soon considerably expanded (see fig. 2).

P. D. Ouspensky, established since 1921 in London and rapidly accepted among thoughtful people as a most interesting man, was crucially important to Gurdjieff at this time. He was giving public lectures on the Gurdjieff teaching in his steady, appealing, somewhat professorial style, attended by men and women of influence who belonged to varied worlds—literary, Theosophical, commercial, medical. Alfred R. Orage met the Gurdjieff teaching through Ouspensky, as did his younger friend Katherine Mansfield and many others who decided, with Ouspensky's decisive agreement, to register as students at the Institute and give it a try. Initial financing for the Institute also came through Ouspensky's connections in London. Who lived at the Institute in those early years? Those who migrated with Gurdjieff from Russia and other stops along the way; a considerable number of impoverished Russian exiles who found their way to the Prieuré and relied on Gurdjieff's generosity; a wave of English participants prepared by Ouspensky; and soon Americans drawn by Gurdjieff and Orage's talks and the public Movements demonstrations of winter-spring 1924 in several American cities. While there was mockery and distortion in some British newspapers—a kind of Hallowe'en rattle of derision and fright—Ouspensky in London, respectable and respected, was the counterbalance. There was no parallel "translator" in France, and no native French apart from Jeanne de Salzmann. Some years more were needed for French participants to find their way to the Gurdjieff teaching.

What was it like to take leave of one's daily life, at least for a time, to become a resident of the Institute? Though Orage sold his stake in *The New Age*, the leading literary journal of its time, and shocked some friends and colleagues by leaving for Fontainebleau, those who knew him best couldn't miss the consistency with his earlier interests in Nietzsche, Theosophy, and speculative cosmology: he was a man in search. His reflections at that time were altogether in character—clear, worldly, brilliant without showiness. "There are men in London," he once said, "who are already as 'clever' as it is

Fig 2: The Prieuré des Basses Loges at Fontainebleau-Avon.
Source: The Gurdjieff Foundation of New York

possible for men to be under ordinary conditions and who are asking themselves whether this is the ultima Thule—whether they have
reached the final limits of their evolution. We believe that there is
something more, and so we are here."[6] Men and women. Recording
later in a notebook a conversation in London with Orage, Katherine
Mansfield wrote: "Let me take the case of K. M. She has led, ever
since she can remember, a very typically false life. Yet, through it
all, there have been moments, instants, gleams, when she has felt
the possibility of something quite other."[7]

Orage once likened the impact of the Institute to the "stop"
exercise which Gurdjieff included in the public demonstrations of
1923–1924: the dance troupe in vigorous movement would freeze
at his command "Stop!" in whatever posture, however transitional
or awkward, they happened to be at that moment. Duplicating a
Sufi exercise Gurdjieff had witnessed and no doubt participated
in during his travels, it could lead to strikingly dramatic moments
on stage. "The institute is just a 'Stop!' exercise for all one's former habits and preoccupations of oneself," Orage offered, "and

it enables us to see ourselves in a new light. The shock may be alarming or depressing, or it may be immediately stimulating." Assessing his response to the Institute program as he had come to know it, he continued, "I feel centuries older, years younger and infinitely stronger; and I do not despair of one day being real and really human."[8]

In New York in the spring of 1924, Margaret Anderson and Jane Heap—cofounders of *The Little Review*—with several friends took leave of their familiar lives with a different attitude, as if they were entering a parable. "People from all parts of the world . . . were living and working in the Institute. Orage and the group that had come to New York were returning with Gurdjieff. And so it was that in June, 1924, Georgette, Jane, Monique and I—as well as several other people who felt as we did—left New York for Paris. We knew the import of our decision: we had prepared to 'cast aside our nets' and follow."[9]

To choose a word that strikes me as factual, Gurdjieff at this time was mighty. He had been known in earlier years as "The Tiger of Turkestan"; it was still so. In these pages I don't particularly want to emphasize his personal magnetism, though we'll need to speak of it time and again: either he brought ideas and practices and a renewed understanding of community that can be useful to many people long after his lifetime or he brought a sort of higher glamour of no lasting importance. The former is indisputably true; the latter was asserted for decades by critics echoing one another—we have already encountered Gurdjieff's "seductive gaze" in chapter 1, the professor's review of Russell Page's great garden and great folly. However, it must be said that, early and late, Gurdjieff's powerful presence—his sun and storms, his awareness experienced by others as a tangible influence—was a key fact and incentive for his followers. He was living evidence of the worth of the way he proposed. C. S. Nott, whom we met in New York and who would soon become a resident at the Prieuré, bears witness with persuasive innocence to this aspect of Gurdjieff's person in the years we're exploring. "Even to sit with him," Nott has written, "while he was talking in Russian with others was an experience. Like one of the Rishis, he was 'blazing with energy,' and one left him revitalized. As a small electric machine can be charged with energy just by being near a more powerful one, so a person could be magnetized by being near Gurdjieff, by his force and 'being.'"[10]

With his small band of courageous pupils Gurdjieff had successfully overcome recurrent experiences of extreme danger in the Caucasus from soldiers and brigands, illness, and prolonged physical hardship. He had correctly interpreted the sociopolitical weather in multiple settings, from Tiflis, seemingly peaceful but vulnerable, to Turkey on the edge of revolution. At last coming into his own as the founder of a school unlike any in the West and implanted in a stable society, Gurdjieff had sufficient resources to pitch the enterprise to a substantial scale. Of course there were risks. But as he said some years later, "I will take 90 percent risk, even 99 percent risk, but never I take 100 percent."[11] An unfriendly British author who witnessed a dance demonstration in New York wrote that Gurdjieff's "general appearance made one think of a riding master."[12] He isn't far wrong, but he might have substituted the words *dance master*—the best of them are nothing if not demanding and rooted in their bodies.

Louise March counts sixty to one hundred residents at the Prieuré in the early years.[13] People would come and go, and they were meant to come and go: the Prieuré was not a monastery. How were they living, for what, and under what "rule"? The last question can legitimately be asked: Gurdjieff gave periodic talks to clarify and enlarge the shared vision of the house, and a steadily growing sequence of aphorisms familiar to all provided a template of values and attitudes and a shared vocabulary. As well, no doubt more important, there were private conversations with Gurdjieff and with some of the most experienced pupils about how to be, how in the course of the day to experiment toward that "something more" mentioned by Orage. The Movements themselves, even for those who for one reason or another did not participate in them, contributed to the atmosphere and meaning of the house. "Once, when I came back earlier [from Paris]," Olga de Hartmann recalled, "I entered the balcony of the Study House to look and see what they were doing in the Movements. Mr. G. was just showing The Consecration of the Priestess. His wife was in the middle as the priestess and, as she was taller than the other ones, it was an absolutely wonderful picture. . . . Mr. de Hartmann was of course at the piano and improvised the music at once as Mr. G. showed the Movement."[14] Katherine Mansfield also took careful note of that Movement, now known as "The Initiation of a Priestess."[15]

A way of life quickly took shape. Within a short time the kitchen had acquired style and efficiency, the neglected grounds were responding to care, a kitchen garden was springing up, there were cows in the barn and other animals on the way. Further, a dirigible hangar from the war just past was being delivered in parts for reassembly as the much-needed Study House where dance rehearsals, performances, and community meetings were planned. The accelerated pace of the Prieuré was intentional; it was a condition of life at the time. Gurdjieff would walk among outdoor teams: "*Skoryy*," he would say in Russian, or "Queeker," his pronunciation of "quicker." This must have been among Gurdjieff's first words of English. The riding master was setting life in motion.

KATHERINE MANSFIELD: YOU SIMPLY HAVE TO WAKE UP

We must now *sonner fort*—ring loudly—at the Prieuré gate, as a sign requested, and hope to find our way in. Some brilliant people, residents for longer or shorter periods, wrote at the time or later how they perceived life and their own lives at the Prieuré. There is far more than enough material to draw on; we need only begin—with Katherine

Mansfield's joyous adventure of discovery, despite her illness, and Orage's utter misery until he grasped what Gurdjieff had in mind for him. Both were among the earliest residents. Permit me to call her Katherine in the next few pages, though I wouldn't dare call Orage "Alfred" (I believe that people did call him Orage). I have long thought about her at the Prieuré and as a writer, a converter of love of life into words that love life; I take her personally, it can't be otherwise.[16] Is there such a thing as sparkling sincerity? She perhaps uniquely possessed it; her letters from the Prieuré to her husband, John Middleton Murry, in England are alive with it. It's the custom, I think a good one, to retain Katherine's insistently casual punctuation. She wrote to him on the day after her arrival (21 October 1922):

"Here" is a very beautiful old chateau in glorious grounds. It was a Carmelite monastery then one of Madame de Maintenons "seats". Now it is modernised inside I mean chauffage centrale, electric light and so on. But its a most wonderful old place in an amazing lovely park. About 40 people, chiefly Russians, are here working, at every possible kind of thing. I mean, outdoor work, looking after animals, gardening, indoor work, music, dancing—it seems a bit of everything. Here the philosophy of the "system" takes second place. Practice is first. You simply have to wake up instead of talking about it, in fact. You have to learn to do all the things you say you want to do.[17]

Like everyone else, she received a work assignment without delay. "I start Russian today, and my first jobs which are eat, walk in the garden, pick the flowers, and rest much. Thats a nice calm beginning, isn't it. But its the eat much which is the job when its Gurdjieff who serves the dish."[18] She had scarcely spoken with him yet. She quickly discovered what it means to have companions not of one's own choosing. "Some of the English 'arty' & theosophical people are very trying. . . . But one can learn to use them, I am sure. Though Im not much good at it yet. On the other hand some of the advanced men and women are truly wonderful."[19]

She was enchanted. Though she found the arty people hard to bear, she was a bit arty herself.

I spend all the sunny time in the garden. Visit the carpenters, the trench diggers (we are digging for a Turkish Bath—not to discover one but to lay the pipes). The soil is very nice here, like sand with small whitey pinky pebbles in it. Then there are the sheep to inspect & the new pigs that have long golden hair very mystical pigs. A mass of cosmic rabbits & hens—and goats are on the way, likewise horses & mules to ride & drive. The Institute is not really started yet for another fortnight. A dancing hall is being built & the house is still being organised. But it has started really. If all this were to end in smoke tomorrow I should have had the very great wonderful adventure of my life. I have learnt more in a week here than in years of life la-bas.[20]

One of her assignments, as noted earlier, was to sit in the kitchen and take in the scene. Gurdjieff must have wanted her to understand something there, though she couldn't fully participate.

Mr Gurdjieff likes me to go into the kitchen in the late afternoon & "watch". I have a chair in a corner. Its a large kitchen with 6 helpers. Madame Ostrovsky the head, walks about like a queen exactly. She is extremely beautiful. She wears an old raincoat. Her chief helper, Nina, a big girl in a black apron— lovely, too—pounds things in mortars. The second cook chops at the table, bangs the saucepans, sings; another runs in and out with plates & pots, a man in the scullery cleans the pots, the dog barks & lies on the floor worrying a hearth brush. A little girl comes in with a bouquet of leaves for Olga Ivanovna. Mr Gurdjieff strides in, takes up a handful of shredded cabbage & eats it . . . There were at least 20 pots on the stove & its so full of life and humour and ease that one wouldn't be anywhere else. Its just the same all through—*ease* after *rigidity* expresses it more than anything I know.[21]

Gurdjieff had assigned two women to look after her needs—Olgivanna and Adèle Kafian—both of whom later wrote invaluable short memoirs of their time with Katherine.[22] Dr. James Young was also in and out; he could fetch firewood for her room, lay a fire, and keep an eye on her state of health. Another measure was taken for her health, based on folk medical tradition: a balcony was built for her in the cow shed, provided with comfortable seating and carpets, and decorated from the ceiling down by Alexandre de Salzmann with a sort of paradise scene of birds and other creatures, many of whose faces uncannily recalled the features of Prieuré residents. There was a toucan-like de Hartmann bird, prominent of beak, among many others. Katherine was to spend some hours each day there, inhaling the rich, possibly healing odor of the cows below. "One has the most happy feelings listening to the beasts & looking. I know that one day I shall write a long long story about it."[23] Gurdjieff called on her there one day.

On Saturday afternoon when I was in the stable Mr Gurdjieff came up to rest, too, and talked to me a little. First about cows and then about the monkey he has bought which is to be trained to clean the cows. Then he suddenly asked me how I was and said I looked better. "Now," he said "you have two doctors you must obey. Doctor Stable and Doctor New Milk. Not to think, not to write . . . Rest. Rest. Live in your body again." I think he meant get back into your body. He speaks very little English but when one is with him one seems to understand all that he suggests.[24]

Needless to say, no servant monkey appeared then or later—Gurdjieff was simply improvising to entertain Katherine.

Sitting close to the fireplace in the manor house salon, as the Study House wasn't ready yet, Katherine witnessed the dances every evening. And she saw things.

> I must say the dancing here has given me quite a different approach to writing. I mean some of the very ancient Oriental dance. There is one which takes about 7 minutes & it contains the whole life of woman—but everything! Nothing is left out. It taught me, it gave me more of woman's life than any book or poem. There was even room for Flaubert's Coeur Simple in it & for Princess Marya . . . mysterious. By the way I have had a great talk about Shakespeare here with a man called Salzmann. . . . His wife is the chief dancer here—a very beautiful woman with a marvelous intelligence.[25]

The life, her life, was far from delightful dawn to dusk; there was the other end of the stick. Like everyone, she had come under a rule, a practice of self-inquiry in community conditioned by Gurdjieff's injunction to her—and to all—to "live in your body again." The society of men and women around her ranged from Alexandre de Salzmann, whom she adored and admired, to others not as welcome. She wrote to her husband:

> I don't know how you feel. But I still find it fearfully hard to cope with people I do not like or who are not sympathetic. With the others all goes well. But living here with all kinds I am simply appalled at my helplessness when I want to get

rid of someone or to extricate myself from a conversation, even. But I have learnt how to do it, here. I have learnt that the only way is to court it, not to avoid it, to face it. Terribly difficult for me, in practice. But until I really do master this I cannot get anywhere. There always comes the moment when I am uncovered, so zu sagen, and the other man gets in his knockout blow.[26]

This is delicious; it breathes her spirit of sparkling sincerity. It also reflects in a strenuously lived version an element of the Gurdjieff teaching that must already have been practiced at the Prieuré: to face circumstances, to face others, to face oneself insofar as possible without yielding to automatic judgments, reactions, and all such. Not long after Katherine's passing, Gurdjieff gave a talk to the community on "separation of oneself from oneself." She was already working on that.

We must take leave of Katherine, but a few more brushstrokes will do no harm. Writing to her husband in late December after two full months at the Prieuré, she said something that soars beyond comment: "You see . . . if I were allowed one single cry to God that cry would be *I want to be REAL.* Until I am that I don't see why I shouldn't be at the mercy of old Eve in her various manifestations for ever."[27]

A few days later, writing to an English cousin, she summed up her experience in a curiously thorough way, as if in valediction.

I am living with about fifty to sixty people, mainly Russians. It is a fantastic existence, impossible to describe. One might be anywhere—in Bokhara or Tiflis or Afghanistan (except alas! for the climate!). But even the climate does not seem to matter so much when one is whirled along at such a rate. For we do most decidedly whirl. But I cannot tell you what a joy it is to me to be in contact with living people who are strange and quick and not ashamed to be themselves. It's a kind of supreme airing to be among them.[28]

Many years later, at his table in Paris, Gurdjieff misheard a toast to a woman named Cathleen. J. G. Bennett recalls, "Mr. G. pricked his ears and said, 'Who? Where?' Madame de Salzmann pointed to Cathleen, and he said, "Oh. I thought you said Katherine Mansfield. She my friend. But she die. . . . She my good friend."[29]

A. R. ORAGE: THE FORMER THINGS HAD PASSED AWAY

Orage's initial experience at the Prieuré was entirely different. Age forty-nine at the time he arrived, he was a rather tall, lanky Yorkshireman (see fig. 3) who hadn't worked physically in years—there hadn't been time or need alongside his outstanding career as a literary entrepreneur, discoverer and protector of new talent, and pioneer of new ideas. As well, he was something of a chain-smoker. "Duliotherapy" was not for him. That was how he was invited to start. A mysterious means cited in the printed program of the Institute to help bring people around to themselves, the Greek roots of the word resolve to slave therapy.[30] Alarming . . . "My first weeks at the Prieuré were weeks of real suffering," Orage recalled. "I was told to dig, and as I had had no real exercise for years I suffered so much physically that I would go back to my room, a sort of cell, and literally cry with fatigue. No one, not even Gurdjieff, came near me. I asked myself, 'Is this what I have given up my whole life for? At least I had something then. Now what have I?'"[31] Olga de Hartmann has objectively impartial, third-party insights to offer; even late in life she hadn't forgotten this vivid scenario.

As a job for [Orage], Mr. G. told him to dig a ditch, not far from the kitchen garden because, he said, the rain from a little hill always made too much water collect. He showed him

Fig. 3: A. R. Orage in the late 1920s. *Source*: Martha Welch de Llosa

the place, and the length and width of the ditch. Mr. Orage had never had a spade in his hands before but he began this project with great zeal. Every morning when Mr. G. went to the kitchen garden to look at how the work was going, he would tell him, "Well, well, very good, Orage." But the third or fourth day he told him, "Look, the edges of the ditch are not equal. You must take a little piece of string and measure across so that the edges will be quite equal." Orage did this, and the next day when Mr. G. passed, he stopped and said, "Orage, it is very good. Now put the earth back in it, we don't need this ditch anymore."[32]

On his side, Orage caps the story: "When I was in the very depths of despair, feeling that I could go on no longer, I vowed to make extra effort, and just then something changed in me. Soon, I began to enjoy the hard labor, and a week later Gurdjieff came to me and said, 'Now, Orage, I think you dig enough. Let us go to café and drink coffee.' From that moment things began to change. This was my first initiation. The former things had passed away."[33] By this closing reference to Revelations 21:4, Orage conveys that, at least in retrospect, he too felt himself to be journeying in a parable.

Orage hadn't been singled out; duliotherapy was the order of the day for able-bodied men and women. Gurdjieff understood that the first thing needed by many of the spiritual seekers who joined the Institute was a return to the body that couldn't be accomplished in the abstract: it needed shovels, spades, hammers, planks, dirt, and straw. A lovely man who with his wife had accompanied Gurdjieff from St. Petersburg through all the trials of migration was a psychiatrist, Dr. Leonid Stjernvall. No longer young when the Prieuré opened its doors, he seems to have had the custom of walking the grounds, observing, and sometimes advising or admonishing. He once approached Stanley Nott, who was breaking up stones. Unlike Orage, Nott was accustomed to physical labor, but that wasn't the end of the matter. "You know," the good doctor commented to Nott, "Mr. Gurdjieff says we should learn to work like men, not like ordinary laborers. Like men, not like machines. Try to save your energy while you are chopping stones. You waste much energy in resenting what you are doing. Make a list of thirty or forty words in a foreign language and memorize them while you are working; at the same time try to sense your body and notice what you are doing."[34] This was the Prieuré, the Institute for the Harmonious Development of Man, and this was solid Prieuré advice.

The emblem of the Institute (see fig. 4), devised in Tiflis by collaboration between Gurdjieff and Alexandre de Salzmann, and eventually published in three languages, reflects the diversity of practical work at the Prieuré—everything from weaving, ironwork, and forestry at lower right to raking, sweeping, and laundering at lower left, with much in between. A mysterious object just to the right of the Gurdjieff portrait called for detective work: a cylinder with a bugle-like horn on top, an early gramophone. At center in the lower zone, an alchemist's alembic, a distillation vessel, reminds that the Gurdjieff teaching concerns transformation of the human and, in point of fact, in the Russian exposition Gurdjieff made effective use of alchemy as a metaphor for human change. Clutter may well have been a conventional image for the alchemist's laboratory—at least Edmund Dulac, the brilliant turn-of-the-century illustrator, thought so: you will enjoy online his vision of the alchemist at work in his edition (1911) of Hans Christian Andersen's *The Wind's Tale*. It may be sensible to consider the clutter of tools across the lower half of the Institute's emblem as suggesting alchemy of another sort: alchemy through attentive work with common tools. I have never known—does anyone now know?—what unhappy person is represented as a head imprisoned behind the strings of a lyre; there is a rosewater sprinkler nearby at left, perhaps some comfort. Is this the singing head of Orpheus, an image revived in late nineteenth-century Symbolist art? That may well be—but why?

The upper zone of the emblem is pure Gurdjieff, a pattern of symbols that can be patiently read. Left and right, angel and devil, she with a sprig of myrtle, he with a palm frond—symbols respectively of love and peace. Menacing but not chaotic, the devil has a strict place in the pattern. That he holds a palm is a curious thing; there are Tibetan tales of Padmasambhava subduing local demons across the country—perhaps they too remained fierce-looking though obedient. At center is a lightly inscribed enneagram into which are fitted the four symbols of the Evangelists, with a dove, symbol of the Holy Spirit, placed in the axis and perched on the enneagram. The head of the symbol of Matthew is well worth contemplating: serene, steady, androgynous. What

Fig. 4: Emblem of the Institute for the Harmonious Development of Man.
Source: The Gurdjieff Foundation of New York

overall are we being told? Perhaps—very perhaps, as Gurdjieff would sometimes say—we are to read the image as a statement of the ideals of the Institute. The human being who can contain and master the energies of angel and devil, embody the wisdom of the Gospels, and allow the enneagram—life itself—to whirl without losing balance is well on the way to awakening. A concluding observation: the circumference is an ouroboros, the snake biting its own tail, symbol of eternity—used, as it happens, in just the same way in one of the prominent emblems of the Theosophical

Society. I have no idea why there is this borrowing, but we have already established that Gurdjieff was mindful of elements taught by Madame Blavatsky.

A fragment of tradition has survived through Olgivanna Lloyd Wright, who would sometimes speak with her husband's architecture students about her earlier life. "Olgivanna danced nightly in the Study House," a student reported, "with its enneagram hovering overhead. On either side of the inner triangle, Gurdjieff had painted an angel and a demon. To move beyond their grasp, he told her, she must learn to master both. Only then would she be able to use their energies to regenerate her own life."[35]

The emblem of the Institute must seem remote now; it speaks a language of symbols from an era and milieu where Christian imagery and a touch of the occult were much more familiar. What should we retain? I would say the serenity of the central figure, the integration of angelic and demonic energies around him/her, and the profusion of means in the lower zone, tools with which human beings can learn, as Dr. Stjernvall put it, to work like a man. And then, the words and thought at the top: to know, to understand, to be. They return us to Gurdjieff's exposition of knowledge and being. They are simple and, as powerfully as any complex symbol, they put the question of what we wish, what we care for.

The stress of Prieuré life, particularly for some of the English, recent arrivals with whom he had spoken, was a matter of concern to Professor Denis Saurat, visiting in the winter of 1923. In his later account of an interview with Gurdjieff (assisted by a translator), an exchange has long haunted me. "Do you know that many of the people here are close to despair?" Saurat asked. Gurdjieff in response: "Yes, there is something sinister in this house, but that is necessary."[36] Why sinister, why necessary? As it happens, in an earlier interview (October 1922), published only recently, the same question received an expansive answer.

Question: How do you explain the despair that some pupils of the institute fall into in the beginning?

Gurdjieff: There exists a principle in the Institute about which I will tell you at once, and then this period of despair will begin to be quite clear to you.

A man generally lives with a "foreign" mind. He has not his own opinion and is under the influence of everything that others tell him. . . .

In the Institute you have to learn to live with your own mind; you have to be active, to develop your own individuality. Here in the Institute many people come only on account of their "foreign" mind; they have no interest of their own in the Work at all.

That is why when a man arrives at the Institute, difficult conditions are created and all sorts of traps laid for him intentionally, so that he himself can find out whether he came because of his own interest or only because he heard about the interest of others. Can he, disregarding the outside difficulties that are made for him, continue to work for the main aim? And does this aim exist within him? When the need for these artificial difficulties is over, then they are no longer created for him. . . .

What is his own . . . cannot be taken away from him. . . . Only when this begins to exist, is it possible for these periods of despair to disappear. . . .

For most of the people now gathered in the Institute, the physical work is indispensable, but it is only a period of the whole plan.[37]

Relations between Gurdjieff and Orage matured quickly and firmly after that first invitation to coffee. Orage continued to toil— there is a photo of two men pulling a heavy cylindrical road roller in a British newspaper, winter 1923, one of them clearly Orage, and another photo of Orage at rest, reading in the Study House.[38] Gurdjieff must soon have realized that Orage was ideally suited to serve as the representative of the teaching in America when the time came: he already had a wide circle of admirers, his intellectual scope and ease in conversation would surely attract thoughtful people, and he was nothing if not a quick study, loyal to the teaching and to the Institute where it was coming to birth. Orage preceded Gurdjieff to New York in December 1923 and remained behind in the spring of 1924 to form and support groups and raise money for the Institute. When Gurdjieff began to write in late summer 1924—his Russian and Armenian text converted to awkwardly literal English by Thomas de Hartmann and others—Orage was for years positioned at the far end of the editorial stream to create a final text. He had help, notably the highly capable Jane Heap and Jean Toomer, but *Beelzebub's Tales*, published in 1950, is still honored as "the Orage translation."

Gurdjieff did not spare him. In time there were grave difficulties between them, thoroughly documented and interpreted in the existing literature,[39] and their relations broke off in 1931. But when Gurdjieff received the news of Orage's untimely death in London, 1934, he wept and said, "This man . . . my brother."[40] The quality of their relation, the subtlety and goodness of their conversation over many years, is reflected in a memory Orage shared with an English colleague at some point after 1931. "'Gurdjieff once told me,' said Orage, 'that he knew my ambition. He said I wanted to be one of the "elder brothers" of the human race, but that I had not the ability it required. 'You not know how to give,' he told me. 'You only let others take. Let them take, you do no good: you lose and they get dependent. Not easy to give. Learn how to give, then you make other people free.' I believe he was right.'"[41] In this conversation they were harking back to Theosophy, familiar to them both, in which the notion of elder brothers of humanity was a central ideal. Paul Beekman Taylor is the only historian to have noticed that Gurdjieff sent out word on the day he received news of Orage's passing that there would be a concert in his memory that evening in one of the recital spaces at Carnegie Hall of Gurdjieff / de Hartmann music Orage had especially cared for and pieces the composers had dedicated to him.[42]

The Study House:
Here There Are Only Those Who Pursue One Aim

Raising and decorating the Study House, a short distance from the residential manor, was the stuff of legend, a super-effort if ever there was one, and Gurdjieff wasn't much interested in standard levels of effort. Katherine Mansfield lived long enough to see the piecemeal arrival and early reassembly of the hangar, and she enjoyed beyond measure an evening in the salon when sixty-three Oriental carpets acquired for the floor and walls of the Study House were passed in review with discussion of their themes and regional provenances.[43] I suppose that every valid teaching and ancient religion has its characteristic setting; adherents know at once and reassuringly where they are by looking around and noting familiar signals. In Zen Buddhism, the unspeakably brilliant system of signals includes austere walls, sometimes ancient timbers, gleaming floors, sitting cushions, an altar, pots of sand with smoking incense, drums, worn wooden clappers. At once you know where you are and begin to remember why you are there; the teaching is already in the objects. Where the Gurdjieff teaching is concerned, it is carpets, rich in color, infinite in design. Do they encode knowledge of human nature and the cosmos? Are we a geometry? Is the cosmos a geometry? Are we paradise gardens, despite our weeds? So it can seem when good carpets are nearby. Some have inarguable authority. The mystery of the center, of progressive radiations from center to periphery, of the containing border, of flashing movement and kaleidoscopic

Fig. 5: Interior of the Study House at the Prieuré.
Source: The Gurdjieff Foundation of New York

complexity, of the flowering Creation: it is all there. One's straying eyes find abstract creatures tucked into the design—birds, sheep, the occasional dragon. Carpets are all very different and all very much the same, like people. If a modest Gurdjieff house cannot afford many carpets, it can always afford one; that is enough to activate the signal. All of this began in the Study House. Strange to say, one of Gurdjieff's most implacable critics in recent literature characterized him early in his book as "an Armenian carpet dealer," as if that clinched his critique in advance.[44] I don't think Gurdjieff would have minded.

There are many accounts of the building and decoration of the Study House (see fig. 5), perhaps best and clearest from Dr. James Young, a participant.

A multitude of activities were . . . set afoot by Gurdjieff. . . . But the *pièce de résistance* was the building of the "study-house."

An area of ground large enough to accommodate an ordinary aerodrome was leveled after exceedingly strenuous work with pick, shovel and barrow. The framework of an old aerodrome was erected on this, fortunately, as I thought, without loss of life or limb. The walls were lined within and without between the uprights with rough laths. The space between the laths was stuffed with dead leaves. The laths were then covered over inside and out with the material out of which the Hebrews made their bricks, a mixture of mud and straw, or hay chopped very small. Stoves were then put in the building and the walls dried and hardened before painting them. The roof was made of tarred felt nailed on to the joists; glass extended all the way round the upper half of the walls. This glazing was improvised from cucumber frames—a really good piece of work. After these had been fixed in position the glass was painted with various designs. The lighting effect was very pleasing. The floor, which was the naked earth pounded thoroughly and rolled, and dried by means of the stoves, was covered with matting, on which were placed handsome carpets; the walls below the windows were hung with rugs in the Oriental fashion. A stage was devised, and a kind of balcony for an orchestra; also two tiers of seats all round the walls, padded with mattresses and covered with rugs and skins, for the accommodation of visitors. A gangway ran between these two tiers of seats and a low wooden railing, which enclosed the charmed circle, reserved for pupils. I have described the building of this edifice to give some idea of the amount of labor that was put into it and to show how it was evolved out of the most primitive materials, with improvisation almost as guiding principle.[45]

Dr. Young has a point about safety; things did happen. The most unforgettable story involved Tchekhovitch, young and bold and weary to the bone. One night late in the construction process he had climbed a ladder to a crossbeam to install electric wiring—and while up there fell into an exhausted sleep. Tchekhovitch recalled:

> Waiting for someone to pass me the wires, it seems I instinctively wrapped my arms around the beam and fell into a deep sleep. I found out later that they had yelled to me several times in order to throw me the wires. Hearing these repeated calls, Mr. Gurdjieff had rushed over and immediately placed people under the beam to break a possible fall. Next, with a finger to his lips, he called for silence . . . and climbed up like a cat. Speaking very softly, he put his arms around me to keep me firmly on the beam. I was awakened by his soft and affectionate voice. It took me a while to realize the strangeness of the situation that made me worthy of such brotherly love. Assured that I had come to, he released his hold and immediately ordered me down. Once my feet hit the ground, his tenderness disappeared and he berated me so severely that I slunk away to my bed and took refuge under the covers.[46]

J. G. Bennett knowledgeably likened the decoration and atmosphere of the Study House to Sufi community houses he had visited in Turkey; I'm sure he's right.[47] But it reflected other atmospheres, as well: those humble glass cucumber frames, transformed by translucent paint into stained glass windows with carpet-like motifs, spoke of French cathedrals; a circular glass fountain, perfumed, with changing colored lights (surely set in motion for visitor days only) drew on Gurdjieff's probably innate sense of theater and of luxe located equivocally somewhere between over-the-top and perfection itself. And then, the Study House was an improvised frame structure, not masonry for the ages. That didn't matter. The interior was, by all sober accounts, a sacred space. Gurdjieff knew what needed to occur there: the practice and presentation of dances and music requiring such attention, such concentration, love, and care, that the atmosphere of the Study House would receive all that—and give it back.

The Study House is long since gone. I don't know that anyone has seriously tried to reconstruct it through photographs and verbal descriptions, of which there are many, offering a patchwork that might be pieced together. But the thirty-eight Gurdjieff aphorisms painted on wooden structural members, over the main entrance, and elsewhere in the interior, have been preserved and published.[48] Like the aphorisms of Pythagoras in their time and place, they spoke to values and attitudes intended to set the order of the house and give its residents food for thought. And again in the spirit of Pythagoras, they were not simply written out in English or Russian, no—they were hidden from outsiders behind the screen of a special Prieuré script devised by Gurdjieff and Alexandre de Salzmann and known only to Institute residents. Tchekhovitch could recall how the aphorisms fit into daily life.

One day Georgi Ivanovitch showed us a phonetic alphabet whose letters were inspired by Persian writing. These letters had been conceived and drawn by Alexandre de Salzmann, and could be used equally well in any language. Using this alphabet, de Salzmann wrote in calligraphy on the walls of the Study House the aphorisms formulated by Mr. Gurdjieff. We spent a lot of time deciphering these inscriptions and pondering how they could illuminate our daily life and our mutual relationships.[49]

It may be that the flowing Georgian alphabet also influenced the Prieuré script—de Salzmann would have known it from childhood. There are still a very few practitioners of this script, to one of whom I am grateful for figure 6.

As much as any surviving object or memory, the aphorisms reflect Gurdjieff's values and those of the teaching. Critics of Gurdjieff

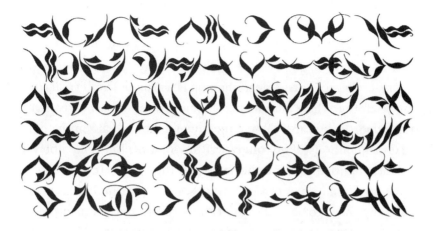

Fig. 6: Aphorism written in the Prieuré script. *Source*: Jim Kendrick

have never ventured far enough inland on what René Zuber once called "*le continent Gurdjieff*" to notice or appreciate the aphorisms.[50] There are far too many to explore here, and like markings on a compass none is dispensable, but we should think about a few. The aphorism illustrated in figure 6 reads, "Remember you come here having already understood the necessity of struggling with yourself—only with yourself. Therefore thank everyone who gives you the opportunity." It is said to have been inscribed on the lintel at the entrance; I don't doubt that, as it sets the terms of the voluntary contract with self and others. People working side by side are not only exercises in forbearance for one another—far from it, there can be strong bonds of trust and mutual appreciation—but when difficulties crop up, even severe difficulties, there is wisdom at hand for the willing. One does one's best to exercise tolerance, to follow with a certain inner distance the vivid intricacies of discomfort; a world of useful self-knowledge lies that way. But the exercise needn't be endlessly self-abasing. Years later in Paris, during the Occupation, Gurdjieff made that clear in conversation with a pupil asking how to respond to a colleague who had stolen from him a box of matches, seemingly a small concern but matches were rare at the time. Gurdjieff said that he could overlook such small reverses—but the time might well come when he would have to go to the petty thief and say, "Please don't steal my matches anymore, I need them; it is wartime. Don't steal from me."[51] Both of these statements—"Thank everyone who gives you the opportunity" and "You stole my matches"—echo in the halls of Gurdjieff houses, no longer written on walls but remembered. Together with another aphorism from the Study House: "If you have not by nature a critical mind your staying here is useless." All things need to be understood anew, reassessed again and again with adjustments made as needed and where possible, in communities where people, even awkwardly but authentically, are seekers of truth. Such communities require quiet, critical minds at work if they are to endure past the first thrilling years.

"Only he can be just who is able to put himself in the position of others"—yet another aphorism from the Study House walls. Throughout his writings and preserved exchanges with pupils, Gurdjieff used all forms of the word *justice* with interesting formality, in effect making it clear that justice is a very high value not ever to be treated lightly. From his perspective, to be just is an objective requirement, however much personal work may be needed on the way toward it. To put oneself in the position of others is an act of compassionate imagination freed from self-concern. One sees the other, feels the other, as if he or she is oneself—or nearly so. This is not an easy thing, but clearly Gurdjieff regarded it as characteristic of what he would call a remarkable man (which we can instantly translate as a remarkable man or woman—that is what he meant, though the language of his day rarely reflected the gender issue). When he turned to writing in the later 1920s and early 1930s, the concept of justice reappeared in one of his most central reflections.

From my point of view, he can be called a remarkable man who stands out from those around him by the resourcefulness of his mind, and who knows how to be restrained in the manifestations which proceed from his nature, at the same time conducting himself justly and tolerantly towards the weaknesses of others.[52]

The three aphorisms we have considered, concerning critical mind, relations with others, and justice, meet here. What continues to astonish me in this thought from Gurdjieff's *Meetings with Remarkable Men* is its simplicity and earthiness. Human beings may be seers of higher worlds, and so on and so forth, but that is not where Gurdjieff's basic values settle. They settle on earth, among people making their lives. There can indeed be seers of higher worlds—we need such people—but first things first.

"Here there are neither Russians nor English, Jews nor Christians, but only those who pursue one aim—to be able to be." Not to dwell overlong on any aspect of the Prieuré, we should give this aphorism our best thought and move on. Its rhythm and meaning echo St. Paul's letter to the Colossians (3:11): "Here there is no Gentile or Jew, circumcised or uncircumcised, barbarian, Scythian, slave or free, but Christ is all, and is in all." Gurdjieff's variant shows where the emphasis lies for him: on the quality of persons. From the perspective of his teaching, work on oneself is initially an individual, earthly, one might even say secular struggle to clarify one's identity and reach toward a new inner order. The Lord is distant and one's responsibility is great. Gurdjieff asked a certain modesty of his pupils. Margaret Anderson has recorded that "God was not mentioned [at the Prieuré] after the day when someone at . . . table succeeded in a direct question and Gurdjieff answered 'You go too high.'"[53] On another occasion Tchekhovitch heard much the same: "Only he who has succeeded by persistent and conscious efforts in freeing himself from the chaos resulting from his own lack of consciousness can be aware of what religion really means."[54] But that is not the end of the matter. Those who are more able to be, who have made the necessary sacrifices and somehow found their way on, may well perceive that "Christ is all, and is in all"—and if not precisely that in our multicultural world, then whatever parallel there may be in their own cultures.

This aphorism returns us yet again to Gurdjieff's exposition about knowledge and being, and to the words heading the Institute emblem. "To be," in the lexicon of Gurdjieffian words and the lexicon of experience, is many-layered and many-sided. At one level it means to be present in this world—*present*, a term and thought likely first introduced in the West in Gurdjieff's writings, now common. It means that one has attained or knows something of the way back to a sense of reality, of "being there." But it means more than that. It means that one cares for and strives invisibly toward depth of humanity—toward conscience and awakened feeling, toward some reserve of goodness and wisdom that can gradually reveal itself and offer guidance. To be is to be fully human at last, not a dreamer, not consumed by self-serving passions, not complacent. Further, it is a matter of contact and acknowledgment, open to whatever we intuit or know to be above us, open to one's fellow human beings, to living things, to all things that support decency of life. When one encounters authentic being in others, it evokes spontaneous respect. There was an interesting and practical man named Gabo in the circle around Gurdjieff later in life, who once explained that he didn't understand Gurdjieff's teaching and didn't much care to understand—but he had the most profound respect for him, all the same.[55]

Gurdjieff later explored more fully the terrain intimated in this aphorism through conversations with Father Giovanni in *Meetings with Remarkable Men*. Readers may recall this striking figure, a Catholic missionary to a remote region of Central Asia whose encounter there with the World Brotherhood, as he called his community, prompted him to settle among them, no longer a missionary. Gurdjieff and his comrade, the archeologist Professor Skridlov, were listening.

> Father Giovanni told us a great deal about the inner life of the brethren there and about the principles of daily existence connected with this inner life; and once, speaking of the numerous brotherhoods organized many centuries ago in Asia, he explained to us a little more in detail about this World Brotherhood, which any man could enter, irrespective of the religion to which he had formerly belonged. As we later ascertained, among the adepts of this monastery there were former Christians, Jews, Mohammedans, Buddhists, Lamaists, and even one Shamanist. All were united by God the Truth. All the brethren of this monastery lived together in such amity that, in spite of the specific traits and properties of the representatives of the different religions, Professor Skridlov and I could never tell to which religion this or that brother had formerly belonged.[56]

For those who were willing to *sonner fort*—to ring with due vigor—at the Prieuré gate, and for future generations who found comparable doors elsewhere, this must be what Gurdjieff had in mind: to work with others toward what he called "the ableness to be"—not least the ableness to be Christian or Jewish, Buddhist or Muslim, or more broadly to know and serve God the Truth. That ableness, so he wished, sets in motion the most demanding values of the religions, gives them a firm home in people and, through them, in society at large. Tchekhovitch noticed in Gurdjieff's room at the Prieuré two large paintings: one of Buddha, the other of Christ.[57]

THE PRIEURÉ LECTURES

In the course of 1923, Gurdjieff periodically gave talks to the community, impromptu in their timing but carefully thought through in advance—in January alone, five such talks. They may have been transcribed at once and circulated among the participants in Russian, English, or both languages; however that may have been, excellent versions survive.[58] The talks convey general principles and attitudes fundamental to work on oneself, in keeping with a thought Gurdjieff confided to a resident at that time, Dr. Maurice Nicoll, a Jungian psychiatrist who in later years in England would found and lead a Gurdjieff school and make lastingly significant contributions to the published literature.[59] The Institute is "a hatching place for eggs," he told Nicoll. "It supplies the heat. Chicken inside must try to break shell, then help and individual teaching possible. Until then only collective method."[60] The talks were "collective method"—and as well, when needed, critiques of attitudes or behaviors in the community that had drifted off course.

As always in these pages we must be selective, but certain of Gurdjieff's themes bear mention. An early and recurrent topic was the integration of mind, body, and feeling, which for Gurdjieff is not an additive process, as if to twine a rope, but rather the basis for a qualitative change in awareness. In what follows from January 17, little more than a week after the sadness of Katherine Mansfield's passing, we should remember that he was speaking to both men and women.

> Until now you have not been working like men, but there is a possibility to learn to work like men. Working like a man means that a man feels what he is doing and thinks why and for what he does it, how he is doing it now . . . and how it is generally best to get it done—whether there is a better

way. . . . The essence of man's correct work is in the working together of the three centers—moving, emotional, and thinking. When all three work together and produce an action, this is the work of a man. There is a thousand times more value even in polishing the floor as it should be done than in writing twenty-five books.[61]

We have already heard Dr. Stjernvall translate this perspective into practical advice to Stanley Nott as he was breaking up stone. Tchekhovitch could recall Gurdjieff's direct reprimands but also his warmth when he knew that he had been understood.

"You see," Gurdjieff once said, "everyone passes by here and no one picks up this piece of paper! . . . And you! Look! Why come back with an empty pail? Think about watering the tomatoes on the way back. Why do you work like a day-laborer? Try to be conscious of the needs and possibilities of the moment. We all depend on each other's work and intelligence." [Tchekhovitch added that] when our minds were clear and alert, and we had become sensitive to every need, Mr. Gurdjieff said nothing more. His presence appeared lighter, more congenial, almost brotherly. A warm smile would appear on his face, and the mood became that of something subtly shared.[62]

Two days later, Gurdjieff asked the residents to look more deeply into the relations among mind, body, and feeling, and the potential for change.

The power of changing oneself lies not in the mind, but in the body and the feelings. Unfortunately, however, our body and our feelings are so constituted that they don't care a jot about anything so long as they are happy. They live for the moment and their memory is short. The mind alone lives for tomorrow. . . . The merit of the mind is that it looks ahead. But it is only the other two that can "do". . . . So far, in the minds of those present there arose . . . a desire to attain something, to change something. . . . There is only this bare idea in the head, but each has remained as he was. Even if he works ten years with his mind, if he studies day and night, remembers in his mind and strives, he will achieve nothing useful or real, because in the mind there is nothing to change.

Turning to the analogy of the equipage—horse, carriage, driver, passenger, in which the horse represents emotional energy, the carriage represents the body, the driver represents the mind—Gurdjieff added, "what must change is the horse's disposition. Desire must be in the horse, and ability in the carriage."[63] The passenger, for the moment, is a changing sequence of I's, not the potential master of the equipage. The Institute's program, its exercises from fieldwork to sacred dances, was designed to awaken and unite the three energies of mind, body, and feeling. United, they offer a foundation for something more, which Gurdjieff called self-remembering, and self-remembering in turn offers openings of another order. The "psychology of man's possible evolution," as Ouspensky put it with succinct clarity, has stirred to life.

On the following day yet another lecture, this time focused exclusively on self-remembering.[64] It is a brilliant thing, providing first a model of close self-observation—of uncovering by direct awareness the multiple strands of the day-to-day self—and then a model of persistent concentration, penetrating to zones of intention, wish, and receptivity that are not day to day. "I must not say 'I' merely mechanically, as a word, but I must note in myself its resonance. This means that in saying 'I' you must listen carefully to the inner sensation." Listening, resonance, sensation: Gurdjieff initiated at the Prieuré an approach to self-awareness and the possibility of fullness of being. It is true that he was a riding master in these years, demanding, urging people on. It is also true that he was a man of spirit. His approach to the deeper dimensions of human being was expressed in a new language unheard before in the West, although many of its terms have since entered the *lingua franca* of contemporary spirituality.

Published only in 1975, the lectures were read for decades in typescript in Gurdjieff houses, and their perspectives passed into the oral teaching, the communities' long conversation among experienced participants, older and younger, and peers. Wherever they are found, oral teachings may be exercises in repetition and progressive loss or, on the contrary, of rediscovery from day to day of what has always mattered, refreshed by new insights and current experience. Valid oral teachings are creatively unstable with all of the resources needed to continue developing but also the potential to stop, to fix in place. This poses an existential challenge; it obliges those who guide oral teachings to be as sensitive as possible to nuance and change while remembering what was said in the beginning. One day a man to whom I and many owe much, Lord Pentland, commented to a group of his pupils that "contributions to knowledge will be gratefully received," as if he were a fund-raiser. It was funny, it was full of life.

Later that winter and spring of 1923, Gurdjieff continued to detail the "collective method" through lectures. Among other things he asked the community to distinguish between genuine thought—quieter, clearer, pertinent—and what he called the formatory apparatus, the mill of mental associations and accumulation of labels that occupy the place of genuine thought. Gurdjieff had immense confidence in the capability of the real mind to guide the process of liberation—for example, to explore and understand the influences under which we live, some life enhancing, others harmful: "Personally I would advise you to try freeing yourselves and to do so without unnecessary theorizing, by simple reasoning, active reasoning, with yourselves."[65] By way of illustration he offered an extended example of active reasoning around the common phenomenon of taking offense: "M. is here and also K. We live together. M. called me a fool—I am offended. K. gave me a scornful look—I am offended. . . . I am hurt and shall not calm down and come to myself for a long time." The reasoning that follows moves toward independence of mind and heart, responsive to others yet self-possessed. "M. called me a fool. Why should I be offended? . . . Must he necessarily be wise? He himself may be a fool or a lunatic. . . . If a fool has called me a fool, I am not affected inside. . . . But if in a given instance I was a fool and am called a fool, I am not hurt, because my task is not to be a fool. . . . So he reminds me, helps me to realize that I am a fool and acted foolishly. I shall think about it and perhaps not act foolishly next time."[66] This is territory in the Gurdjieff teaching—wider in the teaching than these few quoted words suggest—where the Stoicism of Epictetus and Marcus Aurelius finds its renewal, its place in contemporary life.

Recalling this renewal gives me mysterious satisfaction, as if for once the passage of time has not erased all things, all good things. In some recess of self I am a soldier against time; perhaps we all are. The original Stoic teachings, powerful on the page, nonetheless need to dock in lives today, to integrate with a general enterprise of living understandingly. Gurdjieff offered, and offers, the needed conjunction. Whatever else the Gurdjieff teaching may be, it is unquestionably a renewal of the insistent light of Stoicism as taught with dramatic flair by Epictetus and exquisite pensiveness by Marcus Aurelius. To the best of my knowledge Gurdjieff did not mention either by name; they are nonetheless nearby.

Pursuing what he meant by active reasoning, Gurdjieff offered what strikes me as a classic statement concerning two kinds of self-love: "We do not possess ourselves nor do we possess genuine self-love. . . . Self-love is hell, and self-love is heaven. These two, bearing the same name, are outwardly alike, but totally different and opposite to one another in essence. . . . Our aim must be to have self-love. If we have self-love, by this very fact we shall become free of many enemies in us. We can even become free of these principal ones—Mr. Self-Love and Mrs. Vanity."[67] And there the talk ends, though with a parting irony and admonition: "How to distinguish between one kind of self-love and another? . . . Thank God we, who are sitting here, are safe from confusing the one with the other. We are lucky! Genuine self-love is totally absent, so there is nothing to confuse." This is quite like Epictetus—the old master was sparing where compliments and reassurance were concerned. But Gurdjieff offered a sprig of hope. "Active reasoning is learned by practice; it should be practiced long and in many varied ways."[68] In later years he would often say, "Repeat, repeat, repeat." In the 1940s, when a brilliant pupil reported dazzling results from her first explorations of an inner exercise, he could not have been more dismissive. He wasn't remotely interested in what she was saying; it would take a thousand more attempts to reach results of value. The norm of persevering practice was set in place at the Prieuré.

We should touch on one further theme in the lectures of those months: the need to economize energy, to observe and reduce chronic physical tension, and to explore the possibility of conscious relaxation. As always, the teaching was intensely practical; it was about bodies in motion, the mind closely observed, feelings allowed to make themselves known. "Learn—when you sit, when you stand, when you lie down—to tense your right arm or your left. . . . Get up, tense your arm and keep the rest of your body relaxed. Try it in practice to understand better. . . . Relax everything except your legs, and walk. Pay particular attention to keeping your body passive, but the head and face must be alive. The tongue and eyes must speak." Experimenting in this way may seem at first a dreary business, but it becomes engaging and lays the groundwork for a more integrated self-awareness. Gurdjieff tied this study back to his observations a few months earlier concerning M.'s ridicule and

K.'s scorn: "From tomorrow on," he proposed, "let each person . . . begin to practice the following exercise: if you are touched to the quick, see that it does not spread all over the body. Control your reaction; do not let it spread."[69]

The Gurdjieff teaching was not, and to this day is not, a mountaintop teaching: though it asks for sustained individual initiative and has the potential to enrich one's privacy—to create a place of independent reflection and feeling that knows self and world with growing sensitivity—nonetheless it draws on the presence of people together in community to challenge and refine what each one is. "One hand washes the other," Gurdjieff used to say, in this zone of experience as in many others.

THE PRIEURÉ CHILDREN

There was a second constituency at the Prieuré: children. Here is a small batch of them (see fig. 7); there were quite a few more. The children included Gurdjieff's brother Dmitri's family of three girls, who lived in a separate cottage on the grounds, plus the de Salzmann children; Jane Heap's young American wards, Fritz and Tom Peters; Madame Ouspensky's grandson; brave Valentin, Gurdjieff's nephew, sole survivor of the Armenian genocide in his immediate family (he had found his way to his uncle); plus the Stjernvalls' son, Lili Galumian's son, and a few stray others. We would know little about the lives of the Prieuré children and Gurdjieff's way with them were it not for Fritz Peters' memoir *Boyhood with Gurdjieff*. It is pitch-perfect. Fritz, age eleven when he first arrived, would come and go, depending on the will and whim of his guardian and remote parents, but he spent extended periods at the Prieuré under Gurdjieff's paternal wing. They would speak, it seems, quite often. Peters' accounts of those talks, written many years later, and of his many adventures and mishaps at the Prieuré, have an intriguing quality of objectivity as if it all, word and act,

Fig. 7: Prieuré children in winter. *Source*: The Gurdjieff Foundation of New York

had been permanently inscribed in him. To appreciate that flavor, we might read his account of a conversation that occurred after Fritz had disastrously neglected his assigned duty to care for the herb garden and had accompanied Gurdjieff on a mortifying row-by-row inspection of wilting plants.

> He talked to me for a very long time that morning, and empha-sized the fact that everyone had, usually, a particular, recurring problem in life. He said that these particular problems were usually a form of laziness, and that I was to think about my laziness, which took a fairly obvious physical form, as in the case of the garden: I had simply put off doing anything in the garden until someone had taken notice of that fact. He said that he wanted me to think seriously about my laziness—not the outward form, which was not important, but to find out what it was. "When you see that you are lazy, necessary find out what this laziness is. Because in some ways you already lazy for many

years, can take even many years for you to find out what it is. Must ask yourself, whenever you see your own laziness: 'What is this laziness in me?' If you ask this question seriously, and with concentration, is possible someday you will find answer. This important and very difficult work I give you now."[70]

It is tempting to write that Gurdjieff taught the children—those who were willing—in a less demanding or complex way than adults, but that really isn't so. He raised much the same topics, set comparably challenging tasks for inner and outer work. For example, as he did for the adults, he asked Fritz to practice self-observation. I find nothing simplified for youthful understanding in what follows:

He said that it was a very difficult exercise to do and that he wanted me to do it, with my entire concentration, as constantly as possible. He also said that the main difficulty with this exercise, as with most exercises that he did—or would in the future—give to me or to any of his students, was that to do them properly it was necessary not to expect results. In this specific exercise, what was important was to see oneself, to observe one's mechanical, automatic, reactionary behavior without comment, and without making any attempt to change that behavior. "If change," he said, "then will never see reality. Will only see change. When begin to know self, then change will come, or can make change if wish—if such change desirable. . . . If wish to learn to become millionaire, necessary to devote all early life to this aim and no other. If wish to become priest, philosopher, teacher, or businessman, should not come here. Here only teach possibility how become man such as not known in modern times, particularly in Western world."[71]

Gurdjieff raised with young Fritz one of the difficult points in the practice of inner work: not to expect results. Adults can wrestle with this tendency for years or a lifetime; they can question and explore, they can read the Bhagavad Gita on that very issue, so beautifully and persuasively stated—and still allow longing for desired results to fragment their perception of here and now. The paradox is implacable: only through unconditional sacrifice of the image or vision of a desired result—no unstated bargaining, no imagined quid pro quo—can there be receptivity enough for the longed-for result. And even then, who knows? In his own terms and experience, Fritz was asked to understand this.

Over the years until his untimely death in 1938, Dmitri was something like an unwilling foil for his brother Georgivanich, as the Russians familiarly called him. A strikingly handsome man, a bon vivant and spendthrift, who managed to look after a family of three children, Dmitri was temperamentally unsuited to sympathize with much that went on in his brother's orbit. He could be quite funny, exasperated but funny, on that topic. Once Georgivanich had an intense conversation with his brother in Russian in the company of Solita Solano and others, who begged Dmitri—what was he saying, what was it all about? And Dmitri replied, "*Vrai, je n'ai rien compris de tout cela*"—Frankly, I didn't understand a word.[72] On another occasion, a car trip, things were going from bad to worse because Georgivanich often enough preferred things to go from bad to worse (car breakdowns, wrong roads, scoldings). At the height of the deliberate chaos of the day Dmitri sighed, "*Jamais un peu de repos*"—never a quiet moment.[73]

All the same, Dmitri's children were deeply fond of their unpredictable, ingenious uncle, though he could test their patience. One of those children, Luba Gurdjieff, grew up to own and manage a popular restaurant in London where she served Russian dishes with earthy hospitality and an explosive sense of humor. She had begun cooking at the Prieuré. While this is not, and must not be, a book of quotations, it is irresistible to quote Luba about two trips with her uncle during the later Prieuré years. Her first account evokes the joy and terror of car trips, then and later.

> In spring we used to go to the south of France. We always had three, four cars going, with maybe twenty people all together. My Uncle would always drive the car in front. He was a rotten driver. My father was a good driver, but my Uncle was rotten. I don't know how he didn't kill himself. He was a terrible, terrible driver. . . . I would say, "Thank God I'm not in his car." He would drive very slow; then he would go very fast. Then he would pull over by the side of the road and we would have a nice picnic—not just sandwiches, but roast chickens, cucumbers, vegetables. Mama and I used to prepare it all in advance, packing the baskets—wine for the grown-ups and lemonade for the kids, lots of fruit. We always had seleyotka—you know, the salty herrings. Uncle used to like that. We used to have little cakes. We each had our own napkins. It was all quite fun. We would always take the wind-up gramophone with us so we would have music when we ate. Everybody used to swim when we got to the seaside. We took all the dogs with us. It was really an outing.[74]

And so that wind-up gramophone, hidden in the solemn Institute emblem (see fig. 4), turns out to have had recreational use. Luba's tone, so relaxed, irreverent, and appreciative, reflects her family affection. As does the following more excruciating tale of an incident in Cannes, on the French Riviera.

> He used to make it very difficult for us, sometimes. I remember once I was sixteen years old and we were staying in one of the poshest hotels, the Carleton. I had a very pretty dress,

my first evening dress, with flowers. There I was, all nice-nice, with makeup and all that, and my Uncle says that night he's too tired. He's not coming down to dinner. I thought, "Oh, thank God. We're going to have a nice, peaceful dinner." And in the middle of the dinner he comes down with a big tray of watermelon. And he is in his pajamas and dressing gown. He says, "Ay, children, I forgot to give you that for dessert." If you could see us! We were so annoyed. Everybody in all this jewelry and everything, in front of all these posh people, we were very proud, sitting there, and he goes and messes up everything, coming in his pajamas and slippers. Next morning I say, "Uncle, how could you do it?" He says, "What did I do?" I say, "You came in your pajamas, and we were sitting in the dining room." He says, "Well, you put pajama in night time. You can put it in daytime—doesn't matter. It was pajamas. Wouldn't change a thing. You must have a little carboozi." (Carboozi was watermelon.) But he loved children. He used to start all kinds of games. He enjoyed that. He used to hide all kinds of things in the trees and we were supposed to find them. You know, toys, money, pocket money. He used to bring out the gramophone and we would start dancing.[75]

We have encountered this Gurdjieff—Diogenes again—fearless, droll, sometimes terrifying, fortified with childlike naïveté: "What did I do?" It all worked out quite well in the end.

PREHISTORY OF THE MOVEMENTS

We should enter the Study House, where sacred dances and exercises—all that is now called Movements—were being created, rehearsed, and set to music in 1923, nearly every evening, often far into the night. But can we first walk the grounds and converse? We should think over certain points. In the course of Gurdjieff's travels in the Middle East and Central Asia, he witnessed in sanctuaries of various faiths and sects a remarkable living library of sacred dances and rituals. When did he have the audacious thought that such dances—committed to memory, perhaps in time adapted—could form a significant part of a work toward being, toward wholeness and awareness, in the West? A further question: Did it come to mind early that traditional dances and danced rituals might in time show the way toward original choreography, that they represented a language of dance that could be spoken anew? Sacred dance was unknown in the West, though it survived in ancient, marginalized cultures such as the Native American and Australian Aboriginal. In the margin of Western culture there was a text, the apocryphal Acts of John describing the very beautiful circle dance of Jesus and the apostles—but scarcely anyone knew of it. There were wall paintings in Etruscan and Egyptian tombs depicting sacred dance with simplicity and sweetness of line and color. Etruscan painting in particular conveyed a sense of seriousness and vitality—but few knew of such paintings, and what did they have to do with life in our time?

Yet Gurdjieff at some point must have thought the unthinkable: that highly disciplined, often complex dances and rituals set to music could serve as skillful means toward the grounding and gradual awakening of Western men and women who for the most part would have had no prior exposure to dance outside of ballroom, dance hall, and ballet theater. Gurdjieff used to grumble colorfully from time to time about the fox-trot, the dance sensation of the 1920s: it was everything he didn't mean by dance, though at one point in *Beelzebub's Tales* he softens enough to offer a sympathetic portrait of a hardworking, not very prosperous Parisian teacher of ballroom dance.[76] Gurdjieff's redefinition of dance would, of necessity, be total: Dance in Gurdjieff's world would foster the development of attention, of conscious movement and collaboration with others, of fluidity and composure. It would offer participants clues to inner freedom through an immense variety of attitudes well beyond their habitual physical and emotional postures. Dance would become a transformative education.

Gurdjieff's initial sources were for the most part temples, monasteries, remote religious communities. The material was religious through and through. He was anything but indifferent to religions and their larger visions of human nature and obligation—but at some point in his encounter with sacred dance and ritual he must have recognized that the dance materials he might reconstitute for the deep education of Western men and women could convey without words the essence of the knowledge and feeling encoded in them. This was daring; it represented an immense confidence in the power of a special kind of dance to teach—and the capacity of his future pupils in largely secular cultures to learn in a new way. A Turkish, no doubt genuinely learned and concerned man who attended one of the first public performances of the Movements (Paris, December 1923) faulted Gurdjieff precisely on this point in a review article: What right had he to transfer the majestic whirling ritual of the Mevlevi dervishes from its traditional homes in Turkey to a Parisian theater? He could have asked that question about numerous other dances and ritual exercises in the Paris performances. I don't know that Gurdjieff addressed this question at any point, but it is evident that he believed the potential gain to far outweigh any loss, and he could not have been unaware of the encroachment of modernity— of railroads and armies and colonial ambition—on the traditional worlds through which he passed as a sort of Bartók: the composer collected music in the Hungarian hinterland, Gurdjieff collected dances across the Middle East and Central Asia. There is a vast difference between appropriation and collecting seeds to transplant where they can flourish anew. The dances and danced rituals were their own argument for goodness. They were capable of teaching by the way, as if unnoticed, not specific elements of any religion but something to my mind more important and fundamental: a sense of the sacred, nested in a new sense of oneself.

ÉMILE JAQUES-DALCROZE

I have written that the West knew nothing of sacred dance—but there was something, there was someone, all the same, with a natural affinity for what Gurdjieff had in mind: the holistic approach to music education of Émile Jaques-Dalcroze (1865–1950).[77] Curiously, they were nearly exact age peers; that is not the only curiosity. It seems that they never met, although Dalcroze, already well-known, visited Russia in 1913, and is said to have attended a performance of the Movements in December 1923 at the Théâtre des Champs-Élysées. The meeting nonetheless took place, consequentially, through Dalcroze pupils. Born in Vienna to a Swiss family and drawn to music at an early age, Dalcroze studied music in Geneva through the university years and for a shorter period in Paris under major masters, notably Gabriel Fauré. Invited in 1886 to serve as assistant conductor for an orchestra in Algiers, he spent a season there—and it was there that he first heard in indigenous North African music what he was destined to hear: rhythm—complex, non-Western, compelling. We know something of that transformative journey in the lives of other artists: recall Henri Matisse and Paul Klee, both of whom learned color, as if by rebirth, in North Africa.

Dalcroze returned to Geneva with new insights and a discovered mission, though it took years for him to give it shape. In 1898, he was still tentative: "I have taken to dreaming of a music education in which the body itself would play an intermediary role between sounds and our thought, and would become the direct instrument of our feelings."[78] In time Dalcroze found his way to an altogether novel approach to music education: through the body, through rhythmic movement, through listening and physical response. The Dalcroze method was born, uniting three disciplines: solfège (sight singing and immediate pitch recognition); improvisation at the piano or other instrument (in order to creatively support rhythmic exercises); and eurhythmics, as we put it in English (the more comfortable term in his French is *Rythmique*).

Music students of all ages—Dalcroze cared to train the very young—would move to music, respond to rhythm, melody, and dynamics; music would enter through the body and unite thought and feeling. "The goal of instruction in Rythmique," he wrote, "is to guide pupils toward being able to say, at the end of their studies, not 'I know' but 'I experience.'"[79] Dalcroze was aware of an obstacle as pertinent to Rythmique as to Gurdjieff's dances and exercises: "I deny," he wrote with passionate certainty, "that even an artist of genius has the possibility of fully appreciating and soundly judging our rhythmic exercises and their influence if he has not himself rigorously participated in our special approach to education."

As time went on, there were countless rhythmic movement exercises from which Dalcroze and Dalcroze teachers could draw to animate their classes and, despite initial resistance among influential music educators in Switzerland, the new method made its way both in Switzerland and across the world. Today there are Dalcroze schools or certified individual teachers virtually wherever Western music is taught. In 1911, with generous financial and moral support, Dalcroze established his headquarters in a new building designed specifically to meet the needs of his educational methods in Hellerau, a garden-city suburb of Dresden. It quickly attracted dance students and theater professionals from many countries; here it proved possible both to teach the Dalcroze method and to expand its application to include musical theater.

There was a Dalcroze teacher in Tiflis in 1919, known professionally as Jeanne Matignon-Salzmann. It was Jeanne de Salzmann, who as we know took refuge with her husband, Alexandre, in his native Tiflis after the abrupt closing of the Dalcroze school by the German authorities at the beginning of World War I. Introduced to one another by Thomas de Hartmann, who had known Alexandre in pre-war Munich, Gurdjieff and the de Salzmanns formed a lasting bond. A surviving program from the Tiflis State Opera Theatre, dated June 22, 1919, records parallel performances of the Gurdjieff Movements and Dalcroze Rythmique: "Part 1: The Method of Jaques-Dalcroze," including exercises such as "Realization of rhythms, dividing a rhythm," "Independence of limbs," "Solfège, improvisation," and "Pulse/accent"—pure Dalcroze, performed by local young women. And then "Part II: The System of G. I. Gurdzhiev," including seven "Exercises of plastic gymnastics," three "Exercises for ancient sacred dances," the Stop exercise, and two dances from theatrical works Gurdjieff was developing at the time.[80] The distinction between "plastic gymnastics" and "ancient sacred dances" signals that Gurdjieff was already creating new choreography. Gurdjieff's roots were in the dances and rituals of the Middle East and Central Asia; Dalcroze's roots were in music education, and there they stayed through a lifetime of creative work: two very different worlds. But as senior Dalcroze students and graduates interested themselves in Gurdjieff's teaching and in a few instances became lead dancers, Jeanne de Salzmann foremost among them, something of the Dalcroze ethos entered the Gurdjieff repertory through their shared attention to complex rhythms and gestural patterns, and to what has just been called "independence of limbs," experienced for example through a sequence of four varied arm gestures paired with three varied steps. As well, both schools needed resourceful improvisation at the piano to accompany movement exercises. All of this said, the relation between the Gurdjieff Movements and Dalcroze Rythmique needs study by a dance historian thoroughly familiar with both bodies of work.[81]

There is an interesting perch in time, February 1934, when Jeanne de Salzmann's brilliant pupil, the young writer René Daumal, attended what he noted to be a "demonstration" by Dalcroze and his students in Paris. The notion of demonstration, not performance, may well represent another kinship between the Gurdjieff

Movements and Dalcroze: from the 1923–1924 public events to this day, the word *demonstration* designates public presentations of the Gurdjieff Movements. For Dalcroze it meant that he conducted a class in the presence of an audience; for Gurdjieff it signaled a certain austerity, a willingness to share but not for the sake of creating an entertaining spectacle—with one exception, to which we'll soon come. Daumal was bowled over by the immediate responsiveness of Dalcroze students to improvised music and by the fluidity and intelligence of their movement.

> The method of Jaques-Dalcroze differs from all of our educational or gymnastic systems in that it wishes to approach human being as a whole. . . . Jaques-Dalcroze seems to have dreamed of a teaching method that would allow us to weigh sounds, touch numbers, hear movements, sense ideas, conceive feelings, see melodies, and breathe rhythms. . . . The pupil . . . first learns to react at once, by an agreed gesture, to a given musical signal . . . [and] the first result . . . is this observation: "Apart from the few necessary, mechanized gestures of my daily life, I do not know how to make use of my body; I am master neither of my muscles nor of my nerves, I am incapable of even somewhat sustained attention, I have no memory, I am absent from myself." At least, if the pupil in question cares for his own existence.[82]

This is quite fascinating: Daumal is looking at the Dalcroze method and results through a Gurdjieffian lens—and, after admiration, that gives rise to demurral. It strikes him that Dalcroze pupils "possess the supplest and most complete means of expression that a human being can possess," but to what end? "It seems that they can do whatever they want: but it has to be recognized that in general they don't know what to do." Among the younger pupils, Daumal perceives a finely trained expressive faculty used only to express "shadows or conventions of feeling, empty attitudes, nearly stereotypes."[83] Daumal concludes that the work of Jaques-Dalcroze has no aim; it prepares the student for . . . what? He allows only one exception to this charge: the musical training of children, where he gives due credit to the success of the Dalcroze method in Swiss elementary schools. Late in his review article, Daumal alludes enigmatically to teachers other than Dalcroze "who have taken up the best part of his method and use it, among other means, toward the sole purpose, beyond naming, which every human being can pursue with dignity."[84]

This is not Daumal at his best. His multiple judgments pull uneasily toward an undisclosed destination: movement and musical exercises as taught in those years by Jeanne de Salzmann to a group of devoted pupils. He dedicated a separate article to that topic in the same year, 1934, in which he speaks freely and warmly, as a poet and close observer of human nature—first of all his own.[85] But he surely recognized in the methods of Émile Jaques-Dalcroze the source of some of the methods of his teacher. Just as Gurdjieff had a debt to Theosophy, he had a debt to Dalcroze, about whom he learned from the Swiss educator's pupils. Dalcroze didn't teach the sacred, but he did teach the effervescent human and a way from music study to oneself as a whole; not a small challenge and a large accomplishment.

Guided by Alexandre and Jeanne de Salzmann, Gurdjieff tried in 1921–1922 to lease the beautiful building in Hellerau that had once been the Dalcroze Institute; it could have become the home of the institute he had in mind to found in Europe. The negotiation didn't work out well at all; they moved on to Paris—where a chance encounter with Jessmin Howarth, a Dalcroze graduate and friend then training a corps de ballet at the Paris Opera in Dalcroze techniques, led to an invitation to use the Dalcroze studio while it was free during the summer holiday. As noted earlier, only a dance historian will have enough perspective to detail and more richly understand the kinship between Gurdjieff and Dalcroze. But is it too much to say that they were unacknowledged brothers?

MOVEMENTS AT THE PRIEURÉ AND IN PUBLIC PERFORMANCE

Like music, dance is difficult to put into words. We enter the Study House and fall mute. Gifted dance critics can create a parallel text which has its own beauty, but it is not dance. We face that obstacle here. Gurdjieff's first troupe of skilled dancers would have practiced everything from the highly elaborate "Initiation of a Priestess," for which only the music survives—Olga de Hartmann witnessed it one evening from the Study House balcony—to a series of six "Obligatories" with which pupils begin their approach to Movements. Gurdjieff is reported to have said that his entire teaching is in the first of them. I don't know comprehensively in what respects that is so. I do know that the music of the First Obligatory begins with a swirl of four rapid notes rising to a majestic G minor chord of the dominant. It is a call to be and to act—but one holds still, listening, absorbing the energy of the chord, finding oneself. External movement begins only with a second bold chord—and on from there through a sequence of movements and tempi that progressively add complexity and speed. The initial stillness and listening are a teaching, as is all that follows in its demand for relaxed balance to coordinate dynamic movements of the arms, legs, and head. The Movement as a whole establishes a center—it is oneself—while the changing tempi and increasing complexity ask that center to be steady and keen. The music ranges over a sequence of feelings from majesty and gravity to aerial lightness—and back around again. All of this is a shared experience: a class typically assembles in three or four rows of six men and women, with a teacher and pianist. All are responsible to one another.

There is a particular silence and respect in a Movements Hall; one enters the silence with spontaneous respect and becomes part of it. It must also have been so in the Prieuré Study House, the first Movements Hall. It is a place where the need for attention is acutely experienced, and where attention is born. It is a place of effort and challenge, beauty and self-confrontation; of awkwardness and grace, willingness and discovery. One of the sacred dances filmed by Jeanne de Salzmann as a lasting record bears the title "The search for total presence." This is the possibility and necessity. However elusive it may remain, drawing even a little closer to authentic presence in the course of a class is a modest revolution, one's own revolution.

Although I fault Gurdjieff's critics for attacking him and the teaching itself on the basis of scant knowledge and prejudices passed thoughtlessly from one to the next, the same cannot be said of their attitudes toward the Movements, which have been for the most part invisible for decades. There was much notice in British, American, and to a lesser degree French news media in 1923–1924, when Gurdjieff brought the dances to public attention, but in later decades public presentations have been rare—for example, the first public offering by the Gurdjieff Foundation of New York, after a gap of some fifty years, occurred in spring 2017. Yet, since the Prieuré, work with Movements has been nearly continuous in Gurdjieff societies and institutes without calling public notice to itself. There have been many reasons for discretion, perhaps above all a concern that the Movements not drift off from the teaching as a separate performance discipline. An unintended consequence of discretion has been that assessments of Gurdjieff and the teaching by critics (well-meaning or not) generally lack this element, although Movements are integral to the teaching and represent one of Gurdjieff's unique offerings to Western men and women in search of themselves. It is a little as if one set out to describe the Statue of Liberty—the serene face and classical gown, the soft patina from long exposure to the elements—without mentioning the torch held high. In future we can do better.

Movements are dance/music creations; the music composed by Gurdjieff and de Hartmann in collaboration is inseparably bound to each Movement.[86] Thomas de Hartmann has provided an account of the composers' collaboration; others witnessed it. Ever the modest pupil, de Hartmann gave all credit to Gurdjieff—he, the professional musician, merely harmonized the compositions, gave them finished form, followed instructions. But that has never seemed entirely believable; the mutuality must have been richer and deeper. De Hartmann brought to the collaboration everything he had learned as a conservatory student under Rimsky-Korsakov and other vastly distinguished musicians, and his career in pre-revolutionary Russia had placed him in the front rank of his generation. When in his very last days Gurdjieff asked him, through Jeanne de Salzmann, to compose music for the "Thirty-Nine," the Movements he had created during World War II and later, de Hartmann consented and wrote some of the most extraordinary music for Movements in the repertory—strictly in the idiom established with Gurdjieff more than twenty years earlier. I understand through oral sources that he had some hints from Madame de Salzmann, improvised musical elements that had seemed promising in class; a skilled musician, she had accompanied Gurdjieff at the piano when he introduced the new sequence of Movements and fitted them to the class. The music for the "Thirty-Nine" demonstrates that de Hartmann had deeply absorbed and retained the idiom, despite the fact that his independent compositions for orchestra, chamber groupings, and voice were wholly different in style. He had turned back toward Gurdjieff from his own practice of a contemporary style akin to those of his generational peers, Russian and French.[87] In later years Gurdjieff's independent music, meditative improvisations on a hand-operated harmonium in minor scales and Middle Eastern modes without compositional elaboration or finish, created a touching atmosphere and often ended evenings with his pupils in his Paris apartment.[88] The music that flowed from their collaboration, for both Movements and in time a wealth of pieces for solo piano, bears a composite signature: it needed them both.

Margaret Anderson, among others, could recall the excellence of the leading members of the dance troupe at the Prieuré. "Usually Gurdjieff began the evening at the piano," she has written, "composing the music for a new dance-movement which M. de Hartmann scored simultaneously; then the pupils began to work it out under Gurdjieff's instructions, always given in a mental shorthand that sounded far too rapid to be understood. But the woman from Constantinople and several others translated the comments into movement almost as swiftly as M. de Hartmann had made the piano orchestration."[89] The woman from Constantinople may refer to Olgivanna, though she wasn't from Constantinople.

Quick and able as some participants were, the Movements were not and have never been intended for professional dancers. For many evenings, no doubt at the back of the class, young Stanley Nott was contending with himself. Preparing a new Movement, "Gurdjieff called the three teachers to him," Nott recalled, "showed them the movements a few times with explanations, gave Hartmann the melody, and went and sat down. They began to work at once on the gestures; and in a short time, less than an hour, were teaching them to us. But we young pupils had to spend many hours working on them before we were able to do them passably well."[90] The difficulty wasn't just to commit the sequence to memory. "It took me a long time," Nott recognized, "to learn to sense and feel each movement, gesture, posture. Such a simple thing it seemed, to 'sense,' but, being English, brought up on physical drill and army training, I had to be reminded over and over again to 'sense' my body."[91]

Years later, in the 1930s and as it happens in Chicago, Gurdjieff was approached by a pupil who was, in fact, a professional dancer—but she was somewhat older now and fearful that her body would soon be unable to stand the strain of long rehearsals. In response, she recalled, "Mr. Gurdjieff rose from his desk," and moved toward her. "In very emotional tones he said: 'Where I come from, in the monasteries, there are a great many dancers at all stages of development, all ages. But only older dancers permitted to dance in the temples. Only those who have gone through years of apprenticeship. Only older women dance the rituals. And they are all fire, all perfection, their movements are beautiful, performed with precision. All these women are old, over sixty. They dance like goddesses.'"[92]

Gurdjieff's Movements were and are for everyone willing to participate. Arguably, the only professional performers over the near-century since the Prieuré 1923 were the troupe Gurdjieff trained and brought first to the Théâtre des Champs-Élysées and later to American cities, and they were professional only for the duration of the tour. Some of the most skilled and experienced became teachers, but that role too is a study, not a profession. After seeing the Movements at the Prieuré or in Paris, the outstanding ballet impresario of his day, Serge Diaghilev, is said to have invited Gurdjieff to present Movements as a subordinate feature of some performances of his company, the Ballets Russes. Gurdjieff refused. I don't know whether the obstacle was subordination or the transition to professional performance. Whichever it may have been, it was a turning point toward the privacy that has prevailed, apart from rare public offerings, since then.[93]

The program notes for the winter-spring 1924 Movements presentations in New York, like the Parisian program, raise a point not yet explored. The ideas and language take us to the edge of modern Western culture; the audience—and we ourselves—are asked to be receptive to an unfamiliar theme: the two purposes of sacred dance.

Oriental dances have not lost the deep significance—religious, mystic, and scientific—which belonged to them in far off ages. Sacred dances have always been one of the vital subjects taught in esoteric schools of the East. Such gymnastics have a double aim: they contain and express a certain form of knowledge and at the same time serve as a means to acquire a harmonious state of being. . . . Art in that early time served the purpose of higher knowledge and of religion. . . . Ancient sacred dance is not only the medium for an aesthetic experience but also a book as it were, containing . . . definite . . . knowledge. Yet it is a book which not everyone can read who would.[94]

Gorham Munson, whom we have encountered in earlier pages, bears witness to the personal impact of this closing sentence.

How quickly we learned the truth of the last observation. The . . . "obligatory exercises", the initiation of the priestess, the dervish dances, the pilgrimage movement called "measuring-one's-length", the folk- and work-dances, the enneagram dance— all these and many others had a strange impact that can only be described as awakening. The design and the detail were extraordinarily precise, and one could well believe that they were an exact language to convey knowledge. But one could not read it, only feel it; and the feeling was—tremendous.[95]

What he writes is valid to this day for many dedicated participants in Movements classes. Some Movements—there are perhaps two hundred in all—are composed in an open, instantly grasped language: for example, of prayer in movement or of quiet circularity as if worlds were in motion. But as far as I know there is no explanatory tradition interpreting in words what one dances. One has to "see it feelingly," like Gloucester in *King Lear*, and that is quite enough. Gurdjieff put considerable emphasis on what he called the "instinctive sensing of reality," weak in many of us but not irretrievably so.[96] Participants in the Movements are more likely to sense their meaning instinctively than to work it all out in words—for which in any case there is scarcely time and no compelling need. Yet it is true that Gurdjieff stated more than once that dances preserved from very ancient times "correspond precisely to our books." In his autobiography he evokes at length a monastery where he witnessed such dances performed by superbly trained priestesses—he may well have had them in mind when he encouraged the anxious dancer in Chicago. "Everyone in the monastery knows the alphabet of these postures," he writes, "and when, in the evening in the main hall of the temple, the priestesses perform the dances indicated for the ritual of that day, the brethren may read in these dances one or another truth which men have placed there thousands of years before .... And these dances are called sacred."[97]

His description of the priestesses' training dwells on the antiquity of the dances, "at least four thousand five hundred years old."[98] I don't know whether this archeological assertion is to be taken literally, but its import is clear: Gurdjieff had limitless respect for the traditions of sacred dance he encountered and wished his pupils to respect, study, and assimilate them as he had. He prolonged those traditions, gave them place and purpose in life today, and added to them through original choreography created in the spirit long ago established. Among the roles he played during his years in the West—founder and director of an institute, author, and still others—there was one identity he accepted and lived without a trace of irony. It was enough, and said all that needed to be said: "simply a teacher of dancing." Elsewhere in his writings, he enlarged on that a little: "a rather good teacher of temple dances." He hadn't wished to be an author; as we'll soon see, he felt that authorship was forced on him by circumstances. But he had wholeheartedly wished to be a rather good teacher of temple dances.

In the course of 1923, as Gurdjieff and the Prieuré dancers prepared for theatrical performances, we already know that invited guests and journalists were welcomed on some weekends to witness the Movements and acquaint themselves with the Institute. French newspapers weren't terribly interested. One rare notice, searching for a familiar point of reference, described the Institute as a new, Orientalized edition of the nineteenth-century utopian socialist communities championed by the Comte de Saint-Simon and Charles Fourier. Fourier's concept of phalansteries, communal homes for more than one thousand members of a phalanx, provided an easy platform for ridiculing the Prieuré and its founder, as did the quasi-religious fervor of the next generation of Saint-Simonists. "Who would have said, who would have thought," wrote a French journalist, "that the prosaic twentieth century would see an alarming revival of the Saint-Simonian community or the Fourierist phalanstery? . . . So Monsieur Bazard and Father Enfantin have again set foot on earth. Only Father Enfantin has traded his name . . . for that of G. S. [sic] Gurdjieff."[99] Bazard and Enfantin were leaders, somewhat notorious, of the Saint-Simonist movement. In coming decades, French authors and journalists critical of Gurdjieff would mockingly recall the phalanstery from time to time; it seemed an adequate, dismissive parallel. In François Mauriac's lament over Katherine Mansfield's bad judgment, we have already encountered it.

British journalists showed up in force at the Prieuré and, with some exceptions, went home to mock and vilify what they had encountered. "'Nature' School for Society Cranks," reads a headline of March 31, 1923, with the following just beneath: "Weird Music and Flimsy Draperies. In the heart of a French forest certain distinguished British Intellectuals of both sexes indulge in nightly paroxysms of weird dancing and mysticism in the practice of a 'soul' seeking cult inaugurated by a handsome and alluring Greek."[100] The long article under this heading is for the most part shameless fantasy: for example, the Study House is rechristened the "House of Pleasure," and Gurdjieff is described as moving "in flowing white robes through the 'House of Pleasure'. . . . The dancers wear only the lightest and flimsiest of clothing and there is an atmosphere of complete frankness and unconventionality." The costuming was never flimsy or sensual, as the author implies; both men and women typically wore an ivory-colored, rather long tunic and pants of the same material, sashed at the waist in the colors of the spectrum. Gurdjieff himself dressed plainly, no flowing robes. Another British headline reads, "'Dr.' Gurdjieff and His Magical Secret of Life. How to be a Super-Man or Super-Woman by Feeding Pigs, Dancing Weird Dances All Night and Other Fantastic Antics."[101] The balance of the article fabricates an interview with Gurdjieff, who is quoted as saying things he could not possibly have said. Articles in other papers were equally grotesque; one headline reads, "Amazing Scenes at Home of Weird Cult. Princess and Millionaire as Dancing Dervishes. Strange Doings of Men and Women Disciples From All Parts of the World Who Are Learning to Live 200 Years."[102] There is a hint in one British paper that the presence of Orage at the Prieuré lay behind this mocking attention.

> How far the Fontainebleau mystics may have gone on the way to that full development of the mind which is their ideal can be known only to themselves. What the "profane," i.e., all the world minus the little band, can remark is that they have been accorded a measure of publicity rarely given by the Press to any but boxers, criminals, and movie stars. Whether this is due to the fact that among the disciples is to be found one of the most brilliant of living English journalists may be taken as matter for speculation.[103]

The contrast between Gurdjieff's reflections about sacred dance and much journalistic reception at that time dramatizes the cultural disconnect facing Gurdjieff, the teaching, and the dances. He and his immediate circle kept a close eye on the publicity effort—for such it was. Someone at the Prieuré was responsible for a meticulous album of newspaper clippings with occasional marginal notes in Russian and other languages.[104] Looking at this malicious press, a friend of mine asked whether Gurdjieff and the Institute could have been better protected by Orage or others who knew full well the excesses of the gutter press. Perhaps yes, but this must have been one of Gurdjieff's calculated risks—more good than ill might come of it. It's true that particularly in America, despite a degree of nonsense journalism, there were judicious, appreciative articles; so too in England, particularly when Orage's circle entered the fray. We can again rely on Tchekhovitch to provide vivid eye witness.

> The curiosity aroused by our activities grew day by day. Articles on the Prieuré appeared in the press both in France and abroad, and unleashed a veritable invasion of journalists. Georgi Ivanovitch received them warmly and tried to explain the meaning of our search to them. I recall that one day he said to a group of journalists, "I am going to show you some Movements whose purpose is to awaken man's latent inner possibilities, allowing him to open to a new perception of himself and of reality. If you don't distort the meaning of my words, I will gladly give you any clarification you wish." After dinner, we put on traditional costumes and demonstrated a series of specific postures for prayers and sacred dances from various oriental countries. The journalists photographed everything. This invasion of the Prieuré by the press lasted several weeks. A host of articles was published both in France and abroad, but none faithfully passed on the explanations given by Georgi Ivanovitch. They preferred instead to give free rein to the most fantastic interpretations of the meaning of our work. It was so many pearls offered to those who refused

to admit their lack of understanding. This chorus of slander made Mr. Gurdjieff's work seem like a great hoax and its creator, a charlatan—a twentieth-century Cagliostro. We were dumbfounded by the way the journalists, convinced that they had a real scoop for the gutter press, exploited the public's credulity and trust. They managed to distort a work directed toward consciousness until it was completely unrecognizable, either by making it totally absurd or by deliberately turning it into something evil. One day, Mr. Gurdjieff discovered a particularly shocking article accompanied by photographs that gave the impression that the sacred dances were somehow suspect and even immoral. From that day on, he never allowed reporters to set foot in the Prieuré again.[105]

For ten performances of a varied program of Movements, December 13 through Christmas Day, the residents moved practically the entire contents of the Study House to the storied Théâtre des Champs-Élysées, where Stravinsky had debuted *Le Sacre du printemps*.[106] Carpets, the multicolored scented fountain, goat skins and mattress seating, who knows what else. Thomas de Hartmann had orchestrated all of the music, originally piano scores, for a thirty-five-piece orchestra.[107] The program gave due emphasis to the origins of dances and ritual movements in religious communities and regions that must have been unknown to all but a few in the audience. The very first in the program: "A few gymnastic exercises selected from the 35 exercises of a school called 'The Seers.' *This school has existed since time immemorial in large artificial caves in Kafiristan, on the heights of Kidjera.*"[108] In the second part of the program, there is a somewhat similar title: "Devotional Exercises performed by the monks who style themselves 'They who tolerate freedom', and who are called by the people 'They who have renounced.'" The contrasted perspectives are striking, and of course deliberately cited; not just informational, the program reflects some of the values underlying the dances. One also learns, for example, that Eastern Christianity did not wholly abandon sacred dance: "Ritual movements performed by the Christian Monks in the environs of Sessi Madane, Transcaucasia." And that a trance oracle was still functioning at the Hudankr Sanctuary in Chitral at the time Gurdjieff passed through that forbiddingly mountainous region, now part of Pakistan. That dance was called a "fragment of a ceremony" inducing "the magnetic sleep of the priestess." There were village work dances—for example, the "shoemaker," set to delicious music—and what the program calls "popular Oriental round dances." As already noted, the demonstration also included "ritual movements of the Mevlevi Dervishes, known as the Whirling Dervishes." This must have been a very early if not the first presentation of this form of sacred dance, now well known, periodically performed in the West by Turkish Mevlevi communities, and universally admired.

All of the music in the program has survived, and many though not all of the dances and rituals. In day-to-day practice in Gurdjieff houses, Movements are identified by much simpler names, often just a date such as "June 15," likely indicating when Gurdjieff first brought the dance to class. I should add that Internet mapping services are effective only up to a point if one wants to verify place-name information in the program. "Sessi Madane" is unknown to the Internet—but there may be a spelling difference. On the other hand, Mazari-Sherif, noted as a source, is modern Mazar-e Sharif in Balkh Province, Afghanistan.

There was one further element in the program offered in American cities, though apparently not in Paris: "Various exercises for the development of memory, hearing, sight, attention and concentration."[109] A bland description, but the event itself must have been astonishing and—of all things—fun. Gurdjieff found it interesting to train Prieuré residents in techniques for secretly communicating to the stage, as if by magic or occult means, things whispered by an audience member to a roving member of the troupe, for example the name of an animal or opera. In the Study House version of this exercise, Alexandre de Salzmann on stage would almost instantly draw the animal or de Hartmann would perform an appropriate aria at the piano.[110] However did they know? These are two examples; there were other "tricks," "semi-tricks," and "real supernatural phenomena." For Prieuré residents, study of the techniques was an exercise among many others, and it must have been thrilling to bring them into performances. For the audience, the program concluded on a light note. And for us in these pages, we encounter a somewhat trivial but still telling sign of an important aspect of Gurdjieff's complex identity: the magus, the magician. We'll soon open this topic—it too was part of the Prieuré experience.

There were few reviews in French newspapers, evenly divided between appreciation and disparagement. The reviewer for *Le Petit Journal* noted "an ease, a precision, a quickness, a unity . . . an extraordinary self-mastery. . . . Incomplete as they are in view of the vast designs of Mr. Gurdjieff, these demonstrations present to our eyes new visions."[111] Another reviewer, writing for *Le Temps*, sneered as mightily as possible:

> The thing that strikes one most in these movements . . . is the strong effect of the rhythm, a hypnotic effect, for the pupils turn and stamp as if bewitched. They remind one of the primitive Slavs in the *Sacre*, of Nijinsky, and of the mechanical dancers in *Les Noces*. They perform grimly, like a group of convicts, without a smile. They exude a horrible sadness; one is instinctively repelled by the spectacle of Will reduced to nothing by suggestion. At the end of each number the performers seem to collapse inwardly becoming ugly and dull.[112]

He thought it on balance wise to "quarantine" the performers at the Prieuré—they were "phantoms with silk sashes" under the spell of "the mysterious Persian," by whom he meant Gurdjieff.

Preceded by Orage and Dr. Stjernvall, Gurdjieff and the troupe reached New York in early January and readied their performance—their demonstration—while Gurdjieff, much aided by Orage and translators, gave talks to introduce the teaching. For purposes of this book we have no need to follow them to America; much has already been well and thoroughly written (see the bibliography). A few observations, all the same. It was the Jazz Age in America, that has to be faced. There is unmistakable overlap between Mr. Gershwin and Mr. Gurdjieff in a March 1924 headline: "'Get a Hold on Rhythm, by Whirling Much and Often,' says Mr. Gurdjieff." There was also tongue-in-cheek humor—this from a Cleveland paper: "Gurdjieff To Wake Up Sleepy Yankees." And there was unimaginable stupidity. A series of syndicated papers all ran a photo of Gurdjieff arriving by steamship, raising his astrakhan cap in salute, revealing of course his shaved head, with this caption: "Willfully Bald—G. I. Gurdjieff, founder of a cult whose devotees shave their heads daily."[113] Out of shame, it is tempting to end this book immediately.

The serious press in New York, Chicago, and Boston gave the troupe a more favorable reception than in Paris. Gorham Munson was a keen eye witness: "The indisputable triumph of the tour was the program of ancient dances and movements. People who had no use for the ideas of Gurdjieff excepted the dances from their censure; the dances, they said, were strange and wonderful. There had never before been anything like them in America."[114]

Louise Welch evoked years later the uneasiness and yet interest of American audiences.

To most of the onlookers, in spite of Orage's lucid explanations, the idea that dance could be a way of self-study was foreign. In those days, dance was self-expression. The idea of sustained movement as an avenue to self-awareness was difficult to grasp. Moreover—and this was especially puzzling—these dances were obviously not primarily meant to create an aesthetic response.

Instead, those watching were given a glimpse of a moment when the dancers were in touch with unaccustomed levels of feeling and thought. The whole purpose of the dance was the experience of immediate awareness. An audience of newcomers could hardly be blamed for missing this. For the Gurdjieff sacred dance is a very subtle, if at the same time a direct way of making contact with the sources of attention and sharpening the possibility of accurate inner vision. On his first sight of this form of sacred dance, the distinguished Catholic scholar, Jacques Maritain, called it meditation in motion. For some, it was difficult to accept that the dancers, absorbed in the study of attention, made no effort to be appealing. Orage tried to make clear that theatrical attraction was not part of the discipline of these movements; there was no attempt to lure the audience. But if the spectators watched carefully, they could recognize the changes in state brought about by the movements and the dancers' attentiveness to them. This form of the Gurdjieff teaching could both produce and demonstrate the transition from ideas to inner content.[115]

One further New York memory is irresistible—recounting a crash, somehow comical though rewarding, between the high standards of Olga de Hartmann and the underlying goodness of Gurdjieff. After a performance, she recounts:

There was a meeting in Carnegie Hall in which there were a lot of people. Mr. de Hartmann and Ferapontoff translated what Mr. G. said in Russian and Mr. Orage related it to the audience. After the meeting, I asked Mr. G., "I looked out at the audience and saw that half the people were not even looking interested, and looked quite asleep. Why do you allow all these people? Wouldn't it be better to have fewer people, who are interested?" Mr. G. answered me . . . even a little bit angrily, "How can you judge? Perhaps those who seem asleep today, in 20 years something will be awakened in them and those who now seem so eager will forget in 10 days. We have to let everyone hear, the result does not belong to us."[116]

Gurdjieff felt at home and well received in America and visited periodically in the coming decades. He found Americans to be naïve, our culture young—but less spoiled, much less constrained by caste, class, and pretension than Europeans. We were eager to hear the new. While in New York, Gurdjieff gave some of his most reflective talks—for example, "The Two Rivers," addressing human destiny quite unforgettably. "It will be useful if we compare human life in general to a large river which arises from various sources and flows into two separate streams."[117] Remaining in New York, Orage, with characteristic intelligence and ease, attracted groups of people, some of whom in later years became superb teachers of the Gurdjieff material, Louise Welch among them.

AT THE LIMIT

When Gurdjieff returned to the Prieuré in April, life resumed as before. Somewhat hidden beneath the surface was his constant concern to raise and earn money for the Prieuré—for maintenance and renovation, for mortgage and other recurrent payments, for future plans, and for the many dependents who relied on him, not only family but also Russian exiles among the residents. He had business relations in Paris, where he kept a small apartment. He would come and go often; a cheerful photograph shows what appears to be a return to the Prieuré after a business day in Paris (see fig. 8), where he had come to regard the Café de la Paix as his "office." But the way of life he imposed on himself must have been tiring in the extreme. "Sleep little without regret": a Study House aphorism. Where is the limit?

Fig. 8: Return to the Prieuré from Paris. *Source*: The Gurdjieff Foundation
of New York

On July 8, 1924, he reached the limit. Driving home on his own,
he lurched off the road, struck a tree, and was discovered some time
later by a gendarme who rushed him to a local hospital and, finding identity papers in Gurdjieff's pocket, notified the Prieuré. He
had suffered a grave concussion and other injuries but no broken
bones. Attended by doctors from the hospital, by resident Prieuré
doctors, and within days by trusted Russian doctors from Paris, he
was brought back to the Prieuré in a coma that would fitfully last
for some weeks. Ever since, there have been competing explanations of the accident, of which Gurdjieff himself had no memory.
Tchekhovitch was quite sure that a dog had leapt from a passing
car, Gurdjieff swerving to avoid it.[118] Olga de Hartmann was quite
sure of a more elaborate scenario, starting with a car bursting out
of a smaller road onto the main road. And at least a few others
regarded the accident as deceptive, staged to extract Gurdjieff from
the immense burden that the Institute had proved to be. I do not
credit this third solution. There was simply too much grief around
him; the injuries were real, the loss of memory real, the blurred

eyesight real, the very hesitant return to activity also real. And then, in later years Gurdjieff spoke of the accident as transformative in ways that could never have been anticipated. It closed a chapter and opened others. We'll soon listen to his thoughts in that regard.

Olga de Hartmann wrote of that time:

> Now I really experienced for myself the sense and meaning of life with Mr. Gurdjieff and understood the significance of his personality for all of us. I felt as if without him, the forces of life would stop. . . . I felt that his whole life's work would be undone. Such fright overcame me at this idea that, at the same time, another feeling rose up and I told myself: "If God exists, it cannot happen. If God exists, Mr. Gurdjieff lives, so he will not die. Perhaps there will be weeks or months of incapacity, but he will live, because he has to live." I repeated all the time within myself "If God exists. . . ."[119]

The life of the Prieuré darkened and slowed. Every night, two or three of the Russian residents were on their knees in front of Gurdjieff's door.[120]

He slowly recovered. There are vivid scenes from those long weeks—among much else, young Fritz carrying Gurdjieff's chair for him as he walked the property, and bonfires before which Gurdjieff sat at length, as if fire renewed his strength. Jeanne de Salzmann was of the opinion at the time that he deliberately prolonged his convalescence to test the residents' independence: Could they manage without asking his counsel on matters large and small? Thomas de Hartmann agreed with her.[121] Be that as it may, on August 26, some seven weeks after the accident, Gurdjieff dictated a statement to Madame de Hartmann and had her read it aloud to the residents gathered in the salon. It was initially apologetic: "When I walked and spoke with you in the beginning, I forgot everything. That is why, if, during this time, I have done something disagreeable, if

I have offended some of you, I ask you to forgive me. Only a few days ago I began to live as before. . . . Only three or four days ago I began to remember." Then he turned to another theme. He would close the Institute. "There are very few people here who understand. I gave all my life for my Work, but the result from other people in general was not so good. . . . I don't wish to continue as I have done until now. . . . Forgive me. I wish now to live for myself." For the time being he would regard the residents as guests. "In two weeks I will begin a new work. The names of those who may stay will be posted. Others will have to leave. . . . Again, I repeat that the Institute is closed. I died."[122] The moment and his words were stark, though no one would have missed the promise of new work and the hope of a place in it.

Thomas de Hartmann was of course among his listeners. In spite of everything his heart must have been full: Gurdjieff had survived, he was nearly himself again. A few days later, de Hartmann affixed the date August 30 to a new and deeply felt composition for piano, "The Prayer of Gratitude."[123] I don't know if Gurdjieff had a hand in it. An andante in C minor, it is the memoir in sound of that time, extraordinarily touching through the simplest of means. It is also an early sign of the prolific musical collaboration between Gurdjieff and de Hartmann that would unfold in the next few years. No longer focused on the musical needs of the Movements, which Gurdjieff ceased teaching after the accident, the paired composers offered nearly daily in the salon what Orage with Russian flourish liked to call "noo moosic."[124] The four-volume edition of their music for solo piano is without exaggeration monumental. A charge to Gurdjieff's future critics: listen first to the music—there are now excellent recordings—before settling your perspective.

There were some years when I would rather grandly say to myself and a few friends that I was no longer interested in Gurdjieff's ideas, all that had palled on me—but I was interested in Gurdjieff's feelings, therefore in the music and Movements. It was just a way of continuing; one does need strategies. But the point was true: the music of the mid- and late 1920s is a text unto itself, text of another kind, endlessly nourishing.

Despite Gurdjieff's statement, the Institute did not close. Unquestionably, it shed residents who by then should in any case have known better than to rely on Gurdjieff permanently for room and board and a life. He was no longer willing to support them. While recovering, Gurdjieff had weighed I suppose virtually everything. The Institute was a formidable vehicle for his teaching. A nucleus of qualified teachers was taking shape; in time they could and would carry the Gurdjieff material toward future generations. Further, the Institute was generating piecemeal a valid though unpublished literature—transcribed talk by talk—that could in time reach far beyond its walls. But the Prieuré also had limitations, not least that its existence depended squarely on him, a man no longer young and no more sheltered than any of us from vicissitude.

A New Discipline: Authorship

Reluctantly recognizing that he might put much of his teaching, though not all, into written form, he decided to write. After awkward early attempts dictated to Olga de Hartmann from his convalescent bed, he conceived what would become a vast work, the trilogy *All and Everything* with a massive book, *Beelzebub's Tales to His Grandson*, at the heart of it. As there is a chapter ahead on his writings, there is no reason to pause over them here except to note how Gurdjieff lived, now that he had reached the difficult decision to give much of his time to the new and unfamiliar discipline of authorship.

It became, for years, his central activity around which the daily life of the Prieuré resiliently arranged itself. Pupils were welcome as residents for periods of time—Orage in New York ensured that there were quite a few Americans, particularly in the summer months. J. G. Bennett has written that Gurdjieff willingly spoke with people privately to help them set their course of self-inquiry and inner work, and he often participated fully in whatever was set for Saturday evenings. Movements eventually resumed in the Study House under the direction of the lead dancers, with Mr. de Hartmann as usual at the piano. There is charming, though silent film footage of the Prieuré children on the lawn one summer practicing an Obligatory and a stop exercise under the direction of Madame de Salzmann and Madame Galumian; a toddler darts in and out among the older children, no one minds. Provided that they were known to residents, weekend visitors were not unheard of. It was as a humble weekend visitor that the young Lincoln Kirstein came to the Prieuré and left with a vision of possibility and deep regard for Gurdjieff that remained with him for a lifetime; he was the cofounder, with George Balanchine, of the School of American Ballet and New York City Ballet, and in his own right a force in the arts culture of America for many decades.[125]

Though Gurdjieff had at the Prieuré all of the leafy, shaded spots anyone could wish to write in the warmer months, he generally preferred very public places—the Café de la Paix, a local café in nearby Avon, among such places. Car trips resumed when he regained his health, but now when the caravan stopped for lunch or rest he might well take out one of the simple notebooks he used and pick up writing where he had left off. Louise March, whom he had invited to live and work at the Prieuré as a typist and German translator, once asked, "'Why don't you work here in the fresh air in these beautiful surroundings?' I gestured toward the rose garden, the goldfish pond, and the rows of sycamore trees in front of us. Gurdjieff replied, 'I always work in cafés, dance halls, places where I see people, how they are; where I see those most drunk, most abnormal. Seeing them, I can produce impulse of love in me. From that I write my books.'"[126] Dr. Stjernvall would often sit silently beside him for hours as he wrote—playing, it seemed, no apparent role. But Gurdjieff would show him text, and as a native

Russian speaker Stjernvall would suggest edits which Gurdjieff
was likely to accept most gratefully. The picture is a tranquil one:
the author in deep concentration, the bewhiskered editor and old
friend altogether at his service.[127]

Tchekhovitch and others have evoked the way of life in those
years, the hard work but also Saturday evening and holiday feasts
and weekly Turkish baths when the men would relax and joke with
one another along lines unfit for mixed company. (The women also
had their time at the Turkish bath on the property, but there is no
record of their conversations.) Tchekhovitch recalled one of those
sessions in the bath house.

> Mr. Gurdjieff took a special delight in hearing de Salzmann
> tell stories. He laughed so hard that he finally had to say,
> "Salzmann, stop, stop! You're killing us!" One day, a rather
> proper guest was shocked at seeing Mr. Gurdjieff laugh in
> this way. Smiling, Mr. Gurdjieff responded by saying that
> these two hours at the baths were the only rest he allowed
> himself each week, conforming to law. No doubt those unac-
> quainted with inner combat—the "Holy War" that one must
> wage day in and day out with oneself—have not experienced
> these moments of grace and letting go, and so they develop
> a rigid, idealized, and false representation of self-mastery.[128]

There was order in the life, but also—if we are to believe Martin
Benson, who must be believed—an improvised, anarchic undercurrent. Benson was an American veteran of World War I who had
found his way early to the Prieuré. Physically strong, a good farmer
and much else, he was capable of every kind of labor. When I knew
him decades later, he still possessed an improvisatory, anarchic
spirit; many people loved him for that, and for his unstitched wisdom. He called Gurdjieff the "Old Man," a term of respect probably
carried over from the military.[129]

The Old Man called it "the institute," but it was no more institutional than flying a kite. You lived and starved and somehow you lived. For a big party I'd stay up for a couple of days
cutting wood just for the fireplace, for the dining room, and
that was the only warm room in the house. I worked like hell.
No one else has subjected themselves in that atmosphere—just
complete subjection to his rule and law and doing the best
I knew how. The thing that gets under my skin is truly when
people become moralistic. We led an amoral life . . . a *holy,*
amoral life. My life at the Prieuré was out of this world.[130]

There are worlds of incident and detail to savor from later years
at the Prieuré, but in this vein of holiday and feast I must introduce
at this point just one starry thing. Writing about festive Saturday
evening meals after the baths, Gorham Munson could recall various
off-putting Caucasian dishes—"We ate the heads of sheep, including
that delicacy, sheep's tongue"—and recalled as well the round of
toasts in Armagnac, Gurdjieff's preferred alcohol, to a lengthy series
of "idiots." Gurdjieff had created an elaborate, multi-tiered vision
of human types—ordinary idiots, compassionate idiots, squirm-
ing idiots, and many others—to which toasts at such meals were
unfailingly to be offered. Endowing a Georgian custom of multiple
toasts with Gurdjieffian meaning, toasts to the idiots remained in
force to the end, from the Prieuré to Gurdjieff's Paris apartment
in much later years. Among Gurdjieff pupils seeking any available
relief, the term *idiot* has been given an etymologic interpretation
from the Greek, in which it harmlessly means "specific type." But
it cannot altogether escape the common meaning: it also means
idiotic. "Gurdjieff sat at the center of the table," continued Munson,
"and behaved like a fantastic character out of a book, a Rabelaisian
or Falstaffian host."[131] There is the point and word: Rabelaisian.
Gurdjieff was an austere, ruthlessly demanding teacher of temple
dancing—and on occasion festive beyond measure. Rabelaisian, to

be precise. Tchekhovitch knew and appreciated this side of Gurdjieff and had given it thought.

> I realize how difficult it is to express the essential quality that
> infused these moments of relaxation. It was Mr. Gurdjieff's
> presence, after all, that created this light-heartedness and
> genuine letting go of ourselves. He was always encouraging
> us to acknowledge the laws of nature and reminding us that,
> like breathing, the whole of life is the result of two opposite
> but complementary movements: going and coming, expan-
> sion and contraction, involution and evolution. In fact, we
> valued these moments of rest all the more since the days
> before these celebrations were always filled with intensive
> work and extraordinary demands.[132]

We should keep in reserve the notion of parallels between Gurdjieff and François Rabelais (1494–1553), a writer of genius but more
than that: he was a cultural force, an inspired and inspiring example
of intellectual and emotional freedom and humane values in an era
of growing turmoil. He too knew the examples of Pythagoras and
Diogenes. The parallels in authorial mission, literary style, and attitude are strong, although I have not been able to prove even that
a reasonable Russian, Greek, or Armenian translation of Rabelais's
works was available in the earlier years when Gurdjieff was a voracious reader. For now, we need retain no more than the image of
Gurdjieff at table, his Rabelaisian spirit of enjoyment and fellowship.

JULIA OSIPOVNA

We know too little about Gurdjieff's wife, Julia Osipovna Ostrovsky (see fig. 9), but in that respect we are not alone. Olga de
Hartmann described her as "unnoticeable and yet always there,"
and, despite long years together, she and her husband knew little

of Julia Osipovna's life until late conversations with Thomas. Of those conversations nothing has been passed along. She flashes momentarily in Prieuré records and fades back. Katherine Mansfield perceived her as "a queen exactly" in a raincoat as she looked after things in the Prieuré kitchen. Olga de Hartmann was struck by her beauty and majesty during a rehearsal of "The Initiation of a Priestess." And Gurdjieff himself, who would have met her in St. Petersburg, recalled that in a beauty contest, not further described, she had outshone the universally admired beauty of the opera star Lina Cavalieri to win first prize. An online search effortlessly demonstrates that Cavalieri was a striking beauty who appeared in opera throughout Europe, including St. Petersburg before the revolution.

In a number of passages in his writings, Gurdjieff records his love for his wife, most touchingly in his account of sitting between her and his aged mother on a bench at the Prieuré. Though the two women had no native language in common, they had worked out a language of their own and shared much about their lives. It gave him delight and comfort to hear them speak with one another behind him when he leaned toward his work table.[133] The Gurdjieff couple had not had children, and at the time we're exploring it was too late.

The best portrait in words we shall have is from Olgivanna Lloyd Wright's belatedly discovered autobiography. Olgivanna writes there that she was visiting Katherine Mansfield in the cowshed when "Georgivanitch's wife came in to milk the cows. She wore a black dress of an old German style, tight in the waist and around the breast, with the skirt flowing down in rich folds. Her beautiful head was tied with a black scarf. A gentle smile, sad and lovely, was always on her lips. The gray-blue eyes looked into the distance with just a little touch of fear in them. A truly superior face."[134] In a later passage, Olgivanna captures other features of Julia Osipovna's nature: "She loved life and spoke of it in gusty, colorful, intriguing

Fig. 9: Julia Osipovna, The Prieuré, ca. 1924. *Source*: Institut G. I. Gurdjieff, Paris

terms. I communed with her in that realm with exchange of laughter, jokes, and making fun of others. . . . She was much more bound
to life than I was, and her work lay in the direction of freedom from
her passions. But she had so much warmth, generosity, and acceptance of human weaknesses. She resolved tension between herself
and others with laughter."[135] Particularly in these words a fitting
wife for Gurdjieff is recognizable. I don't know why she retained

her maiden name Ostrovsky, but in a brief typed document from the Prieuré years, which has recently come to light in an archive, she signed her initials: J. G.

At some point in the winter of 1925 she was diagnosed with cancer. She received hospital care, but "surgery and treatment were useless," Olga de Hartmann recorded, and she returned to the Prieuré, where her husband deployed every means within his reach to lengthen her life and bring comfort.[136] Madame de Hartmann remembers him spending much of his time in her room. Everyone contributed: Thomas de Hartmann had an upright piano brought to her room, and once, charmingly, Julia Osipovna made a request of him when her husband was spending the day in Paris. "Since Georgivanich is not here, would you play Chopin for me?" she asked.[137] She was Polish by birth. As she well knew, Gurdjieff had quite severe judgments of Western music. Much of it struck him as sentimental, associative, subjective, not even remotely an inscription of essential knowledge— his foremost demand where art was concerned. De Hartmann seems to have had the whole of Western music stored in his mind; I'm sure he complied with guiltless pleasure.

Gurdjieff suffered to witness his wife's steady deterioration, "this now stooped and sallow-faced woman" walking toward him with the help of a cane.[138] He wrote later that each time he saw her walk with difficulty, "there arose in me a feeling of revolt and my heart pounded like that of a balking horse."[139] Soon she was confined to her room. Speaking with his young pupil Fritz Peters, Gurdjieff made it clear that he was helping his wife through his own vitality.

He said that his work with her was extremely tiring and very difficult "because I try to do thing with her which almost not possible. If she alone, already she be long time dead. I keep alive, make stay alive with my strength; very difficult thing.

But also very important—this most important moment in life for her. She live many lives, is very old soul; she now have possibility ascend to other world. But sickness come and make more difficult, make impossible for her do this thing alone. If can keep alive few months more will not have to come back and live this life again. You now part of Prieuré family—my family—you can help by making strong wish for her, not for long life, but for proper death at right time."

At that moment in the conversation, Gurdjieff converted its gravely personal topic into a teaching for Fritz that reaches past Fritz to readers decades later. "'Wish can help,' Gurdjieff continued, 'is like prayer when for other. When for self, prayer and wish no good; only work good for self. But when wish with heart for other, can help.' When he had finished, he looked at me for a long time, patted my head in that affectionate animal way, and sent me to bed."[140]

She was living through him, he told Fritz; "it took almost all of his daily energy."[141] What does that mean? I have lingered over this altogether saddening passage in the life of the Gurdjieff couple and the Prieuré in order to ask this question. Olga de Hartmann's unpublished memoir sheds light.

> She stayed in a big room at the end of the Ritz corridor in the Prieuré and two young people looked after her. Mr. G. came once and sat near her window in an armchair. She could not swallow anymore, even liquids. I had just entered the room when he told me, "Give me a half glass of water." He held it in his hands about ten minutes and then told me to give it to her to drink. I couldn't avoid telling Mr. G., "But you know she cannot swallow." He repeated, "Give it to her to drink." What could I do? She was his wife. So I lifted her head and tried to give her to drink. And can you imagine, she drank it

all and after that, perhaps for nearly a month, she was able to swallow liquids. Once when the doctor came to see her and stayed to dinner with us, he sat near me and told me, "She should have died a month ago. I cannot understand how she continues to live."[142]

Years earlier, when Thomas de Hartmann lay nearly dying of typhoid fever in the Caucasus, Gurdjieff had intervened. "One day I became conscious," de Hartmann recalled, "and I saw Gurdjieff bending over me with the sweat pouring down his face. All his force seemed to be directed at me. He gave me a piece of bread and went away. I sat up and began to eat it, and I realized that he had saved my life."[143] There was more than one incident of this kind in years to come: Gurdjieff as magus, here *magnetizing* water, to use the standard occult term. Where such things are concerned, I have no inclination to doubt the recollections of pupils whom I have trusted many times over on other topics. Inner work of the kind taught by Gurdjieff stores and concentrates energy and allows some gifted ones to heal others by infusing life energy absent or at low ebb—or by using water as a means of transfer. It was simply so. Further, it was not limited to Gurdjieff. Several of his closest pupils developed something like the same capacity in later years. I have never heard this outcome described as a necessity or even much discussed; it must be one of the results that Gurdjieff regarded as "mathematic," coming about in certain people as a consequence of much else.

He was well aware that greater energy entails greater responsibility. The dance theater piece most closely associated with Gurdjieff, *The Struggle of the Magicians*, pits two schools against each other in a Middle Eastern setting: schools of the Black Magician and White Magician. Never produced in full, the theater piece survives only in part—lovely fragments of music, a number of dances, the written scenario. The White Magician prevails, although the scenario ends not in triumph but with the White Magician's prayer: "Lord Creator, and all you His assistants, help us to be able to remember ourselves at all times in order that we may avoid involuntary actions, as only through them can evil manifest itself."[144] It isn't beautiful language, but the thought has staying power.

Gurdjieff chose not to be present in the very last days before his wife's death. He had given all he possibly could. He asked to be called, in Paris, when certain physical signs appeared, and so it was.

The death of Madame Ostrovsky in June 1926 is a watershed moment. Life at the Prieuré returned afterward to the norm of those years—Gurdjieff was writing, there were car trips full of incident, pupils continued to arrive for stays of a month or more, particularly from America, and Gurdjieff made several visits to America. But the centrifugal forces that would whirl apart the Prieuré and its people were beginning to make themselves felt. By the spring of 1928, Gurdjieff had come upon the fact that the quality of his work as a writer depended on two essentially predictable factors—persistence and patience—but also on a wholly unpredictable factor: the suffering caused, in his first three years as a writer, by the illness and deaths of his wife and mother.[145] He had in effect written against that suffering; it had intensified his ability. With the ruthless logic he would on occasion bring to bear, he decided "in the future, under the pretext of different worthy reasons, to remove from my eyesight all those who by this or that make my life too comfortable."[146] He would prune his life of ease.

At least in the short term, the human cost of this decision was considerable. Gurdjieff's boon companion, Alexandre de Salzmann, took his distance and now lived for the most part in Paris, where he found work in interior design and theater. There was this much providence in his Parisian years: he met the young, overwhelmingly gifted writer René Daumal and served as his first mentor in the Gurdjieff teaching. For her part, Jeanne de Salzmann remained at the Prieuré with her two children. Gurdjieff tried peaceably to persuade Thomas and Olga de Hartmann to live independently, but their loyalty was unshakable until, during a private conversation in a café, Gurdjieff so upset Thomas with a harsh accusation, likely an unfounded accusation of sexual perversion, that the composer rose and fled. Olga had to search him out in nearby crowded streets. The couple retreated to the home they had recently established in Neuilly with Olga's parents. Thomas urged Olga to continue going to the Prieuré—she was needed—but for him it was finished, and soon Gurdjieff confronted Olga in a way that prompted her also to step back completely. Thomas said of Gurdjieff, "He will always be my teacher, and I will follow his teaching, but I wish never to see him again." Olga's retrospection, written late in life, is poignant: "Except for this tragedy that Mr. G. had provoked, I would have been very happy living in our new house. . . . I didn't know what had happened in the café, but never asked my husband so as not to make him nervous again. He had almost had a nervous breakdown but, happily, his music and perhaps also myself in my happiness to arrange our new house helped to pacify him finally. All this occurred in June 1929."[147]

And then there was Orage, with whom Gurdjieff broke in 1931; Madame Ouspensky, who joined her husband in England in 1931, while retaining the highest regard for Gurdjieff; Jane Heap, whom Gurdjieff encouraged to live in Paris and found a group; and no doubt a number of others. I don't presume to understand the pattern. The documents report what they report, but the events push against the boundary they set. Where Thomas de Hartmann is concerned, the dismissal strikes me as cruel, though an oral source preserves that Gurdjieff with Jeanne de Salzmann drove to Neuilly soon after the event and discreetly waited in their car until Thomas returned home, perhaps from an errand: "He's all right," Gurdjieff said to his companion.[148]

Rosemary Lillard, a young American Dalcroze student, Texan by birth, a skilled pianist, and an early participant at the Prieuré—later to marry Stanley Nott, whom we have encountered—was asked by Gurdjieff to leave the Institute. I don't know when this occurred or the motive; the tale reached me through oral sources for which approximation is enough. Somehow she and Gurdjieff found themselves seated together at the Avon railroad station, where they conversed approximately as follows. "You insist that I leave?" she asked. And he: "Yes." She: "Well, sir, we have all been guinea pigs helping you understand how to work with Americans and English, and scientists kill their guinea pigs when the experiment is over. So you should kill me. Or let me return to the Prieuré." One touch of Texas . . . she returned. In later years many participants in the Gurdjieff teaching knew and appreciated her.

Alexandre de Salzmann and A. R. Orage died in 1934. Several others among the unwilling exiles resumed relations with Gurdjieff in later years, and for their part Thomas and Olga de Hartmann became formidable participants in the teaching after Gurdjieff's death in 1949. Thomas's death in 1956 in America, where they had made their home in that decade, marked not the end of attention to the Gurdjieff/de Hartmann music but something more like a new beginning. Thomas played and informally recorded the music, sometimes with a composer's freedom—how did all those unscored notes find their way in? And musicians who had known and worked with him kept the flame bright.

Gurdjieff's ruthless will in distancing many who had been close to him is evident in something he said to Martin Benson. He had had another auto accident on the way to Vichy. He and Stjernvall and others in the car, badly banged up, had received local medical treatment and returned to the Prieuré—Gurdjieff with metal staples stabilizing his abdomen. He insisted that Benson remove the staples (no harm done), and the next morning Benson noticed him hobbling with a cane toward the Prieuré gate. Benson insisted on calling a cab. Gurdjieff already had in mind to resume writing at a nearby "low dive," as Benson puts it. "Benson," Gurdjieff said while they waited for the cab, "I'll tell you something, my aim is to finish *Beelzebub*, and not even death will stop me."[149] This is neither Pythagoras, the lofty teacher, nor Diogenes, the ironist; it is Gurdjieff. As it happens, he was advancing that day the sweetest, most nostalgic chapter in *Meetings with Remarkable Men*, on his father.

MUCH IS WASHED DOWN: THE END OF THE INSTITUTE

We are nearing a moment of valediction. Dependent for funds on American pupils and Gurdjieff's own business ventures, typically around Parisian restaurants but seizing other opportunities as they appeared, the Prieuré could not long survive the American stock market crash of October 1929 and the subsequent Great Depression affecting Europe no less than America. Soon after Gurdjieff's first auto accident, Orage in New York shared thoughts in a letter to Jessie Dwight, his future wife, that shed light forward.

> Sometimes I think G has an unfortunate destiny *against* which he fights as lesser people try to fight against circumstances. Nothing appears to go right for the Institute of its own accord, it makes no progress, and its pupils seem to stand still. Judged by results, in fact, it seems a failure, and yet, I suppose, if only it can keep its footing, it will one day become what G means it to be. It is like building a bridge in a torrent. Much is washed down before the foundation is really laid, but in the end there is something to build upon.[150]

There was, in the end, something to build upon: the Institute as a model of dedicated community, the energy and texture of life there, the Movements and music, Gurdjieff's writings and transcribed talks, the character of the buildings themselves from Study

House to manor house, both of them not unlike others to come as the Gurdjieff teaching found a later welcome in many countries. J. G. Bennett reached a similar assessment, referring particularly to the period when he had been a resident at the Prieuré: "In spite of the obstacles, . . . Gurdjieff accomplished something that had never been seen in Europe before. He created conditions for work that enabled scores of people to discover and verify for themselves the potential for transformation that is latent in every human being."[151] This too could be built upon in later years; it was the heart of the matter.

The end for the Prieuré came in May 1932. There were too many bills to pay, and no money to pay them. Louise March, whom Gurdjieff had long since taken to calling "Sausage," so wished to help. James Moore records a simple conversation: "'Can I do anything for you?' whispered Sausage hopelessly. 'Now only money, money,' Gurdjieff replied. 'One hundred thousand francs I need at once.'" There was no such sum, and even the coal merchant had lost patience. Witnessed by Louise March and recounted by Moore from varied sources, the last days at the Prieuré seem to have blended anguish and acceptance, depending on the moment. There was a tranquil meal, concluding with Gurdjieff's harmonium music: life as it always had been. But that was not the sole mood. Gurdjieff came to the Monks' Corridor with a suitcase to collect typescript copies of his writings. March recalled:

I hear him talking to others in a loud commandeering voice. When he asks where Miss Sausage is, I open my door instantly. He says, "Mees, where your *Beelzebub*? Must go into trunk. Quick, quick. Every page must get in. Nothing can stay." Then he leaves to collect Madame de Salzmann's and Lili [Galumian's] copies of the book. The devils seem to push him. I sense something terrible. . . . When I meet Madame de Salzmann in the hall she says, "Do quiet yourself." I make the effort and reach a sort of calm.[152]

When the time came to leave, the residents had few possessions to take with them. The terms of repossession by the mortgage holder must have stipulated leaving Institute furnishings behind. It fell to Jeanne de Salzmann to rescue the music stored in a steamer trunk. Was Gurdjieff willing to leave it behind or had he been counting on her, a musician, to look after it? For some days Martin Benson remained at the Prieuré with just one companion. "At the end I was the only one there," Benson recalled. "I was in charge of the whole goddamn place. It was a fifty-eight-room château, on fifty acres! . . . And then I left. . . . Mr. Gurdjieff gave me a party in Paris."[153] Soon Benson was on his way back to America. Gurdjieff settled for the time being in a room at the Grand Hôtel, just steps from the Café de la Paix where he surely resumed writing as in the past. Among other things he had a text under way on the history of the Prieuré, later familiar under the title "The Material Question."[154] An early draft carried a different title, an unedited expression of Gurdjieff's feelings: "The History of the Arising, Existence, and with Terrible Agony the Death of the Institute of Harmonious Development of Man, Founded by G. Gurdjieff."[155]

There were several important retrospections on the Institute, none more so than Gurdjieff's own. Years later, J. G. Bennett offered an insightful critique focused on the early months—the months of "skoryy, queeker!"

No description of the external life at the Prieuré can give any adequate idea of what happened there inside people. They could see for themselves that miracles were possible and were occurring before their eyes. They could see people as they really were behind the habitual masks and patterns of outward behavior. . . . But . . . there was something not right. It was too frenzied; we were all in too much of a hurry to "enter paradise at all costs by next week," as Gurdjieff put it. . . . Few, at that time, were ready to accept that the process of transformation takes time, and that each stage must be completed if the next is to go forward properly. . . . Looking back, it seems that Gurdjieff was still experimenting. He wanted to see what European people were capable of. . . . As I see it now, we did not really grasp the profound change of attitude toward ourselves that is needed before the process of work can act freely in us. We were perhaps misled by Gurdjieff's insistence on effort and yet more effort. This insistence was probably needed with Asiatics and even Russians [but] . . . the British . . . in 1922 still had that puritanical streak that makes us believe that what is good for us must necessarily be hard and even unpleasant.[156]

This was a pupil's view, with the ring of truth. There was another, Gurdjieff's own, focused not on the Institute as such but on its director: on himself. It took some years for this view to emerge or at least find its words; we hear it first in the summer of 1936 when Gurdjieff and three members of the Rope were spending time at his "summer office," the Park Café in Vichy. He was thinking back to the auto accident of July 1924. "Yes, all is different since accident," he said. "Then I die, in truth all die. Everything began then from new. I was born that year, 1924. I am now twelve-year-old boy, not yet responsible age. I can remember how I was then—all thought, feeling. I was heavy, too heavy. Now everything is mixed with light."[157]

It was not a passing assessment. Nearly two years later, again with the Rope, he restated that "my past was till accident, then I begin my real life."[158] And even very many years later, in 1948 among American pupils joining him in Paris, "he was speaking of the days long ago, not only of the Institute but even before all that. He said in speaking of those faraway days, 'Before I too heavy.'"[159]

And yet . . . the brilliance and courage of the Prieuré years are unmistakable, never to be forgotten, and the creations of that time, from the teaching itself to the dances and music and more, still possess untapped potential. Denis Saurat, the French academic who visited the Prieuré in 1923 but published his views only in 1933, had asked Gurdjieff, "Why did you come to Europe?" Gurdjieff's response: "Because I want to add the mystical spirit of the East to the scientific spirit of the West. The Oriental spirit is right but only in its trends and general ideas. The Western spirit is right in its methods and techniques. Western methods alone are effective in history. I want to create a type of sage who will unite the spirit of the East with Western techniques."[160] The goal as stated is still fresh, carried not only by Gurdjieff houses but also by other teachings in the West which have reached, by their own paths, much the same sense of things.

The physical Prieuré was no more resistant than anything else to the weight of time. Edith Taylor, a resident for some years, returned to the Study House long after its abandonment and later recorded her feelings: "To this day the Study House holds for me a sacredness that no church ever could. On my last visit to it, so many years after my first, tears came to my eyes to see such magnificence in ruins; the carpets chewed by rats, the offal of dogs and cats and the smell of rotting wool nauseated me; windows had been broken and the supports of the roof had given way under the weight of several winters' snows."[161]

Seeds break up, they keep no beauty of their own. The dismembered Prieuré was a source of seeds that brought life elsewhere.

"You remember at Prieuré, Miss Gordon? . . . You must remember all your life. Who was not there miss too much."

CHAPTER 5

Lux in Tenebris: The 1930s

I have lost a source. The words recorded in my notes are memorable, the comment that enlarges on them is written in Russo-English, which had been mastered by the women of the Rope. Perhaps, then, this fragment lies somewhere in their vast record of conversations with Gurdjieff and belongs to the 1930s. "G. proposes a new toast to a newcomer: 'May you do good all the mornings of your life.' And explains at length how if do good in morning, then all day go well." The morning sunlight, the goodness and hope in these words, convey the steady undercurrent of benevolence in Gurdjieff's person and teaching. But between 1931, when it had become evident that the Prieuré might fall, and 1938, when a seemingly modest event signaled a new beginning, we will need to search out *lux in tenebris*, light in the darkness.[1] There was light; there was also darkness. Gurdjieff's own recognition of his changed estate is reflected in an exchange with Louise March—translator, secretary, and friend—in March 1931. You'll recall that his name for her was Sausage. It was the last day of a New York visit; he would soon board a ship for Paris. "Before he left," she wrote, "my heart was almost torn out of me as I read 'The Mountain Pass' aloud to him. 'Why you cry?' he asked. 'Sausage, now difficult see me.' He indicated his shabby jacket. 'Easy for you when I was king.'"[2] These two remembered moments bracket the years ahead.

When the Prieuré closed in May 1932, its few residents necessarily took in hand their lives. Dr. and Mrs. Stjernvall with their son Nikolai found a home in Normandy and kept in touch with Gurdjieff over the years. Jane Heap followed Gurdjieff's advice by founding a group in Paris to study the teaching, and she resumed frequent contact with Gurdjieff when he reestablished himself in Paris. When Heap moved to London in 1935, she proved to be a most engaging teacher; certain of her pupils were destined to influence the next generation. Jeanne de Salzmann, who will reappear in a uniquely important role some years later, lived successively in Évian-les-Bains on the south shore of Lake Geneva, later in Geneva itself, and in 1934 moved to Sèvres, a suburb of Paris, where she assembled a small residential community in a house of modest size. In Évian and Geneva she earned her livelihood as a teacher of movement and music disciplines; an article by her pupil René Daumal reflects that moment.[3] At Sèvres the situation was different: her companions there were dedicated students of the Gurdjieff material, some also destined to influence what the teaching would become.

And Gurdjieff himself? He shared with the Rope a colorful way of thinking about pleasantness and adversity. It was a sort of sarabande, a descending litany based I think on the Persian regard for roses and acknowledgment that no good rose lacks thorns; roses figure in Persian proverbs. "Roses roses," it begins. Then "roses rose. Rose rose, rose thorn, thorn thorn, thorns thorn and thorns thorns."[4] Thorns have their good use as what Gurdjieff called "reminding factors." Solita Solano recorded in her journal for those years that her friends Kathryn Hulme and Alice Rohrer "returned from a motor trip with him, haggard with fear. K. reported he said, 'Which would you choose—all roses, roses or all thorns, thorns? One for inner life, the other for outer? If both thorns you choose, an intentional contact can be made.'"[5] It had long been Gurdjieff's teaching that intentional suffering is transformative—suffering fully accepted and known in all of its dimensions, physical or moral, and suffering deliberately chosen as an encounter with oneself and source of new insight.

For Gurdjieff in the 1930s there were thorns of both kinds and few roses. Materially speaking he had little money, although on occasion more than enough: then he tended to splurge on the Rope or other close people through car trips or robust meals at restaurants. Solita avoided him on certain days: "Today I'm keeping out of his way, it's rent day and God help anyone who approaches when he must have money, for he speaks of nothing else and it makes me nervous."[6] His work as an author had advanced; by the early 1930s he must have been well along in *Meetings with Remarkable Men*, the second part of the intended trilogy. Orage's last gift to him, in 1931, was an edition of one hundred bound copies of the typescript of the first part, *Beelzebub's Tales*, to be sold for ten dollars each, a good sum at the time.[7] Although the book would continue to be edited and somewhat enlarged until its publication in 1950, it was already substantially settled—and massive: as finally published it numbered 1,238 pages. This first edition of the *Tales* was surely rose, not thorn, though its circulation would have been limited to Gurdjieff's American pupils and well-wishers, few in number. Gurdjieff made several trips to the United States between winter 1931 and spring 1935, but whatever he had wished from those trips—not least, reliable sources of funds and possibly relocating the Institute—did not work out satisfactorily. The Orage group in New York remained for the most part fiercely loyal; that was important for the future. As well, Gurdjieff renewed contact with Olgivanna Lloyd Wright and spent part of the summer of 1934 at Taliesin East, in Wisconsin, where his breathtakingly colorful relation with Frank Lloyd Wright began.[8]

One of the most gifted and arrogant men in America, Wright understood that he had encountered at least *nearly* his match in all respects. His articles in the local newspaper, July through September 1934, as captured in Paul Beekman Taylor's invaluable documentary collection, pay generous homage to Gurdjieff and convert him into a Wright-like personage. "Taliesin was much honored last week by the visit of Georgi Gurdjieff, the noted philosopher and leader of the famous work at the Prieuré Fontainebleau," Wright noted in July. Some weeks later, no doubt many experiences later, he again reported.

[Gurdjieff possesses] a massive sense of his own individual worth . . . a man able to reject most of the so-called culture of our period and set up more simple and organic standards of personal worth and courageously, outrageously live up to them. Notwithstanding super-abundant of personal idiosyncrasy Georgi Gurdjeef [*sic*] seems to have the stuff in him of which our genuine prophets have been made. And when prejudice against him has cleared away his vision of truth will be recognized as fundamental to the man men need. Real men who are real forces for an organic culture of the individual today are rare. I venture to say that one might count them on the fingers of one hand with the thumb to spare.

At Gurdjieff's departure from Taliesin, Wright must have felt constrained to assure the fellowship of architects around him and the general public that, as Taylor reports, "there would not be a Gurdjieff center established at Taliesin."[9] Yes and no. In point of fact, Olgivanna shared elements of the Gurdjieff teaching with the community, saw to it that Movements were taught, and shaped community life somewhat along the lines of life at the Prieuré.[10] It couldn't get out of hand—Frank had his limits—but it was unmistakably so.

Where was the center of gravity in these years? It was not in America, although several visits in the 1930s gave rise to new expressions of the teaching and endless incident. The center of gravity was in Paris: in Gurdjieff's own small room at the Grand Hôtel and later in more spacious apartments, in the modest hotel suite of Solita Solano and her companion, Janet Flanner, on the Left Bank, in Kathryn Hulme's room in the same hotel, in restaurants, notably L'Écrevisse, the Crayfish, where Gurdjieff was particularly at home, and in the Café de la Paix, where he was a regular client well understood and appreciated by the staff. It was a narrow circuit, supplemented from time to time by trips to Vichy and elsewhere.

We should make the acquaintance of a new cast of characters: the Rope, who formed a close circle around Gurdjieff in the mid-1930s in Paris when there were scarcely any other pupils. A circle or retaining wall. They received him with awe and love. He in turn offered what he knew and understood. They tolerated and learned from his stormy nature and managed not to judge him harshly or permanently, though at times they would turn away from him, and he from them. He was a lion in winter; they knew that. What no one could know was how long winter would last; there was perhaps no other season. Nearly all of the women of the Rope were lesbians; Providence must have a sense of humor because no one was more resolutely male than Gurdjieff. Sexual relations were a necessity for him—we'll speak of that in time. But the new circle around him offered nothing. They loved him in another way, and he didn't mind once he had grasped that the women of the Rope were as resolutely distant in that respect as he was resolutely male. And one of them was nearly a daughter, not by blood but by affinity.

I must acknowledge here that two books by William Patrick Patterson provide a wealth of material about the Rope and their conversations and adventures with Gurdjieff.[11] I have worked from archives, in part the same archives he has published, but his publications make it easy—how rarely one can use that word where Gurdjieff is concerned—to know a very great deal about this long moment and its rough but brilliant teachings.

Elizabeth Gordon, English, long at the Prieuré, was elevated by Gurdjieff to be the "Mother Superior" of them all after Jane Heap left Paris in 1935 to live in London. Heap was nonetheless a full participant in the Rope when she could be, and it was she who had brought together in her Parisian group several other members, including Georgette Leblanc as well as Kathryn Hulme and Alice Rohrer, both San Francisco–born, Alice a well-to-do fashion designer. Margaret Anderson, Heap's cofounder and coeditor of the famed avant-garde *Little Review*, had also been a resident at the Prieuré for some period. Louise Davidson, a friend of Kathryn Hulme's, was a participant. And Solita Solano, born Sarah Wilkinson in Troy, New York, soon enough reborn by her own choice as the free-spirited novelist, journalist, and poet known to all as Solita Solano (see fig. 10). Since 1922 she had lived with Janet Flanner, familiar to readers of *The New Yorker* as Genêt. Flanner's "Letters from Paris" in that magazine and other journalism over decades set a standard for clarity, worldliness, wit, and quiet wisdom; she was inimitable. She also knew every writer and artist in Paris and had access to everyone else, or so it could seem. She was *not* a member of the Rope. When first introduced to Gurdjieff, she mentioned to Solita (so I will call her) that he was a "handsome, aristocratic old gentleman."[12] Some good time later, she asked Solita: "When is that damned Asiatic bugger going away?"[13] Where Solita was concerned, he would never go away. Gurdjieff remained central to her life, and the two women had a fully honored pact not to interfere with one another's lives.

The lives of Jane Heap and Margaret Anderson had ignited early. By the time they became Prieuré residents in 1924 they had already played together a leading role, through the *Little Review*, in the development of Modernist literature and art. Kathryn Hulme (1900–1981) was as yet undeclared, so to speak. Cooperating with Solita, she would prove to be a formidable chronicler of incident and teachings around Gurdjieff in the 1930s, and a strong public future lay ahead. Her semifictional novel, *The Nun's Story*, published in 1956, became a best seller and a perfectly lovely film starring Audrey Hepburn. Some years later her book *Undiscovered Country* (1966), based on the private Gurdjieff chronicle she had

Fig. 10: Solita Solano, ca. 1928, portrait by Berenice Abbott.
Source: Berenice Abbott Archive, Ryerson Image Centre.
Published with permission.

amassed with Solita, was immediately recognized as a unique and eloquent participant's witness. For Gurdjieff she was "Krokodil," a large, appetitive creature in his circle of pupils. Solita Solano, known to Gurdjieff as "Kanari," had no public career comparable to Kathryn Hulme's, although she was a well-published journalist and novelist. However, her Gurdjieff chronicle, filled with personal reflections, and her lifelong, practical loyalty to

Janet Flanner strike me as accomplishments leaving nothing to be desired. "My life with Janet," she once wrote, "—she's the only family I've ever had."[14]

Why did Gurdjieff want the company of the Rope? Solita would wonder about that; it was never consistently evident. But this much was clear: he needed readers and listeners to measure the impact of *Beelzebub's Tales* in English, and the Rope was unreservedly willing. "I don't know what he wants of us," Solita wrote at the beginning of November 1935, "but I sense that we are in test tubes now for something he wants to know about his book. He watched us last night as never before and the room was charged with his dynamo and our super-effort. Never have I known or imagined such vibrations . . . It was really life without a body, though our bodies were *in extremis*."[15] In those months marathon readings were the norm. A week after this first entry Solita noted, "Last night we read from 8:30 to 3 A.M. without a break." On that occasion Gurdjieff issued a somewhat threatening forecast which in fact did not come to pass: "He said he plans to write on for two months, finish last book, then start classes. After that we can never see him alone, only from a distance; how we are with him now, is accident. Reading second series now, the portraits [referring to *Meetings with Remarkable Men*]."[16] In fact, for years more he remained closely linked to the Rope, and with some of its members to the end of his life. Solita was apparently most responsive to the *Tales* as they were read aloud, and her responses most interested Gurdjieff. "I seem to go into a state when I'm listening to the readings," she confessed. "The girls say he leans forward and watches me and hardly takes his eyes from my face and that if I knew how he was watching I never could keep my mind on the book. . . . That is what they tell me, I have not seen it because I do super-concentration. They tease me and call me teacher's pet."[17]

It was undeniable: she *was* teacher's pet. In a letter to Kathryn Hulme she shared how that felt. "Did I tell you that in the street

(I walked home alone with him—to hotel for reading) he said, 'You wonder why I am so good to you?' I said, 'Yes, why?' He said, 'I not tell you yet,' and smiled under the electric light like a father. He said, 'Is it bad for you that I good to you?' I said, 'No, I am sure not.' He said, 'I think so too.'"[18] What a fine bond, lightly declared. Of course, this was Gurdjieff: he made life difficult for Solita and for all of the women roped to her. "You very dirty," he told her, "but got something very good—many people not got—very special."[19] It's unclear to me what that was, as she had many strengths. Gurdjieff said that she had will. It must have been that. "Maybe I'm the guinea pig he needs," Solita speculated, not very trustingly. But still, she wrote, "What I'm learning! My head feels as if it were growing. Never did I think I would have such an opportunity."[20] But every stick has two ends, this stick no exception. Solita wrote:

No, I don't go toward Gurdjieff with active pleasure. It's the dentist all over again. There just is literally nothing else to do—but decay in life or die. Once you believe what he says, what alternative have you? Can't think of one. If you say you believe and don't do it, you're a liar and a criminal to "God". Of course, people say they believe but mean they would like to, if they have time one day they will get around to thinking about it and in the meantime the rewards are titillation. I know because I did this emotionally and mentally with the G. ideas for seven years and it was marvelous and nothing like the dentist chair I am now in and see I must stay in.[21]

The formula through these months, and ultimately years, was conversation, readings mainly from the *Tales*, intense provocations causing tears or laughter, and then rigorous inner exercises, some-times supported by alternative medical treatments. Among these elements, conversation and exercises strike me as the most essential. Exercises taught by Gurdjieff have as a rule been little published, little discussed, and those who have nonetheless chosen over the years to publish and discuss leave an invisible tarnish where they have done so. Exercises are skeletal except in conditions that give them flesh and force. The same needn't be said of Gurdjieff's ideas, writings, conversation, and teaching style: they have their place in the long history of teachings and belong openly to that part of our culture concerned for millennia with inner development. Pythagoras and Diogenes, Stoics and Sufis, Christian desert fathers and mothers could easily recognize kinship. But the exercises he offered his pupils, like the "empowerments" in Tibetan tradition, come under a stricter rule. They pass orally from person to person—"from mouth to ear," as some traditions put it—and the flow of insights and substantive change to which they can give rise depends on concentration and discretion. Absent sustained focus among a certain number of concerned people, an exercise even of real merit and depth easily becomes words on a page. Some say that exercises separated from a setting of that kind can be dangerous; I don't know that this is so. I do know that they lose much. Like butterflies pinned in a collector's field journal, they can be gaudy and intriguing, but they lived elsewhere. I should add that the Gurdjieff literature is not self-policing except in the barest sense of copyright protection: materials are published from time to time that lack validity or serious care.

As Solita could recall, Gurdjieff did not put too fine a point on all this. He was about to depart by car for a few days. "We went to Café to say goodbye, but car was out of order (already) and he invited all to the flat for lunch. After he gave us new exercise. 'If ever you tell this, terrible punishment for one who tell will happen. Don't know how or why this happens, but always is so, like a law.'"[22] Another certainty of Gurdjieff's, previously mentioned, is the importance of repetition. "About your exercises," he told members of the Rope, "you will do not one time, not 100 times, but 1001 times you will do and something will happen. Now is your imagination, but sooner or later will be fact."[23] Speaking with Solita, who had a particularly austere regimen of inner exercises, Gurdjieff stated a fundamental truth in Russo-English that may mask its importance. "'Every day struggles,' he said, 'little by little make data and from this data your future depends. You must think of yourself as a baby you take care of and lead by hand. After you do, necessary you rest twice as long as you have done exercise. Be passive afterward.'" At that point his affection for Solita shone through. "I asked," she recorded, "if that meant sitting still or could I do my work on the typewriter? He laughed. 'Oh, yes. You passive then. You well asleep then.'"[24]

Not to be a nuisance, I too will leave a tarnish by exploring an exercise he gave to Elizabeth Gordon in these years. The account is from Kathryn Hulme's papers.

He tells about inner vision—something very important in this work. A. has this faculty psychopathically. He tells her she must do it exact from opposite: 'Do this only when you have conscious wish to do—as now is, you do automatically. Just do opposite way around.'. . . And he tells Gordon, she must begin make data for this kind of thing. How begin—look at an object, then suddenly shut eyes and go on seeing it without any break. Any break in attention when shutting eyes, means you must begin again. Must without break in attention go on seeing inwardly exact details of what last saw. . . . And this all makes for inner vision, which becomes power in time. . . . Was time, thirty years ago, when I could split that table with thought.[25]

We have heard Gurdjieff twice refer to the collection of data, of direct impressions that ground the search for consciousness and being in experience. The language is from *Beelzebub's Tales*—he often refers to data in its pages—but here he ties it practically to "every day struggles." The fractured table is a reminder of Gurdjieff the magus whose concentrated energy allowed him to move past assumed boundaries. On occasion, I think mostly for their entertainment but also perhaps to keep his identity intact in these lean years, he would boast to members of the Rope about his amazing powers in years past. "Around your body is electrical envelope. On quality, quantity, of this material depend if people like or dislike you. Once I had this so strong I could push ship across ocean—and back again."[26] The method of propulsion is Rabelaisian hyperbole, and there are comparably fantastic propulsion systems in the *Arabian Nights*; Gurdjieff often enough refers in the *Tales* to Scheherazade's immortal storytelling. His initial point, however, coheres with his teaching from the Russian exposition forward about hidden though influential aspects of relationship.

Speaking again with Elizabeth Gordon about an exercise, he clarified the ethic governing their relation as teacher and pupil. Her diligent practice would bind him to her. "By telling you this," he said, "I have made myself an obligation to you and I must be your slave, at your service at any moment you command me. But if you do not, I have obligation to stop."[27] A few days later he added that exercises are not an intellectual matter; they need something more, for which he found in his mobile English vocabulary just what was needed. "Must not 'philosophize' about it. Do with faith like monk. Not try to know with the head but with SURE-ing."[28]

Gurdjieff himself came under the law of exercise. In the 1930s, he earned some part of his living as a healer using hypnotism, alternative remedies, and in one reported instance massage to help his patients. He took the occasion of discussing these activities with the Rope to teach a fundamental practice, deliberate foresight—and again rattled the English language to coin a word meaning lawful, requisite, inescapable. Solita is our author here.

Before lunch he tells us how now comes a time for him when he must do inner work as well as outer-world work, and that today he has gone around like the proverbial rat-on-the-wheel. Tells how, a few days ago, when "was quiet in mind" he made plans for the great activity necessary, down to smallest detail, even including a certain kind of massage which he will make daily for a friend because he needs physical exercise also. G: "Today I make this massage, stomach massage, truly with almost end of my force, should not do, but must do, is part of my task. Every little thing I planned, and here I now tell one most important thing, one law-able thing: if thing you must do—some work, some task—you must plan ahead of time, you never can do at the time, but if make exact plan before you must do, then is as if have aim and all prepares for this. Now each day, wish not wish, I will make this massage because plan was made, special combination with friend who now expect it each day—this I do not for him, but for myself, for the physical exercise necessary with inner exercise I do now."[29]

By the 1930s, Gurdjieff was no longer in physical appearance the indomitable riding master of earlier years. The accident, perhaps the loss of the Prieuré, and certainly the passage of years had taken their toll. In 1934, the year he visited Olgivanna Lloyd Wright, he was glimpsed through a New York restaurant window by Claude Bragdon, the architect and speculative thinker who had seen to the successful publication in English of Ouspensky's first book. Bragdon recalled that Gurdjieff "had grown fat, he looked untidy; time had turned his long, black ringmaster's moustache to grey; but he was unmistakably a personage, and the old, arrogant, undaunted look shone forth from his eyes."[30] Gurdjieff once said, "Only two things not spoiled by age—Armagnac and carpets."[31] He would be an exception to this ironclad rule, but that remains to be seen.

Exercises and conversation. Solita rejoiced when there were fewer readings and Gurdjieff consented to teach more formally. "He has begun to talk to us like a teacher. He sat on his big divan cross-legged, we sitting like a class before him. Today he talked for an hour and a half, continuously, 'the search for a soul.' I remember but a fraction. . . . (My habit was to rush out to the café across the street every day and write down everything while still fresh in mind. K. also, when she was in Paris, did the same. We then would combine our recollections and establish sequences.)"[32] Writing to Kathryn Hulme—her "K."—she shared the excitement of that time and contrasted it with the Prieuré years when Gurdjieff was writing. "How I wish you and G[eorgette] were here. Never has he been so accessible, at the Prieuré no one could talk personally with him or ask a question. He talks *all the time* and teaches in every sentence only I don't always know what he means. But what a vibration in the air! You learn something just from feeling him near."[33] Gurdjieff's view of their relations naturally differed, with gentle irony. The account is again from Solita. After a pleasant lunch with three of the women, he thought to mention a personal weakness. "Everybody has many wants, I have only one. I need only one thing. . . . Is my organic weakness of mind, I had this even when young. Is because I waste my time trying to make people understand. So everything I have—except. Why I have all except is because I have knowledge. Now about this weakness that consists in trying to give understanding to people—this weakness is only this much. (He measures off a quarter of an inch between thumb and forefinger.)" Loyal Solita commented: "Then that means you are just *that* much lopsided, Mr. Gurdjieff."[34]

They had had a conversation a few months earlier touching on some of these themes. It was surprising in more than one respect. "He told me today never to say 'in the world' that he is teacher and I pupil. Said 'I used to be also idiot, but finished when my accident. Now I writer and you reader. If I special thing for you do, you not speak. You not pupil—you a weakness.' He laughed."[35] It is difficult to look within Gurdjieff: What was his experience? "My inner world is my inner world," he told the Rope, as if shutting a door.[36] Yet here in these reflections about a new role—not teacher but writer—and the need for discretion about what he nonetheless taught, there are signs of internal reconsideration. As well, he unequivocally repudiates what he was before the July 1924 accident: "I used to be also idiot." From my perspective he is far too hard on himself, but that is my business not his. Gurdjieff's conversations with the Rope, and particularly with Solita, offered the privacy and warmth he may well have needed to reconsider and in time find it again possible to "make exact plan," as he put it. That they were women, not men, must be noticed; their warmth reached him. Good fortune at a time of misfortune.

His inner world was unrevealed except—except when some internal issue or insight struck him as worth sharing. One of the best-known examples from these years was recorded by Kathryn Hulme. As usual, members of the Rope had been at table with him. "Lunch," she wrote, as if striking a refectory bell.

> G. tells us about the new possible car deal wherein he will get a new car and maybe pay nothing. Asks if any of us have a special saint to whom he can burn candles. Gordon says there is a saint special for granting requests, but G says that he knows about that, he wants a saint that might be indulgent for one of us. G: If not, I could just as well take my own saint—Saint George. He very expensive saint. He not interested in money—or merchandise like candles. He wish *suffering* for merchandise, *inner world thing.* He interested only when I make something for inner world; he always know. But *suffering is expensive.*[37]

The words are warm and touched with resignation rooted in the world from which he came, Russian and Christian. "One of us" he said—by which he meant them all. It has occurred to me that the Rope had one undisclosed member: Gurdjieff himself. Here he implies as much. And then, he surely didn't need coaching as to which saint might do, but raising the question allowed him as a resourceful teacher to evoke the role of intentional suffering in the lives of people striving to realize themselves. And further, he evoked the holy watchfulness of St. George—"he always know." The intuition that we are seen by an intelligence and probity far beyond us insistently recurs in spiritual tradition, from Psalm 139—"Lord, thou hast searched me and known me"—to Václav Havel's conviction in our own day that we are known and judged by what he called "Being." Gurdjieff was summoning the Rope to this timeless sensibility through the great matter of obtaining a new car.

Gurdjieff had certain major themes—expensive insights—he pursued with the women of the Rope; we'll look at a further example. But in conversation with him in these years, the ostensible topics were often common and nearby: traits of character and patterns of events. Seen through his eyes, they acquired the quality of teaching; became, however modestly or dramatically, enlightening. He was devoted to daily life, our natural arena of experience, and warned the Rope with some severity not to abandon it. Here it is Solita sounding the refectory bell: "Dinner. G—is only way in life: everything must go back to as is in life, otherwise is psychopathic."[38]

I happened on this topic recently with a woman, now elderly, who had known Gurdjieff well in the late years. "*Il n'aimait pas les gens qui planaient*," she said—he didn't like people who glide, presumably at lofty, dreamlike altitude. Work on oneself is conducted at many altitudes; the point must be to learn to be poised and alert at them all. Today we might speak of the "re-enchantment" of daily life; Gurdjieff cared about that. Sometimes he would cast this value in terms of moving from a habitual chair to a new one still at some distance. "You are all now out of one chair but have not the data yet for sitting next chair. All you do seems to you like pouring from empty into void, all meetings with people and such things. Later when you have data, you will go back and do this same thing and it will mean something."[39] One further point about gliding: Gurdjieff had a native sense of solidarity with ordinary people who know how to do something well. He sometimes spoke of putting people "in galoshes," a Russian expression meaning that they had erred in some way and deserved nothing better. It was not the best place to be. "I can put everyone in galoshes," he told members of the Rope, "spiritualists, occultists, theosophists, all. . . . But I not know yet how put in galoshes shoemaker, carpenter."[40] And he never would know.

At the beginning of this chapter we heard Gurdjieff speaking with members of the Rope about roses and thorns, inner and outer life. It was a recurrent theme, as if nothing could be accomplished until inner and outer had been distinguished, separated, then reintegrated in a new, more knowing way. Failing that, in Gurdjieff's uncomplimentary view, we have the attention of monkeys. "Man has automatic . . . attention," he told the Rope. "Every man has a certain amount. This must be put to work, be concentrated. During a certain exercise, contact must be established with the outer world while inner world attention intensifies. This gradually makes clear the difference between the two worlds, will teach you to separate them, not look on things like monkeys, you all going out to the object and identifying with it. Then you will not live in the outer."[41]

On another occasion, as recorded by Kathryn, he framed the challenge in a more complex way. "One thing," he said, "make you rich for life. Richer than your Mr. Rockefeller. There are *two* 'struggles'—inner world struggle and outer world struggle, but never can these two make contact to make data for third world. Not even God can give this possibility for contact between outer world struggle and inner world struggle, not even your heredity. Only *one* thing: must make *intentional contact* between outer world struggle and inner world struggle. Then can make data which crystallize for third world of man, sometimes called world of soul. Understand?"[42] The Rope must have questioned him closely.

He found opportunities, sometimes oblique but telling, to return to the theme. Once for example in the round of toasts, Margaret Anderson was unexpectedly silent. "You must have good wishing for her," he said (I don't know to which woman he was referring). "Must drink health to her." Margaret replied, "Already I have said it, in my mind." And Gurdjieff: "Is cheap thing. In your mind. Many things can happen in your mind, we not know about. You must make effort, *show* your wishing—with your whole presence, with *you* in it."[43] It was an event located somewhere between the two worlds, inner and outer.

At another time they were discussing the British king, a topic to which Gurdjieff returned as he disapproved of the late 1936 abdication of Edward VIII to marry his American love, Wallis Simpson. He wasn't often concerned by daily news, but in his view a king should remain a king, once a king. Jane Heap was saying that she sometimes forgets to stand up "when they play 'God Save the King.'" "Must remember there is king and stand up," Gurdjieff commented. "This is organization, and you must respect it. Outward you must do. Man has two worlds. Outside he must ceremony make like others. But inner world is yours—all man has is inner world, his independent place. There you can tell your king is merde and be sorry you have such king."[44]

Gurdjieff returned one day from Rouen in Normandy, where he had old Russian friends, and was soon with the Rope. "Ekh, Ekh . . . So tired," he said. "Last night Rouen not sleep, trains pass. Today long drive. But in one way is good thing be so tired. Can feel now what nonentity is body. Can look through and see is 'sheet,' can look and find in middle a pearl—the small earned active part—your I. This gives a happy feeling, is good part of being so tired—to look through and find this pearl—your earned part."[45] A precisely phrased lesson in which daily stress and deep identity cohabit, it conveys more effectively than any conceivable manual the push and pull, and redemptive happiness, of knowing the two worlds—and no doubt living from a poised midpoint.

But we need to pause over Kathryn Hulme's transcription of "sheet." What on earth? Both she and Solita had a hard time with Gurdjieff's liking in these years for the word *shit*, and in French conversation *merde*. There is no outstanding report from the Prieuré about his use of ugly language, and no great emphasis on that in reports from later years, the 1940s, but in the 1930s he would pepper his language with rough expressions. He had long since declared opposition to what he called "bon ton" language and manners; in his view they capture people's minds and behavior in automatic patterns that need gradually to yield to freely attentive minds and the light of conscience. As the exponent in our time of Diogenes' wild goodness and detachment from the expected, he was on solid ground. His rough language was an unmistakable antidote to upper-altitude gliding. But Solita and Kathryn were tolerant, not appreciative. "I'm so used to 'stink' and 'merde,' etc., that I'll be saying them soon," Solita reflected.[46] "His figures of speech are unprintable sometimes."[47] In their near-daily chronicle, they found their way around the problem, Solita by writing *merde* when Gurdjieff routinely said "shit" in English—the French is common in daily speech and carries scarcely any charge—while Kathryn adopted the spelling *sheet*. They got by as they could; the rose had a thorn.

Gurdjieff's rough language gave rise over the years to anecdotes. He particularly liked from time to time to shock his well-educated, well-mannered, and utterly loyal pupils. Louise Welch, prim in manner, superbly well-read with stores of memorized poetry in her mind, was an occasional target. Once he said something awful and turned mischievously toward her at table to ask what she thought. Bravely—she would tell this story with brave gaiety—she replied, "Very refreshing, Mr. Gurdjieff!" It was much the same in later years with Jeanne de Salzmann, a woman of tangible dignity; she would shiver slightly, an almost imperceptible shrug, that is all.[48]

There was always alcohol at Gurdjieff's table from earliest days to last, typically Armagnac, sometimes flavored vodka. Judging wine best suited to what the French delicately call *lavement,* he had no interest in it. The ritual toasts to the idiots were a daily reminder of the general human tragicomedy and of one's own. Each person who returned regularly to Gurdjieff's table was asked to choose his or her idiot and was thereafter saluted as such during the round of toasts. In Russia, at the Prieuré, and in the 1940s there seems to have been nothing more than good-natured chat among his pupils about the purpose and quantity of alcohol: the consensus held that it allowed Gurdjieff to see more quickly behind the façades of those who sought him out, and participants had the right—though he might reproach them—to drink modestly or not at all. That was somehow settled, and if it was a game with risks, people knew how to play it. Legend maintains that no one got drunk at his table.

Again the 1930s differed. At times Gurdjieff was drinking quite heavily, sometimes to excess even for him. At least once in Solita's hearing he made clear that he had his reasons: "Now because such day I will drink Armagnac. In mornings with such troubles as now, I make nervous, make elephant from fly. But with this Armagnac fly is not elephant. Fly is—fly."[49] He was training Solita to be acutely observant of herself and all things—"Continue your studies, Kanari," he said to her in the late 1930s, "and remember, *photograph everything on your mind.*"[50] Naturally, she photographed him. "Puzzling moments for one who understands nothing," she reflected in autumn 1935. "Like wondering why an aware being knocks over same bottle put in same place by his elbow three times in succession, thus spilling favorite drink, Armagnac. Why after glass is filled he tilts it while talking (this always happens) so that favorite liquid spills over his coat and trousers. Is this a lesson for us in what not to do? We don't need it. Everyone was called merde last night except Louise of whom he takes no notice whatever."[51] "When tight," she noticed—another photograph—"he uses merde in English every other word, calls everyone that, waiters too. Pretty hard to take but how one watches to learn!"[52] Solita's puzzlement is easily explained: the master was drunk. She had her personal calculus about this. "Yes, he's drinking again," she wrote to Kathryn in January, "but I'm glad because he talks much more."[53] She knew, as well, that the situation could abruptly change. "He stopped drinking three days ago. From one to four bottles of brandy a day he cut off everything. Had several crises and fell down twice in the street. No time for cinemas, radio—where is our beautiful status quo? Then life was what G. calls . . . 'all roses, roses' or 'spring days.'"[54] She got by as she could; the rose had a thorn.

Drawing on a private archive to evoke this aspect of the difficult 1930s, I am doing Gurdjieff's critics' work for them. There is no good reason to pass over in silence the anguish of those years. There was so much more—formidable teaching, formidable clarities, unique relationships and events—but there was this, too: a periodic struggle for balance at a time when much was askew and wanting. Gurdjieff taught, so to speak, *against* that situation. "Man must at all times mathematically hear, mathematically understand, mathematically answer," he told the Rope. "Only this is life. Always he must be with his I. Only then is he man without quotation marks. No matter what he have in surroundings—people, noise, alcohol—he must always mathematically understand; never lose self even when drunk. *He* can be drunk, but never his I be drunk."[55] He had many ways of expressing this personal ethic. "Fulfill your obligation with consciousness," he said within Kathryn's hearing. "If you wash plates, your obligation is to wash plates. If you doctor, obligation is to cure. If you are a writer, obligation is to write. Not important what you are, big man or small man, not important what you do. Only important how you do it."[56]

Gurdjieff refused the constraints of convention except when it suited him, and he moved with ease in multiple, unlike worlds. For Peter Brook, the famed theater and film director who probably knows as much about Gurdjieff as he definitely knows about Shakespeare, Gurdjieff possessed Shakespearean dimension:

nearly every play of Shakespeare has royalty doing what they do, amorous or murderous, and a subplot peopled with men and women of the trades, taverns, markets, brothels, underworld. Gurdjieff offered his version of inclusiveness in an invitation to Solita one evening after dinner. "Kanari, come with me now for promenade in taxi." "Where?" "Oh, low place, I tired." "I think not, Mr. Gurdjieff." "Trouble with you, Kanari, you always look for high thing. Must have both in life." "Have had low thing, am late for high thing." "Oh, go, go then. Devil with you."[57]

I'm aware that there may be more plentiful evidence of rough language and conduct in the 1930s because the scribes to whom we owe much, Solita and Kathryn, were on duty. But earlier and later there were quite enough scribes; the memoir literature is large. Best to conclude, then, that this period is specific. Why? Why such unrest? Why the mixture of brilliant teachings with something that reads as anger, desolation? The question has no standard answer; I don't even know whether it has been asked. But we should understand what we can of this passage in Gurdjieff's life and the life of the teaching he introduced. Of course there is a limitation: we can know only so much of Gurdjieff. "Everybody imagine," he once said to the Rope, "that he has knowingness for life, but for this knowingness he is nonentity. Life is big thing. What he have is one small piece."[58] What small piece do we have?

The reduction in his circumstances, that he was king once but by outward measures no longer, is the central fact. Once he had lived in a spacious manor at the edge of a royal forest; once he had guided an international community of dedicated pupils; once he was a choreographer and dance entrepreneur whose art had interested no lesser a personage than Diaghilev, who with Stravinsky set the era's dance culture in motion. What a fall.

But there were wisdom and magic still. They shine through the anger and desolation. Gurdjieff had thought about the alternations in lives and expressed his thought in what I take to be a classic text, originally a talk in New York, 1924: "The Two Rivers." In one of the rivers, individual drops literally go with the flow; they cannot influence their location in the river and the fate toward which they are moving. In the other river, so near to the first that a resourceful drop can jump across to it, the drop is "in a different world, in a different life": there, what Gurdjieff calls "the law of alternating progression," prevails. "A drop comes to the top or goes to the bottom, this time not by accident but by law. On coming to the surface, the drop gradually becomes heavier and sinks; deep down it loses weight and rises again. To float on the surface is good for it—to be deep down is bad. Much depends here on skill and effort. . . . Of course . . . you cannot cross over merely because you wish. Strong desire and long preparation are necessary."[59]

He, too, spared none of its hardships, had come under the law of alternating progression. He would rise to the top again and flow toward blessings—the same man, a different man. It would be naive to assert, as if all is for the best in a best world, that the light and darkness of the 1930s was a purgation, a grinding transformation foreseen and needed. Who knows? But we need to trust someone's perceptions at the time, and to that end I nominate Cecil Lewis, cofounder in 1922 of the BBC, the British Broadcasting Company, a decorated ace pilot in the wars of 1914 and 1939. He had known Gurdjieff early and late. These lines were published in a book in 1993, when Lewis was in his mid-nineties; they refer to Gurdjieff as he encountered him after World War II.

G. has changed almost beyond belief. My 25-year-old picture was of a sort of tiger-tamer, with a whip in one hand and a revolver in the other. I could scarcely think of Gurdjieff without expecting a look or a word to make me jump. Now there is a much older man who has built up something that is essentially "good", who has suffered very, very much. Then we were the material from which he was making something for himself. His business was not to do anything for us. Now he is helping in a godlike fashion. Not that the tiger-tamer cannot be called up. I am sure he could put on a role that would shake the streets. But that is not his work now.[60]

Between the tiger-tamer and the old man helping others in god-like fashion lay the decade of the 1930s, its darkness and light. It would be an error to give too much emphasis to either. There were many luminous episodes in the period, innumerable moments when the spark of life and truth between the women of the Rope and their stormy teacher was all that mattered, fulfilling beyond measure. "Life . . . life . . .," they remembered Gurdjieff to have said, "truth, sometimes I even like . . . much material for rejoicings and satisfactions."[61] A reluctant acknowledgment; acknowledgment nonetheless. On occasion there was also pungent humor of a kind common to Gurdjieff and his distant predecessor, Rabelais. I will spare you the opening round of a conversation at the Café de la Paix about novel money-making schemes—suffice it to say that he and members of the Rope were working out a new sort of sausage business. It had something to do with horse and chicken meat. "G. says he has plan for even better business—instead of using chicken, will use a sparrow. Could use a canary, but canary expensive because sometimes sing a little. One horse, one sparrow—good business. But even better—could use one horse, and one *venereal louse*. With such combination as this would make most money of all."[62] Do you see what I mean: Surreal? Rabelais and few others would dive into a topic of this kind with such mock seriousness.

And then there were times of greatest kindness in which all was well with the world and with the little world of the Rope. In Georgette Leblanc's telling, Christmas Eve 1936 was such an occasion.

Extraordinary reunion at his flat tonight. Another age—a patriarch distributing treasures. The little apartment was full—his family, friends of his family, the concierge and his family, old servants from other days. The Christmas tree, too big, too high, was bent against the ceiling and its stars hung down. The distribution of gifts was a true ceremony. Fifty or more large boxes, numbered, occupied a corner of the salon. Gurdjieff, standing in front of a table, glasses on his nose, held a list in his hand. To each box that was set before him he added notes of a hundred or five hundred francs; then he called a name corresponding to a number and presented the box, making the brief gesture that signifies "Don't thank me.". . . At ten o'clock supper was served. On each plate was an enormous piece of mutton, a stuffed Russian roll, pickles, peppers preserved in oil—all the things I hold in horror; but superb desserts were spread out—cakes, fruits, candies of a thousand-and-one nights. We left at midnight and other people took our places. The Russian maid said to me, "From one o'clock till dawn the poor will be coming."[63]

What did the maid say? Gurdjieff had by then begun looking after the neighborhood poor, who were certain of their welcome at the top of the back stairs leading to the kitchen. Perhaps that Christmas Eve they joined him in the salon. From the 1930s to the end of his life he offered a soup kitchen for the needy, often Russian exiles, others also. Typically he prepared the food himself, spoke with each person to learn how one or another was doing, provided warmth where needed but also counsel—"is my weakness," we have heard him say. In later years Tchekhovitch might be helping him and saw what he saw.[64] "I hope with all my heart," Gurdjieff once said to members of the Rope, "that there will rise in all of you feeling for humanity."[65]

CHAPTER 6

Là-bas, rue des Colonels Renard

Wagram 53-46. Should you need to call, this was Gurdjieff's tele-
phone number on the rue des Colonels Renard, where he lived
from autumn 1937 to the end of his life.[1] Nearly anything from that
place and time, even this obsolete code, evokes nostalgia in those,
decades later, who acknowledge Gurdjieff—nostalgia leaping over
the fact that we didn't know him to settle among the pupils, friends,
and family who did know him. Surely there are one or two places
left in the salon, or room to stand if not sit around the table in the
next room. We might be needed in the chain of people silently
passing plates of food—that was the custom—from the kitchen to
forty or fifty others crowded into dining room, salon, foyer. Oxygen
is already long since exhausted, but that doesn't seem to matter.
Gurdjieff rarely if ever opened the shutters, windows, or curtains:
his flat was a place apart, even a time apart. Somehow everyone is
all right. So, too, Gurdjieff. He is at home and well.

The title of this chapter, drawn from René Zuber's journal, carries a charge in the seemingly plain words *là-bas*—words first owned,
so to speak, or given definitive color by Charles Baudelaire in his
poem "L'invitation au voyage" (1857):

> Mon enfant, ma soeur,
> Songe à la douceur
> D'aller là-bas vivre ensemble!
>
> . . .

Là, tout n'est qu'ordre et beauté,
Luxe, calme et volupté.

. . .

Tout y parlerait
À l'âme en secret
Sa douce langue natale.

Without fretting over line breaks and translation-resistant words: "My child, my sister, imagine the sweetness of going there to live together! There all is order and beauty, opulence, calm, and delight. All things there would secretly speak to the soul its sweet native tongue." *Là-bas* is the place apart, distant and ideal.

Strictly speaking, the rue des Colonels Renard didn't qualify. It was centrally located in Paris, not at an exotic distance for Gurdjieff's French pupils during the war years and after. Today you might want to stop in a café at the intersection of avenue Mac-Mahon and the rue des Acacias, where he often had his coffee and surely looked from time to time past a receding row of street lamps toward a flank of the Arc de Triomphe not far off. At some point he turned that view into a parable about the distant aim toward which one might well be toiling and the many smaller aims and thresholds, requiring meticulous attention, that precede it. His apartment was nearby on a street like any other. Yet it was là-bas. Years after Gurdjieff's death, Zuber accurately measured the distance: it was another world. "Here in my house," Gurdjieff stipulated, "all must be quintessence. Rest you do at home."[2] There was a further rule, captured by François Grunwald, whom we have met: "Here there are no spectators."[3] Like Zuber, he was a wholly reliable participating witness. Zuber was among those who for decades after Gurdjieff's death shared the responsibility not only for preserving the spirit and letter of the teaching but for advancing it, refreshing it, tying it to life as life changed.

Across the divide that separated P. D. Ouspensky in England

Fig. 11: Jeanne de Salzmann, ca. 1964, detail from a larger photo.
Source: Martha Welch de Llosa

from Gurdjieff in Paris, the friendship between Ouspensky's wife, Sophie Grigorievna, and Jeanne de Salzmann remained intact and played a consequential role. When Madame de Salzmann visited the Ouspenskys' home and teaching center outside of London in 1936 or 1937 to compare notes about Movements practiced at the Prieuré with another old friend and colleague, Jessmin Howarth, Madame Ouspensky advised her "to go and live close to Mr. G. again. At the time he seemed to have quite small groups."[4] It took time, apparently, for this advice to bear fruit, and there may well have been other causes but in 1938, according to Zuber in conversation, she arranged for Gurdjieff to meet the group of men and women with whom she had been working for some years. An extraordinary company, it included the writer René Daumal and his American wife, Vera, Jeanne de Salzmann's daughter Nathalie and her husband, Philippe Lavastine—he a scholar, editor, and in time a public speaker of formidable gifts; René Zuber, a professional photographer and soon filmmaker; and then Henri Tracol and his wife of those years, Henriette, later known as Madame Lannes; possibly also by that time the young lawyer known after her marriage as Pauline de Dampierre. In the next few years they would be joined by Michel Conge, a physician and war veteran; the writer Luc Dietrich; Solange Claustres and Marthe de Gaigneron, both destined to be lead dancers and Movements teachers in years to come, and still others. Not a complete list, but close enough, of the generation of French participants in the Gurdjieff teaching who, guided by Jeanne de Salzmann (see fig. 11), cooperated with participants in Britain and North and South America to shape its future after Gurdjieff's passing.

Zuber tells the story of that first meeting at the rue des Colonels Renard. All hands settled at table for lunch and exchanged amiably for a time when suddenly Gurdjieff exploded with anger. He said that Madame de Salzmann hadn't properly transmitted the teaching to them, that she had been a nullity and as a result they themselves were nullities. He used every rough word in his international collection of rough words. Then silence. The pupils were stunned. Daumal slowly rose from his place and went around the table to stand behind Madame de Salzmann's chair. He said: "Sir, if Madame de Salzmann has taught us badly, that must be because *you* taught her badly. Where I'm concerned, I tell you it has been an unbelievable privilege to work with her. Like all of us here, I am her loyal pupil." New silence . . . Then Gurdjieff turned to Madame de Salzmann and, in a complicit voice, said in Russian: "Jeanne, you have *one* pupil."[5]

Despite this dramatic introduction, she had many more gifted pupils than that, who thereafter met regularly with them both. This first meeting marked the symbolic though not calendrical

end of the 1930s for Gurdjieff. Jeanne de Salzmann's high intelligence, sensitivity, calm, and unquestionable loyalty generated
a new atmosphere. Even Solita hadn't been able to bring a sense
of peaceful arrival to Gurdjieff: she was daughter, not colleague.
Jeanne de Salzmann brought—or restored—a vis-à-vis that had been
missing, though who would have known that it was missing. She
had become a wise colleague, younger of course and ever so clear
about her debt to him, but mature and capable with light of her
own. Everything began again, began anew. Gurdjieff did not yield
any part of his fiery temperament—but she was there now, cool,
observant, playing a role somewhat like Marpa's wife in the classic
Tibetan tale of Milarepa, making sure that his pupils, reproved and
perhaps even sent flying, landed on their feet, ready to return to the
rue des Colonels Renard where the teaching and the teacher had
new life. That was not her only role; she touched nearly everything
lightly, shared with Gurdjieff the inevitable burdens of teaching,
met privately with pupils to help them, gave Gurdjieff a confidante
with whom he could exchange in Russian to clarify perspectives or
translate both his own and his pupils' more complex statements.
As well, she naturalized the language of the teaching; for years it
had hovered in a middle state of Russo-English and Russo-French,
expressive and exact but a little unstable. Now it spoke flawless
French. Her return did not signal to Gurdjieff that he might retire;
on the contrary, after a gap of some fifteen years he initiated a new
cycle of Movements in a rehearsal studio at the Salle Pleyel with
the promising and able group she had brought to him, augmented
by newcomers. She was the irreplaceable friend to Gurdjieff. A
man whom many Gurdjieff students knew well in later years, Lord
Pentland, evoked their relation in strikingly beautiful words, perhaps echoing Pauline de Dampierre: "Gurdjieff was the creation,
Madame de Salzmann was the benediction."

Friends have told me that what I have written here and in later
paragraphs of Jeanne de Salzmann is hagiographic, that I should

straighten things out by saying something about shortcomings or errors. I know of one or two errors and know of accusations, I think misconceived and unjust, leveled against her conduct of the teaching in the decades to come. Yet there are people whom one is simply grateful to have known.

We should encounter something more of her independent identity before returning to the rue des Colonels Renard. In the years now concerning us, one of the best places to look is Luc Dietrich's account of an early conversation with her, January 1939, at the Paris apartment of his friends Philippe Lavastine and his wife, Nathalie, still known then by her childhood name Boussik. Madame de Salzmann had already understood that Luc played fast and loose with women, and fast and loose with truth, and there had been an incident between them. He was also immensely promising—somehow one knew that though evidence for the moment was thin. She asked Luc whether she could say everything that was on her mind in front of his friends. "She insisted," Luc recalled.

Are they enough my friends, do I care enough for them as friends to permit them to hear what we are going to say to one another? I acquiesce. I really cannot do otherwise. I would like to remember for my whole life what I heard that evening. I would like to see again those three grave faces grouped around the light. Madame de Salzmann says one last time: "Excuse me if I'm sincere." And again says: "I'm going to give you something because you made a positive gesture toward someone I love and respect. Had that not occurred, we would be done with one another, there would be nothing between us. Whereas now we will be either friends or enemies, but we cannot remain as before.

"Good talker, bad actor. You must take your own measure and kill the old man in you.

"*You prostitute everything with your words.* You talk too much and without thinking. In the end you dirty everything with your words: you and your secrets, your *mother*, your *friends*, your *girlfriend*. You discuss the woman you love with everyone and so you dirty her, everyone touches her through your words, everyone sleeps with her through your words.

"You were offered truth and what did you send as an ambassador to receive that truth? A prostitute. You must take your responsibilities. Up to now you have not been a man, you have been a false friend. And then you lie all the time. Your lies disgust me.

"You have done everything possible to make a girl of twenty-three your slave. You wanted to use her, but she was stronger than you. You were infantile with her. You tried to strip her of her confidence, her confidence in herself, and that is a bad thing.

"With Philippe and Boussik you have been a false friend: you have evaded your responsibilities. You have brought them nothing. You can continue this way, you'll have many friends but no true friends, and you'll soon be disgusted and nothing good will come of it. What you give has no value. You give what you have too much of, what you no longer want. You give your garbage. That isn't giving."

Madame de Salzmann spoke for an hour and a half, and when she had finished, she said: "There. And now you are more a friend than before."

I accompany Madame de Salzmann to the Gare Saint-Lazare. . . . As soon as I reach my room I write down everything she said so as to lose nothing. . . .

Remember this evening, 29 January 1939. Sunday between ten-thirty and midnight.[6]

French culture has specific echoes. Here Dietrich is likely to be recalling, even instinctively, Blaise Pascal's written "Memorial" of 1654 to the Night of Fire, his life-changing, ecstatic experience of certainty, joy, and peace "from about half past ten in the evening until half past midnight."[7] The precision about timing is comparable, and Dietrich's word choice—*me remémorer* for "remember"—has a formal, religious quality, as if the new memory must settle everywhere inside, flesh of his flesh. This too had been a Night of Fire. Jeanne de Salzmann's relentless truthtelling marked the beginning of Dietrich's serious participation in the Gurdjieff teaching as her pupil and soon enough among those she introduced to Gurdjieff. One who knew him well told me long ago that Dietrich proved something: that a rose can grow on a dunghill.

Sometimes I write Jeanne de Salzmann rather than the formal—and more customary—Madame de Salzmann in an effort to wring out of our growing acquaintance with her any trace of stiffness. She was indeed, in deed and word, formidable. She carried in her own person the complete teaching; she was both contained and radiant. That the Gurdjieff teaching remains alive today worldwide, rather than a brilliant lost thing, is owed in large measure to her. She understood how to take blazing fire and place it in hearths without reducing it: fire is still fire. But all of this duly noted, she was to the end of her many days—she died at the age of 101—welcoming, warmly human, endowed with a mobile intelligence so at ease with itself that one rarely stopped to admire it, as if it were a spectacle. It wasn't a spectacle, it was a voice. "Madame de Salzmann had the attitude and bearing of a queen," François Grunwald wrote of her in the years that now concern us. "Her very simple way of being and direct way of expressing herself without artifice or emphasis added further to that distinctive sense of royalty. One was immediately drawn by her suppleness and ease of movement as much as by her words free of evasion. Her beautiful face, her dark and benevolent eyes called forth respect."[8]

Tcheslaw Tchekhovitch can add his word here: "In the first few years, I was not really aware of Madame de Salzmann's role. However, toward the end of Mr. Gurdjieff's life, it became clear to me how important she was for him. He solemnly stated more than once, 'Whoever seeks a relationship with me must come through Jeanna. I have entrusted the continuation of my work to her, and she has my complete confidence. She has never let me down.'[9] Gurdjieff typically added that extra syllable to her name.

I have no idea of the appearance of Gurdjieff's earlier apartments in Paris, but his home on the rue des Colonels Renard, where he and Madame de Salzmann met their pupils through the coming war and its aftermath, has remained largely intact. Once while there I had the impression that it is "the crèche of humanity"—those are the unanticipated words that occurred to me, as if it was the birthplace and shelter of something other and greater, belonging to the human race as a whole though unknown. Apprehensive readers are likely at this point to think that your author has at last capsized in the Sea of Nostalgia and must be rescued, but give me a moment to clarify before sending the lifeboat.

To visit the apartment today, seventy years after Gurdjieff lived there, is like entering a sepia-toned photograph: some objects in ceramic and glass retain vivid color, but much has coalesced toward warm uniformity, not displeasing but settled, as if timed by a slow clock. The apartment isn't large—it has long seemed a miracle that fifty or more could join Gurdjieff there. Foyer, salon, dining room, modest kitchen with back door, two bedrooms down a hall, and the pantry or "office" where Gurdjieff met pupils for private conversations, often over coffee, sometimes with his harmonium nearby for music. What strikes everyone who visits, then and now, is the collection of framed paintings thickly lining nearly all walls from wainscot to ceiling, in the manner of nineteenth-century museums. Why did Gurdjieff possess and display a vast collection of paintings of indifferent quality, ranging in theme from landscape and still life to sacred Christian subjects and the occasional nude or

Fig.12: The pantry at rue des Colonels Renard.
Source: The Gurdjieff Foundation of New York

Modernist abstraction? We can ask Fritz Peters to respond to the question. After military service in World War II, Peters found his way to Gurdjieff in a state of greatest need.

When I arrived in Paris again, I telephoned Mr. Gurdjieff and he made an appointment to meet me at a café later that morning. After we had met and while we were drinking coffee, we were approached by an elderly woman who proceeded to have a long conversation with Mr. Gurdjieff in Russian.

I understood enough of their conversation to gather that it was primarily concerned with problems of health, finance, and the difficulty of obtaining sufficient food in Paris at that time. The black market, I knew, was flourishing, and while food was available, it was tremendously expensive. At the conclusion of the conversation, the woman opened a package, wrapped in newspaper, and held up a small oil painting for us to look at. Mr. Gurdjieff asked her various questions about it: when she had painted it, and so forth, and finally bought it from her for several thousand francs. She thanked him effusively and I gathered that, thanks to his purchase, she would be able to afford to eat for a few more days.[10]

From one perspective, the art collection—considered by some connoisseurs to be the worst art collection in the world—was pure philanthropy. Rather than humiliate indigent older people, mostly Russian exiles, by giving them charity outright, he had built a reputation as an art collector always interested to see their own paintings or works in their possession. From a second perspective, which reached me through oral tradition, he considered his art collection to be one part of a domestic diorama illustrating the idiocy and grandeur of the human race; it was a collective symbol. On occasion he improvised about it, *style Rabelais*. J. G. Bennett has written that once in the late evening when few stayed behind "he boasted of all the pictures, their amazing age (plus de 4500 ans! for a poor copy of a Dutch painting), the enormous prices he paid—how they were all stolen out of museums which are left only with copies, etc."[11] Gurdjieff relaxing after a rigorous session with his pupils is unmistakable.

The difficulty of observing details in the apartment is that "here there are no spectators"—true to this day. No one is there as a tourist. It remains a meeting place, though I have noticed alongside my own discreet discomfort, as I have tried to scan and remember details, the discreet discomfort of others similarly interested. Details matter because Gurdjieff constructed a symbolic world from the paintings throughout the apartment and, in the salon, from hundreds of small objects which sum to a statement about the variety of humankind and the tiers of reality—all the while retaining a certain coziness, the well-used quality of the home of an older person. We'll return a little later to the salon.

As far as I know, only one space has been renovated since Gurdjieff's day: the pantry or "office" (see fig. 12) has become a library. We know its original condition from a handful of photographs and descriptions. Dr. Kenneth Walker (1882–1966), a distinguished British surgeon and author who had met the Gurdjieff teaching through Ouspensky, found his way to Gurdjieff's apartment after Ouspensky's death in 1947. His books *Venture with Ideas* and *A Study of Gurdjieff's Teaching* are among the keenest in the literature. Walker was resolutely free and "simple honorable," as Gurdjieff would sometimes define a value he cared for, in his regard for Gurdjieff, the teaching, and the company he joined at the rue des Colonels Renard.[12] For some reason the doctors closest to Gurdjieff in the later years—among others, the cardiologist William Welch in New York, the internist Bernard Courtenay-Mayers in London, and the leading urologist Pierre Aboulker in Paris—shared that characteristic with Kenneth Walker. I admire this; it offers a model for a future in which the Gurdjieff teaching, no longer viewed by intellectuals as marginal, is understood as a cogent inspiration for lives of service. Walker has written:

> Beneath the daily routine of the rue des Colonels Renard there ran a strong current of purpose, a current which would every now and then break through to the surface and reveal itself. This was particularly likely to happen when two or three of us were invited to take coffee with Mr. Gurdjieff in his own private room. This sanctum was situated in the very heart of

his flat and it was actually the storeroom from which emanated the odor of spices which always pervaded the hall. The
walls of his room were traversed by tiers and tiers of wooden
shelves, all overladen with every conceivable form of grocery:
innumerable cans; boxes of candy; bags of flour and sugar;
packages of oatmeal, currants, and raisins; bottles of brandy
and vodka. . . . At a small table, pressed up against a rampart of
shelves mounting up to the ceiling, sits Gurdjieff, with a large
chocolate fish, covered with shining tinfoil paper, swinging
just above the level of his immense head. Madame S. is seated
there at his side ready to interpret for us difficult passages in
his mixture of French, English, and Russian, while the rest of
us sit around him on small canvas-topped stools or upturned
grocery boxes. Lise has deposited the tray of coffee bowls on
the table. . . . It is an occasion either for music or for a private
talk, and we sit there sipping our coffee—the sugar must always
be kept in the mouth and never be put into the bowl—and
listening to his music or else to his words.[13]

The code of discretion we have already encountered still applied.
Walker continued:

If we had been invited to Gurdjieff's sanctum not for music
but for a talk, the conversation was always of a very private
nature. "This that I tell you," he would say, "is for you alone
and it must not be discussed with other people. I ask you to
do this and then later, when you come next time to Paris, you
can report to me what you find." He would then outline some
psychological or physiological exercise and would give us very
precise instructions on how this exercise was to be carried out.
While imparting these instructions he would speak with the
exactitude of an old and experienced physician prescribing
treatment to his patients, choosing his words very carefully

and talking in grave and convincing tones. At such times his words fell on our ears with immense weight for they seemed to be backed, not only by his own wisdom, but by the authority of a long line of unseen and unknown teachers. . . . How strange that the message should have reached me in such surroundings, amid bags of sugar, and bottles of spices, packages of raisins, and canned meats. But was it really so strange . . . ? It is well known that wisdom is to be found more often in the world's byways than in its busier streets.[14]

A newcomer to Gurdjieff's circle, Dorothy Caruso, widow of the great tenor, was also invited to sit with Gurdjieff in the pantry. Shall we collect her perspective?

After lunch he invited me to have coffee with him in his store-room. There, in the midst of fruits and sweets and wines, with slender sausages of camel's meat, bunches of scarlet peppers and sprays of rosemary and mint suspended like a canopy above, as I watched him pouring coffee out of the battered old thermos bottle, I suddenly felt as young and trustful as I had felt when Mother Thompson watched over me in the Convent. Years of worldly experience fell away and I was a child again. Gurdjieff offered me a piece of sugar. "You want to ask me something?" he said. . . . I could not quickly think of any abstract or esoteric question, so instead I blurted out what had troubled me ever since I had been going to his house. "Everyone here seems to have a soul except me. Haven't I any soul?" He didn't answer immediately, or look at me. He took a piece of sugar, put it into his mouth and sipped some coffee through it. Then he said, "You know what means consciousness?" "Yes," I said, "it means to know something." "No. Not to know something—to know yourself. Your 'I'. You not know your 'I' for one second in your whole life. Now I tell and you try. But very difficult. You try remember say 'I am' once every hour. You not succeed, but no matter—try. You understand?"[15]

He was again speaking of the pearl, the earned part, as he had years ago.

The pantry can be understood in two ways. It was Prospero's cave, the intimate place where roots and leaves and foods from the world over gave comfort and a due setting for the old magician, a "colleague of life," as Gurdjieff once named himself.[16] And it was a symbolic representation of all and everything—precisely as he had entitled his trilogy of writings. This being said, we should also keep in mind an observation by Rina Hands, a British pupil who later founded a group for the study of Gurdjieff's teaching in Australia. "I know, of course," she wrote, "that everything that takes place here may be said to have layers and layers of meaning and that if Mr. Gurdjieff asks you to pass the salt, even that may have a special significance for you, but it also means he wants you to pass the salt."[17] In that light, the pantry was a pantry, but also "all and everything."

The salon at rue des Colonels Renard, where meetings and readings took place, and where the overflow of people sharing in lunch or dinner could find a spot, has its full complement of paintings and two remarkable assemblages—a neutral word for things not neutral at all. The first of these is a tall glass cabinet with glass shelves populated by innumerable porcelain figurines again representing all and everything, in this instance the all and everything of human being. Shepherds and farmers, dancers and merchants, dervishes and monks, villagers and courtiers—as cheerful as can be. Owing to their miniature size, one has the impression of seeing them from great height, as if perceived by Gurdjieff's literary hero, the reformed and wise Beelzebub, who typically studies us by telescope from afar. It must have taken Gurdjieff considerable time to assemble this immense though miniature cast of characters, surely as much for his own delight as for the instruction of pupils. It's good to have something to shop for as you make your way through a city. Gurdjieff's American pupils, Edwin and Dorothy Wolfe, had a similar collection of figurines they displayed in their home at Christmastime, and for Christmas 1948 brought it to Gurdjieff's hotel rooms during a late visit to New York. "When we had all the figures in place," Wolfe recalled, "Mr. Gurdjieff happened to come out of his bedroom. He came over to look at what we were doing. He stood for some time looking at this Christmas parade of angels and animals. His face broke into a wide smile. Then like a happy child he said, 'Where you find such thing?'"[18]

There was a second assemblage in a back corner of the salon, this one nearly defying description. Due to the sound rule prohibiting spectators, there is scarcely ever a moment to assess and memorize it. My description, like Kenneth Walker's in Gurdjieff's lifetime, is subject to error. Walker: "The opposite corner of the room was occupied by a large structure of mirrors and gilt, a piece of furniture which a child would have adored. Everywhere on its many plat-forms of mirror could be seen gay little figures, men and women being drawn along in droskies, mounted soldiers, galloping Arab sheiks, Nubians on camels, dancing ballerinas, everything that one could wish to find and still more to be discovered. . . . If the wires were plugged in and the current switched on it would sparkle with dozens of tiny lights. . . . I had no time to examine anything more in the room."[19] Let's try again: imagine an enormous chandelier flowing from ceiling to floor; imagine strings of sparkling crystals falling past a sequence of progressively larger mirrored platforms on which tiny figures are dynamically living their lives—doing all of the things we do, but smaller.

The crèche of humanity: such all of this was and is. Such tender-ness for humanity, for what we are in our first innocence. There is no reason to believe that Gurdjieff had it in mind, but my thoughts go to Proverbs 8, where Wisdom comes before God, "rejoicing in

His inhabited world, and my delight was with the sons of men."
There is more still in the salon, but enough has been said to summon something of the unique interior world where Gurdjieff in his last decade offered a new statement of his teaching and resolutely embodied it—for it was never just words.

Occupied Paris and the Post-War Gathering

Safely among his pupils in New York in the spring of 1939, Gurdjieff decided to return to Paris despite their pleas that he remain with them, far from the European war that seemed increasingly inevitable. Perhaps in conversation with his first teacher, Henriette Lannes, Grunwald understood Gurdjieff's reasoning. "In a period rife with conflict, his ideas and convictions had a better chance of penetrating the minds and hearts of human beings."[20] Gurdjieff had mentioned to Solita three years earlier that he didn't fear such things: "I accustomed to revolution, for me is simple thing, is familiar. All life I have had."[21] Grunwald offers a further insight: Gurdjieff's teaching in 1939–1949 was "still more intense than during the First World War and the Revolution in Moscow"—less intellectual, closer to life experience, and concerned above all with life experience. All records, published and archived, confirm his judgment, to which Gurdjieff added a thought: "In this group," he said—meaning the French pupils with whom he met regularly during the war, "I inscribed in a living way the Third Series of my writings."[22] Readers familiar with Gurdjieff's trilogy, *All and Everything*, well know that the third book is, by any reasonable assessment, unfinished. Apparently he set it aside in 1935, never to take it up again. Further, he had promised a rather different book than the one actually written; a number of tantalizing hints in *Meetings with Remarkable Men* about the third book were never fulfilled. Yet they were fulfilled: through the men and women with whom he worked closely in the war years and after.

Gurdjieff organized for a long war. There were several elements of strategy. Be it legend or fact, he is said to have persuaded food shops from local grocers to elegant emporia that he had oil wells in Texas; after the war, he would promptly pay his debts. This proved to be true: among his "oil wells" were British and American pupils joining him after peace returned to Europe. But he had other sources. "I have only one purpose," he told Fritz Peters as they looked back over their wartime experience, "existence for self, for students, and for family. . . . So I do what they cannot do, I make deal with Germans, with policemen, with all kinds idealistic people who make 'black market'. Result: I eat well and continue have tobacco, liquor, and what is necessary for me and for many others. While I do this—very difficult thing for most people—I also can help many people."[23] That he helped many is beyond dispute. Henriette Lannes said as much to Grunwald after the war. "Every day he would prepare meals for mid-day and evening," Madame Lannes recalled, "feasts for fifty people, sometimes more. He was an extraordinary cook who knew how to delight his guests with delicious Oriental dishes. During the war his home was the only place where I could eat properly; it still is. I believe that without him, I would have died of hunger."[24]

That was not the end of strategy. He also needed to be able to meet his pupils safely, without interference or worse from the Nazi occupant. There were generally two meetings, Thursday and Saturday, the younger group and the older, and Movements classes in a rehearsal studio at the multipurpose Salle Pleyel, a fifteen-minute walk from his apartment. Eight or more men and women coming regularly to his door would surely look suspicious—but nothing ever happened. He must have been protected, to have been known to the authorities as an apolitical, elderly philosopher posing no threat. According to Paul Beekman Taylor, protection and generous funds throughout the Occupation were provided by a wealthy French woman, grateful to him for curing a potentially fatal medical disorder that had dogged her life. She was the wife of the owner of luxurious hotels where highly placed Nazis enjoyed the best of Parisian lodging, food, and ambiance.[25] Thanks to her and others—notably Gabrielle Franck, a pupil and well-to-do art dealer who saw to it that Gurdjieff had funds—he was well and safe, and the life of his circle continued.[26] It has even been said that during the Occupation there were meetings attended without incident by Resistance workers and Nazi officials, interested for the moment not by the war but by Gurdjieff. Why not? The strategy was complete. His pupils had similarly worked out protective schemes. Pauline de Dampierre once said that she had befriended all of the policemen stationed along her walk home from the rue des Colonels Renard. They would greet her.

After the war Gurdjieff slipped up, but not for long. He had somehow come under suspicion by the French police for illegally hoarding foreign currency. They called on him, searched the apartment, found a stash under his mattress, and hauled him off to the station. As he was leaving, he said to those around him, "Good hiding place, *hein?*" I do love this story.

The way of life in the years ahead included conversation and exercises as in the 1930s, and shared meals prefaced by readings from Gurdjieff's works, not unlike the 1930s. In addition, there were regular Movements classes with Madame de Salzmann at the piano; Gurdjieff promised new Movements, which were to be their own, to the able class poised to work with him. There were other differences from the 1930s. Earlier, records were spontaneously kept by Solita Solano and Kathryn Hulme; he may never have seen them. Now, meticulous verbatim records of meetings were kept at his instruction and immediately typed in several copies, to be safely stored but also shared with group members such as René Daumal, whose health did not permit him to stay at length in Paris. These transcripts were known at the time by a disarmingly informal name, *causeries*—talks. Daumal once had a *causerie* tied to the handlebars of his bicycle as he was pedaling I know not where, and somehow lost it. He and a friend spent the night retracing his route but failed to recover it. By arranging for transcripts of meetings with the French groups, both under the Occupation and later, Gurdjieff must have recognized something that I have never heard put into words—perhaps that he was again making a commitment to teach comprehensively, as in Russia, but this time on the basis of inner and outer life experience: no theory, no diagrams, total attention to what one is, to the practical meaning of what he called "conscious labor and intentional suffering," to what remedies can be brought to bear. All of which should be noted down; it had a future. After the war, when the British and Americans found their way back to him, he was quite abrupt with J. G. Bennett, an informed thinker with exacting intellectual tools at his command. "I told him a little," Bennett recalled, "about the paper on Unified Field Theory and how it fits in with his 'Law of Falling'. He would have nothing of it—'Mathematik is useless. You cannot learn laws of world creation and world existence by mathematik.'"[27]

But in writing of these easily grasped differences I am postponing what must be said about the most telling difference: Gurdjieff himself and the influence he radiated. He was old now, not the riding master of the Prieuré, not the troubled genius of the 1930s, but a man and teacher whom his closest pupils tried—in vain, they often felt, but they tried—to understand and characterize (see fig. 13). "He seemed to be filled with an experience—almost incommunicable—" Zuber recalled, "which would set him at an unbearable distance from the common run of mortals."[28] Grunwald perceived much the same.

My ineradicable impression is that Mr. Gurdjieff was made of another clay than the rest of us. I felt him as come from another planet to convey something that our earth-bound intelligence

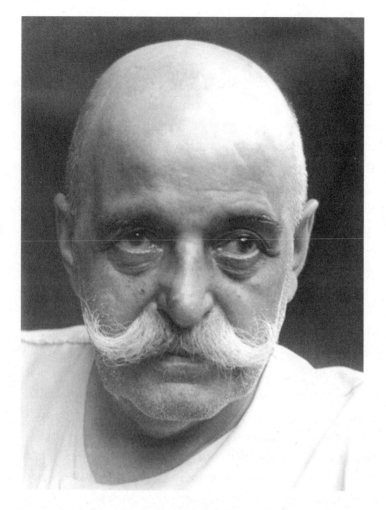

Fig. 13: Gurdjieff, 1949. Source: The Gurdjieff Foundation of New York

cannot easily encompass, and above all to share the immense force which emanated from him until he left us—a force, yes, which people whom he met received in very different ways, as they could. . . . Certain people saw in him a luminous angel, others the devil in person, an accomplished rogue, an altruistic saint. I, François Grunwald, constantly felt a goodness, a generous source of inner energy free of all sentimentality.[29]

At the rue des Colonels Renard, changes in awareness and one's sense of oneself were a matter of vivid experience. Such experiences were among the most potent lessons Gurdjieff offered; they reached far inside, demonstrated possibilities, inspired search and effort. The catalyst was his state, not confined to himself but invisibly radiant and capable of creating a field of awareness for others in which they could explore what it is to be more awake at last. It had nothing to do with drugs, nothing to do with the consumption of alcohol. Further, his state was natural to him. He surely had to renew it, but it was in and of the man. It was not selfish, not a display of superiority but rather a foretaste of one's own best, of one's own awareness taking its first few breaths of freedom. The way opened from there, a way to be traveled by one's own efforts, though in good company.

A striking feature of the awareness and emotional depth Gurdjieff made possible for others is that one instinctively felt more normal, more oneself, and incomparably more self-possessed, as if one had been living in a dream and had awakened. In Gurdjieff's practice, awakening is toward oneself, not toward a superhuman something; and the human self, the microcosm, is understood to be endowed with possibilities that need a lifetime to discover and nurture. Elizabeth Bennett, who lived and helped in Gurdjieff's household for some months in the post-war period, measured the distance between herself and him—and reached a sensible conclusion: "He was . . . quite clearly a different kind of being from any of the rest of us, and I might have expected to be disheartened by the gulf between us. But on the contrary, when I was in his presence I felt full of hope and optimism and I simply knew that 'if he can do it, I can do it.'"[30]

As I write, I feel that I am stammering, although the experience of individual awakening and of the shared field of awareness passed across the generations from Gurdjieff and, through his pupils, reached my own generation. There is something here that prefers experience to words. Yet questions press forward, not least a question we have already encountered: Was Gurdjieff opening the way to religious experience or cultivating in his pupils a religious sensibility? Among those working with him in the 1940s, some had sufficient religious background to perceive their experience at the rue des Colonels Renard in a religious light. Annie Lou Staveley, an American introduced to Gurdjieff's circle by Jane Heap, contributed a remarkable memoir in later years. "In the Church of England . . . Morning Service," she has written, "there is a point where the priest chants, 'O God, make clean our hearts within us.' Of course, the teaching of Christ . . . is largely about just this cleansing of the heart [but] all this ritual has become today only empty words. In the presence of Mr. Gurdjieff many could and did experience such a prayerful wish."[31] She also recalls occasions when Gurdjieff would join the English-speaking group in the salon during a reading from one of his works. "In his presence one had the sense of being fed a new food, a food for which one had been starved all one's life. . . . His glance would pass over us, resting a moment on each of us. . . . One was able to listen better for his being there and as his eyes rested on you, you experienced without knowing what it was, the meaning of the word 'blessing.'"[32]

But he didn't insist on the development or reinforcement of a specifically religious sensibility. It was a matter for each pupil's privacy. In the new cycle of Movements he created in these years there is a magnificent and invariably touching "Prayer in Four Parts," but it is not a creedal statement. It is an experience with few words, acknowledging through dance the biblical truth that the fear of the Lord is the beginning of wisdom but also returning one to oneself as a vigorous human creature. Worship alternating with an ordered swirl of activity: what a lesson in breadth of sensibility, set to unforgettable music. Yet one leaves the class again on one's own, toward one's own life and sense of things. I'm nearly certain that Gurdjieff was interested in developing in his pupils the capacity for religious experience but always rigorously grounded in practical work toward awakening and being. To become, however gradually, a man or woman "without quotation marks," as he often put it, was first and last in importance. To borrow from Jean-Paul Sartre, the Gurdjieff teaching is a humanism. But it lays the internal groundwork for authentic religious sensibility.

During the war Gurdjieff once shared with his French pupils a vow or prayer which he must have wished them to adopt as their own.

I wish to be, I can be, I have the right to be, I have the ability to be. I swear to myself that this will never be for my personal profit, but to help others. I wish to be, to help others. This is to be understood as a vow.[33]

That it is a vow must mean that it remains to be accomplished. Nothing better communicates the seriousness of work with Gurdjieff in the 1940s, and the sometimes unstated goals of his teaching—and surely of all valid teachings. One's own movement toward being is good and necessary for oneself but even better, so to speak, for others, whom one is finally capable of helping with the psychological subtlety yet directness of gesture that are attributes of mature awareness. And that in turn creates what Gurdjieff in the *Tales* calls "reciprocal feeding": he or she who helps is helped. Somewhere here is the basis for a renewed social contract, but that is a topic for another day.

It is strange that one of the most recently published memoirs, François Grunwald's, which found a willing publisher only in 2017 though completed many years earlier, is among the most perceptive and rich in incident. Who would have expected news at this late date? Jewish, fortunate enough to have fled Austria as a young man after the Nazi Anschluss, serving in the French Foreign Legion and later in the Free French forces fighting northward through Italy, he found his way after the war to Henriette Lannes and in due course to Jeanne de Salzmann and the circle around Gurdjieff. Marrying into a French family that owned an extensive apple orchard in the château country south of Paris, he was a wholesale apple merchant when he first met Gurdjieff, but he ardently aspired to become a physician. Hampered by a war injury to his hand, he would in time train as a psychiatrist—and it was already that sensibility he brought to the rue des Colonels Renard. He was a man with eyes, with heart, far from the only one around Gurdjieff but a brilliant observer and expressive writer. Grunwald gave close thought to what he perceived of Gurdjieff in a passage worth quoting in full despite its moderate length. He was striving to articulate the distinction between Gurdjieff the man and the influence he brought to others.

The table was set. In front of him—he was seated on his sofa— were thirty or more little glass dishes containing Russian hors-d'oeuvres (zakouskis) and cups of sour cream and various sauces. People of a certain age or invited guests occupied most of the chairs around the table; Madame de Salzmann facing him, beside her Madame Lannes and I standing behind Madame Lannes, squeezed in among all the others around the great rectangular table amidst a press of people extending into the salon and as far as the foyer.

He was sitting perfectly upright; an irresistible calm emanated from him. A silence progressively made itself felt, becoming more and more dense; a majestic grandeur confined by no material or psychological limit circulated in the space, inner as much as outer, and established itself in us. One's attention became keener as all sensation of time disappeared. Each one of us, better and better established in himself, herself, was looking at him.

Today I am convinced that what we clearly experienced as an inner majesty did not emanate from his person as such, rather that he was a channel, a way of access to a "higher" which, without the least doubt, he rendered perceptible. His presence was the necessary transformer, permitting the plunge into a vastness, an immensity in which my own thoughts no longer importuned me as they ordinarily do, but withdrew. He offered passage to that inner grandeur, and that is why I venerate him.[34]

To this unique account, Grunwald added a footnote of sorts that conveys in a wonderfully droll way Gurdjieff's own sense of what occurred at rue des Colonels Renard.

Of course I wouldn't know how to describe, explain, or comment on what he gave access to. That being said, one day he did approach this inexpressible something, which escapes all words, through a story that seems a priori entirely banal. "During great 1943 massacre," he said, "war everywhere, I try to eat in a big brasserie, place Clichy. I look at menu, see 'onion soup.' I very happy, like onion soup. Order from waiter and rejoice in advance. Big steaming soup bowl, I taste, no taste of onion! Call waiter and say: no taste of onion, no onion in this! And waiter answer: 'It's wartime, monsieur, no onions, it's onion soup without onions.' I astonished; reflect much. Always everywhere, onion soup without onions! You come here, rue des Colonels Renard, only place where onion soup has onions."

René Zuber sat at the same table as Grunwald, perhaps readier than Grunwald in later years to recount with gusto the occasions of tumult around Gurdjieff—but no less sensitive than Grunwald to what lay within it. Zuber has written:

When Mr. Gurdjieff was nearby, it was impossible to sleep in peace. Nobody was safe from being tripped up and sent flying. It is a wonder that there were not more broken bones. His table, at the end of a meal, when a great silence fell to make way for the questions of his pupils, resembled the mat in a judo club. The master, his head shaven like that of a samurai, waited calmly without moving. The "Monsieur, may I ask you a question?" that broke the silence was something of a ritual, comparable with the salutation of two judokas bowing deeply to each other. At that moment the respect that filled the room reached its peak.[35]

No distinction has generally been made between the life of Gurdjieff's groups during the war and the post-war period when the British and Americans returned. But there was a distinction all the same, as recounted by Yahne Le Toumelin, a close participant in those years. At the time my wife and I met her, she had long since become a Tibetan Buddhist nun who had worked with several outstanding Tibetan teachers. "When you go Tibet?" Gurdjieff would sometimes ask her; that must have been her evident destiny. Her years in the Himalayas and later in central France near a Tibetan meditation and study center had not dimmed her memory of Gurdjieff. She was a friend of Luc Dietrich's, whom she mentions here.

Our little Parisian group before the Liberation had passionately loved a mysterious unknown person who promised us fabulous inner liberations, without reference to a system—a person of voluminous magnetism along several dimensions, utterly different from the cultural stars of that moment in the intense, because perilous, climate of the Occupation. It was difficult to face him, as if we were approaching an electric dynamo. A sort of psychological Attila, a great breaker of concepts, an unclassifiable meteorite, he denounced the tricks of the ego, demonstrated with volcanic eruptions the misfortune of our automatic mental habits, even intelligent ones (all idiotic in one way or another). He offered us his attention, his friendship, in a climate of emergency due to the "terror of the situation" and to his advanced age.

Mr. G. responded to our little group with fraternal tenderness for Luc, paternal tenderness for me. He returned tirelessly to his fundamental advice: conscious effort, intentional suffering, struggle against one's own negative principle, through the practices of remorse of conscience, relaxation, and "remembering."[36]

This summary of focal points in Gurdjieff's approach to the French groups during the war is helpful; several are already familiar, others not. With painstaking editorial care, the preserved transcripts from the 1940s will be published in coming years. Transcripts from the year 1943 were published in 2017 under the direction of the Institut G. I. Gurdjieff, and a range of other transcripts have been published with no indication of editor or source.[37] Madame de Salzmann once referred to life and teaching sessions at the rue des Colonels Renard as *bouillir dans la chaudière commune*—"boiling in the common pot": that seems right.[38] Something of what Grunwald meant by Gurdjieff's fidelity in these years to life experience, and what Madame de Salzmann meant by heat, is evident in the following response where Gurdjieff is speaking with a member of the French group.

For every man working for his liberation, every minute lived now must serve to repair what was wrong yesterday and to prepare for what will be tomorrow. I must experience remorse for what was wrong yesterday and stay there, in front of this material. Only there will I find the strength necessary to act differently, the strength which will allow me, little by little, to change my being. And this must be a task for every instant. . . . I can only start from this material, from things experienced, felt, which are for me a certainty. I must go deeply enough into myself to find this certainty, to a place where I am no longer swallowed up by the outside, a place where everything is quiet. I must remain there and make desperate efforts in order to stay inside myself, in order to identify less with things and people. I must choose—decide inwardly—come to understand what has real value for me, and live according to what I have understood, to serve what I have recognized as having real value for me. And this decision has to be constantly renewed; it is necessary to convince oneself of it again and again.[39]

We have spoken often of conversation and exercises. By conversation I mean nothing casual. At the rue des Colonels Renard, whether grave or comical or both in rapid succession, conversation was an act of attention, the whole of oneself receptive, the whole of oneself searching for honest words. It too was an exercise, the most common—we all converse—and at times the most brilliant. In Gurdjieff's response just below to another member of the French group, the place of exercise is clarified: the problem posed and understood, one or more exercises can be practiced as a further source of insight.

> *Question:* I quite understand about the struggle against negative emotions, but what bothers me the most is a very frivolous side of my character which makes jokes—even about my own troubles. It prevents remorse and pity from arising in me. How to get rid of it?
> *Gurdjieff:* This shows that you don't know what you are looking for. You are interested in these questions without your instinct participating. You said it very well. I understand why you are not advancing, why you are stuck in one place. Up to now, your instinct has been isolated. It has never taken part in your work. You have sensed that. Your inside has never

been interested in the things we are working on. Something in you stays apart and watches. Everything in you works—the head, the feeling, but not the instinct, which should be there but does something else instead. I will give you a series of exercises.[40]

This is not Gurdjieff's first mention of what he called "instinct," almost certainly linked to his emphasis on "the subconscious" as the sheltered place of human authenticity. The notion of instinct appears in the *Tales* in one of his most memorable formulations, the so-called second obligatory striving, one of five, incumbent on all: "To have a constant and unflagging instinctive need to perfect oneself in the sense of being."[41] Instinct must be an inarticulate, half-aware turning toward one's good, even when mind and heart show scant interest. It offers no conversation; it is not transactional. It moves its creature, willy-nilly. This explains in part why appointments with Gurdjieff were kept, despite the "volcanic eruptions" that surely awaited.

"I will give you a series of exercises." These words must often have been heard. The transcripts exclude detailed accounts of exercises; they remain part of oral tradition, although some written records exist. Alongside conversation with Gurdjieff and Movements classes, they were an essential means of exploration. What is a human being? What is he/she made of? What is feeling, freed from scattered emotions? What is mind, freed from scattered words and images? What is the experience of unified intelligence—thought, feeling, and body at last assembled? What real, experiential elevation is possible for human beings, and what blocks the way? Gurdjieff gave many, many exercises to his pupils in the 1940s, more I believe than could be practiced and assimilated. He may well have looked at the times—war, Occupation, grave uncertainties—and kept in mind his advanced age: How much longer could he live and teach? Better to store them with his pupils than leave them unsaid. Hearing in America about her teacher's approach to exercises in this period, Solita Solano was dismayed. From a letter to her friend Margaret Anderson: "For this complicated exercise, we used to be given preliminary exercises. . . . About six exercises really are almost necessary FIRST—and I do not understand why he gives an advanced one. Must mean he feels time is running out—a terrible thought!!"[42]

Yahne Le Toumelin was perturbed by the arrival of the Anglo-Saxons, beginning in 1946. She felt that they "called on him for the continuation of a system instituted in the 1920s"—and that may well have been true at first contact with some of Ouspensky's pupils. In London for decades (and in the New York region during the war), Ouspensky had taught the first Russian exposition, the one to which he had been exposed and to which he gave such lucid form in his books. It is nonetheless true that many others of differing experience arrived at the rue des Colonels Renard after the war: members of the Orage group from New York, Jane Heap's London group and J. G. Bennett's group centered near London, a number of French Jewish pupils who had lived in hiding, I'm sure still others. The intimate circle of the war years needed to open to a larger intimacy—and this occurred virtually at once. Annie Lou Staveley's account of the arrival of Jane Heap's English group is the perfect illustration: "We were ready to go to Paris the very moment travel became possible. We were the first of his people to reach him from the world outside France and he welcomed us. 'Do not be afraid any more,' he told us—he standing invisible to us in the dining room while we struggled into hats and coats in the foyer. 'You are at home here. I am your new father!' That was after our first meal at his table when we were already almost overwhelmed with new impressions. As for me, I believed him absolutely."[43]

There was no longer a noticeable difference between life in Gurdjieff's circle in Paris and in New York: there were now many Americans in Paris, and still more British who could come and go more easily. Teaching days and meals were reorganized—there were "English days" and "French days," sometimes an English reading in one space at the rue des Colonels Renard and a French reading in another. Movements classes were mixed, with members of the French wartime class serving as *répétiteurs*—rehearsal teachers— for the newcomers. Gurdjieff continued to create new Movements ranging in tone from serene prayer to mind-challenging complexity and physical demand. He was good-hearted—sometimes—about the talent reaching him from distant places. To Basil Tilley, a classic Englishman appreciated by many in later years, he offered an amiable critique: "You first cousin to elephant. Necessary to become first cousin to cat."[44] There must have been many elephants, but there were enough cats.

Annie Lou Staveley could recall the classes of those years.

Sometimes we were permitted to join in a Movements class at the Salle Pleyel, and sometimes told to sit and watch. On [one] occasion we were to watch from a kind of balcony. At that time Mr. Gurdjieff was composing what were called . . . "The 39 Movements". He had a class among his French pupils so well trained, so finely attuned to his needs that it was a wonderful thing to watch. He needed only to indicate, say, an arm movement and the class literally snapped it up as a seal might snap up a fish. Sometimes a whole sequence of positions would be worked at for hours at a time, only to be discarded the next day. Eventually, one Movement or another was given a name or number, though many worked on at that time I have never seen again.[45]

That sounds peaceful. But there were other days recalled by Rina Hands, the future emissary to Australia. "Mr. Gurdjieff commences to take the practice and for two hours we toil like mad, are cursed—just as in the reports of old. Then that astonishing old man gets up and demonstrates; it was like a miracle—he became young and light of foot, although holding the piano. We began to learn—it is just dawning on me what it is about when he rises, and changes everything—giving a demonstration. He then changes all once more, and amid the groans and contradictions of everyone we proceed."[46]

Those groans can be heard in nearly every memoir of the period—groans and something more. The Bennetts were good on the groans: "Movements at 6, a practice with Solange, and from 7 till 9 with Mr. G. He was very fierce with us, and everything we did was wrong, until we did his favorite No. 17, the Multiplication. Obviously this has for him some quite special significance, and luckily we did it well tonight. He smiled and said if only we did all the Movements like that."[47] Multiplications are complex pattern dances representing the circulation of the Law of Seven embodied in the number series 142857 and in the enneagram. Despite this off-putting description, they are a joy and challenge to study and execute; passing before and behind one another in a dynamic pattern of changes, the participants in a class engage totally, with the support of music that makes audible the quality and feeling of the dance.

Groans—but at other times something else. Grunwald was there on one such occasion: "A perfect sense of harmony seemed to guide the gestures of this old man whose suppleness and unexpected grace, mixed with the beautiful, rhythmic music, brought profound joy. A certain disorder quickly prevailed in the last rows but no one minded, we were transported, and the expression on Madame de Salzmann's face, ordinarily sober, radiated a mysterious joy. Quite other were the Saturday classes when we learned to correct what we were doing and to refine our attention."[48]

Gurdjieff was *creating* in these years—that word pronounced with strongest emphasis by a friend who had participated in the classes. And because he was creating, said our friend, he was relentless. She would become in time a truly inimitable teacher of the

Movements—but at that time, like everyone else, she was struggling to keep up. Once Gurdjieff invited her to meet him at a café after class; of course, she kept the appointment. "If you continue to dance like that," he said to her, "you would be better off learning to knit socks." It was for the sake of Heaven, but it was hard. Once he entered the rehearsal studio where the pupils were waiting, took one look, and sighed, "Panaktikoum"—so a listener heard—and added, "they monsters in pots in Berlin museum."[49]

Outwardly plain with a mild speech impediment, inwardly a keen observer with a gift for words, Irmis Popoff was an interesting woman whom we knew in her older years in New York. She has written of classes in the late 1940s:

> Through the Movements, he bared their souls to his dancers, he unmasked them, forced them to see themselves in their stark nudity, at the same time he lifted them up . . . , providing them with these charts to higher places in themselves from which they could begin to do his work. . . . It was on the floor of the Movements Hall that he became alive with the fire that burned in him; he rose magnificent before our very eyes, dictating movements, changing rhythms, spotting mistakes, lashing orally while we stood at attention, ready to follow his every gesture; changing from one number to another, giving fast explanations on the spot, never compromising, demanding more and more effort, playing no favorites, urging understanding.[50]

Such experience was no small part of life in Gurdjieff's world in the New York winter of 1948–1949, and in Paris throughout the decade. It was not to everyone's taste. One of my professors at university, a well-known poet, literary critic, and caring teacher, told me that he took part in Movements classes in New York during Gurdjieff's last visit. Here two unlike strands of narrative willfully intersect and crash. It happens that Gurdjieff nearly always kept a supply of "bonbons"—hard candies and other sweets in paper wrappers—in a coat pocket. "When he came across a mother with her child," Tchekhovitch recalled, "he always offered a bonbon to the little one. If the child offered it to his mother, he gave him two more. But if the child did not offer anything, that was all he received. If the mother hid the sweet to give to the child later, she was offered more too. In the district where he took his regular walk, he was . . . known as 'Monsieur Bonbon.'"[51] An example of eccentric goodness, of benevolent play, a children's soup kitchen.

One evening after a Movements class in a rehearsal studio at Carnegie Hall, Gurdjieff reached into his pocket, took out handfuls of bonbons and scattered them across the floor among the class participants, who dived for them without shame or hesitation. The still nimble Dr. Welch was among those diving—years later he told me that he didn't mind at all. The young professor looked at this spectacle and did mind; he drew the line there and soon after took leave. One day I told this unfamiliar story to Lord Pentland, the first and long-serving president of the Gurdjieff Foundation of New York. "Yes," he said after I had completed the tale, "you even have to sin."

We must turn back from New York and bonbons to the rue des Colonels Renard. J. G. Bennett, often in attendance with his pupils and his future wife, Elizabeth, beautifully evoked daily life there as a "strange, satisfying environment, at once ritually stylized and perpetually fluid."[52] The Bennetts' coauthored book, *Idiots in Paris*, provides one of the most warmly observed accounts, and Elizabeth Bennett's much later independent memoir is no less rewarding. Gurdjieff's special name for her was Transparente. She confessed that she was physically thin at the time, but the name still seems a grand compliment. "She transparente, *hein*? Nearly."[53]

Gurdjieff's table was organized on two principles: a traditional hierarchy based on closeness to him (senior colleagues and family) and on age (elders in places of honor), but also a system of relations resembling a municipal sewage system. The latter needs more explanation than the former. A few preliminaries: the Directeur, a role exercised by many in the course of time, was responsible for memorizing the sequence of toasts to the idiots and offering them at the proper time. He or she was linked to the Verseur, who poured and replenished drinks. One further role, the Procureur, charged with taking verbatim notes of formal meetings. After these three, the sewage system. Égout, meaning "drain" or "sewer," as the Bennetts explain, was typically an esteemed person to whom Gurdjieff passed extra food and tidbits.[54] If overwhelmed, Égout had the right to pass the surplus to Poubelle on his or her right; *Poubelle* means "dustbin" or, in common usage, "trash can." There were two further elements in the system, Bouche d'Égout (sewer outlet), who received extras from Gurdjieff, and the highly specialized Égout pour Sweet, always a young woman responsible for consuming Gurdjieff's dessert if he didn't want it. There was no personal disparagement of the individuals involved; on the contrary, the system was lighthearted and served Gurdjieff well as he aged and needed less nourishment. There was always abundance; as the years passed he drew on it sparingly.

There were moments of simplicity and charm. "At lunch today I watched Mr. G. making his bowl of salade," recalled Elizabeth Bennett, who often served as Directeur. "This never loses its charm for me. I love to watch his gravity over the whole proceeding, the way he hunts about among the bottles in front of him for the exact sauce or condiment he needs. I love seeing him solemnly pour in the whole contents of a bottle of chutney, mixing it all together, slicing up the cucumber, with his curiously bent fingers, adding the cream, finally sitting back, with a satisfied little grunt, looking around the table and saying, 'Who fresh come from England?'"[55] And in the kitchen there were moments of charm and instruction. Zuber was nearby. "He . . . cooked like a gourmet with the knowledge of a scientist. 'That, special Georgian dish, little chicken, rice and onion, must eat with fingers', he would say. 'That, Kurdish dessert; when suitor proposes and has been accepted, next day he sends this dish to future bride.' He cooked scientifically, like a dietitian who foresees the action on the organism of each dish, each flavoring, each spice. One day I ventured a remark on this subject. 'In fact, Monsieur, cooking could well be a branch of medicine?' which brought the response, 'No, medicine branch of cooking.'"[56]

The toasts to the idiots, as noted before, were a custom based on a traditional Georgian model to which Gurdjieff often added thought-provoking commentaries. About hopeless idiots, for example, within Grunwald's hearing he clarified the hope of the hopeless: "If no hope, only then always continue to work, work inwardly without hope of result. Work always yield profit, often later, great result then, great profit, greater than any hope."[57] On another evening, within the Bennetts' hearing, "when we reached Hopeless Idiots G. was very solemn and . . . spoke about 'this small aim' not to perish like a dog, and how everyone must have this. Everyone must have the wish 'not be taxi', but to have real owner, not a succession of passengers."[58] The assembled pupils' experiences wove themselves into the patterned recitation of the idiots—as the following report from Dorothy Phillpotts makes clear.

Little by little, as I became used to sitting receptive in this pool of quiet, I could feel a clear wish rising to the surface of my consciousness, a gentle movement in the direction of truth which finally represented itself quite definitely as a real prayer—something I had hoped to regain years before, but with all my seeking had never found. This recognition so filled me to the brim, that I was obliged, half turning in the direction of Gurdjieff, to look upon him with a quite new gaze before inevitably looking down again, away from his presence. More came to me now, almost unbearably, than the simplicity of the prayer . . . but what I had been given for the present was really more than enough. Aware that I had been brought to the very brink of a conscious possibility in which there was a strange combination of both suffering and rejoicing, I then heard the toastmaster again, "To the Health of all Hopeless Idiots."[59]

Gurdjieff's attention to all and everything and everyone at table led to what we might today call teachable moments; principles emerged naturally in the course of things. Once, for example, he turned to the person responsible for the toasts, who must have been wool gathering. "Director! Always do only one thing at a time, that of the present moment. But do it well, be in it entirely. . . . Too bad if meanwhile business worth many millions waits at the door. . . . Man is always doing seven things at once; if he does as I say, even for one little thing, the other six will look after themselves."[60]

We must not be voyeurs at Gurdjieff's table, but there were so many incidents, so many flashes of teaching, that we should listen in a little longer. "One night Mr. Gurdjieff was talking about self-awareness," recalled Rina Hands, "—how, in whatever we were doing, we should pause from time to time to say *I*, to say *I* not with the head alone but with one's whole mass. He lifted up his hand, looked at it and said, 'It is like this, even my thumbnail say *I*.' The extraordinary thing was that you could almost hear it doing so."[61] She remembered just as vividly a brief remark that reflects the independent richness of inner life, once established. "We should understand," Gurdjieff said, "that there are two kinds of glad—glad that something happens and glad from inside. Those who have not known this glad, that is not depending on outside, are idiots."[62]

What were these twice-daily gatherings, lunch and dinner, readings and conversations, again and again? They were a Gurdjieffian renewal of the symposia of ancient Greece, of the Early Christian agape, of the *tish* or table where the first generations of Hasidic rabbis and their disciples gathered for conversation. There must be comparable gatherings in Sufi circles and elsewhere. In the field of awareness at the rue des Colonels Renard, in the certainty of both danger and generosity that prevailed, conversation touched on all things from lofty to lowly, with sweet paradoxes in between. For example, this sweet paradoxical story, which seems to have puzzled even the distinguished pupil who recalled it. "I sat at the table at lunch," he reported. "[Gurdjieff] was very far away from us all, though he suddenly returned in order to tell us a silly story about a 'flying elephant'—how once he saw an elephant sit down on a prickly pear: it leapt up and turned so many somersaults that when it had finished there was nothing left but the tusks."[63] A model seeker, this elephant.

It won't be possible to capture everything said, every experience at Gurdjieff's table in the 1940s, or even the essence of everything said, everything experienced—of course not. In that regard I have felt governed by lines from a letter of Emily Dickinson's:

> To attempt to speak of what has been, would be
>   impossible.
> Abyss has no biographer.

Nonetheless, before capitulating we can turn in a number of directions. There was concerted teaching at every gathering, recorded both by the Procureur and by participants such as Kenneth Walker, who heard well.

There were two other words, besides conscience, of which Gurdjieff made constant use, the words duty and responsibility. He said that on arriving at a certain age every man had certain duties to perform; he must justify his existence by service to his fellow creatures and to his Creator. . . . I recall very vividly an evening on which he inquired my age and, having learned that I was the oldest person present, except himself, he turned to the others and said: "You notice that I do not treat everybody in the same way. I treat seniority with respect and so also must you." Then speaking directly to me he added: "And you on your part must discharge your responsibilities as an older person. When people apply to you for help you must give them what they expect of you, for you also have to make payment. Always bear in mind that every age has its appropriate duty to perform." It was indeed a general principle . . . that the more senior the standing of the member of the group, the more was expected of him; a lapse that could be pardoned in another person could not be pardoned in him; an effort that was sufficient elsewhere was not sufficient for him. All manifestations of personality and of self-love in an older person were received with a special scorn. And it was with man's personality that Gurdjieff was always at war, for it was this that prevented his making contact with the deeper and more real parts of his being.[64]

If this was Gurdjieff's essential message to older men and women, he also had messages for the young. One especially pleasant and characteristic story concerns Paul Beekman Taylor, now a retired professor of Nordic languages and much appreciated author on Gurdjieff, then a young man in Gurdjieff's circle by virtue of his mother's participation. The incident occurred one evening at table during a car trip to the south of France; quite a few pupils and family members had caravanned with him.

Before [Gurdjieff] went he held up his half-eaten segment of melon and said who could clean this so that it could be painted—tomorrow he wished to paint this skin and give it as a present to a friend—who would prepare it for him? Paul said he would, and Mr. G. said Eve [Paul's sister] could help him and if they did it properly he could have 1,000 francs. When we left the dining room Eve and Paul were sitting at the table still, with their heads together over the melon skin. . . . Paul came back with his melon skin and showed it to Mr. G. They bent over it together, very solemn, and then G. said, no, it wasn't quite good enough: nothing yellow should remain. Paul went solemnly off to fetch a razor blade and Mr. G., watching him go, laughed and said, "See now what education he have. Until now he knew nothing, he only knew how to eat and shit. Never he work with this," tapping his forehead, "now this his first *labeur*." When Paul came back again after an interval, the skin was perfect: Mr. G. folded it and put it in his pocket and gave the 1,000 francs—"not forget sister."[65]

He took much the same approach to very young people—for example, at the end of a Movements class in Paris. The tale is told by Elizabeth Bennett, one of the brightest explorers of the abyss.

One night, at the end of the Movements class, Madame de Salzmann's two little grandsons were there, Serge and Olivier. And when Gurdjieff said, "Who work, eat. Come dinner, nine o'clock," Olivier piped up and said, "Can I come?" Gurdjieff said, "Have you worked?" "No," said Olivier. So Gurdjieff said, "Then work now. Hold your arms out sideways for two minutes." So the child held his arms out sideways and we stood around—his mother, his grandmother, Gurdjieff, and some of the Movements class. There he stood, brave as a lion I will say, and after about a minute and a half, he said, "Can I put my arms down now?" and his mother and his grandmother said with one voice, "No!", so he went on and finished his two minutes, and came to dinner.[66]

Gurdjieff was rigorous concerning parents and children. He asked parents to treat their children as a sacred trust. In the lean years following the war, when food was rationed in Britain and expensive in Paris, he would speak with parents—of all nationalities—in strenuous terms. To have children in one's care is to have a work in life, a work on oneself. When he says, "You finish now" in what follows, it should be read as "You are finished now," your personal needs come far behind a child's needs.

> "Now you understand what I tell." He was very emphatic. "You have children. You finish now. You make a task, sacrifice for children. What you would like eat yourself, give children. Be good mother. If you rich I would not say this, but something different. But children cost much . . ." Quite free now, I began to reply, "But I must do good work now in order to be a good mother, a good example." Gurdjieff, however, interrupted me quickly and started by repeating himself. "You must make a task. Be mother. You die—you sacrifice for children. You do this exact and work will come into life. You never do this before. Necessary learn sacrifice."[67]

As we said at the beginning of this exploration of the 1940s, Gurdjieff now relied in part, and strenuously, on life experience. His teaching built, and builds, from the inside out and from the outside in—from "the place where everything is quiet," as we have heard him say, but also from the challenges of daily life, here caring for a child in a time of scarcity.

The baby in question was a new arrival, and Gurdjieff was vulnerable to the charms of the newborn. Until Dorothy Phillpotts needed to take leave from lunch to feed her infant daughter, he hadn't understood that she had brought the child to Paris.

"What? Baby is here?" said Gurdjieff, his voice rising at the
end of the question, "Two, three days and I not see? Please," he
beckoned with his head, "baby my weakness. Bring tomorrow,
lunch. . . . First we will have Christmas tree." "The baby's only
six months," said Bennett. "All babies like tree," said Gurdjieff.
I arranged to bring her at two. . . . When we said good-by he
said: "That baby, she my pupil. She understand everything,
all *Beelzebub*. You not understand, but she understand." Not
recognizing myself, I handed him the photograph of Caroline
in her christening dress which he said he would keep, adding
with great satisfaction, "She my youngest pupil."[68]

Gurdjieff once said—I have no idea when—that he only liked
people "under five and over fifty-five."

Respecting the abyss of time, we have nonetheless looked in two
directions, toward older and younger. An inviting direction remains:
the private reflections of good people. I'm thinking particularly of
the journal kept by René Zuber in which, for decades after Gurdjieff's
death, he would periodically reflect about the man and teaching.
Words said long before at the rue des Colonels Renard would return
in a new light—for example, Gurdjieff's insistence on the need to
"outwardly play a role, inwardly not identify." It can easily seem an
injunction to play at life, to withhold sincere commitment, but it is
much more difficult and interesting than that. The injunction is to
take one's place in life fully, to occupy with understanding, commitment, and even love the roles great or small that fall to one—and yet
not be swallowed up. In a journal entry of late 1971, Zuber had this
in mind: "All human beings, whether we like it or not, are prisoners
of our internal cast of characters. At every moment we unconsciously
play a role. Mr. Gurdjieff told us to play our roles voluntarily, i.e.,
consciously."[69] In this way it might be possible—again borrowing
from the journal—to "live one's life as an awakened witness to it."

Hidden not far from these reflections is Gurdjieff's recurrent emphasis on the need for direct perception of "I am." From this all things could flow, including compassion and service. Zuber had this teaching in mind decades later and intuits in terms I've not seen elsewhere the fulfillment of "I" at a level far surpassing it. "He who says 'I' as completely as possible places himself at the foot of a great ladder, of which the other extremity—invisible—touches the ocean of the uppermost heaven . . . where there is no longer I."

A beautiful reflection: I don't know where to store it—down here among us all, or somewhere in the untouched heights where it may keep better. René Zuber's journal speaks to the future of the teaching after Gurdjieff; there would be men and women of quality to think it, live it, and guide a new generation.

Saying Goodbye

Saying goodbye to Gurdjieff at the rue des Colonels Renard was a unique exercise: Who knew what might happen as one looked into his face a last time before taking the boat-train to England or a return flight to America? Dorothy Phillpotts, the mother of young Caroline, shows one way to go about it. "The prospect of departure having softened the noisy mind," she has written, "and for the time being wiped away all ambition, one sat on one's heels at the door of the salon or even, somehow quite naturally, knelt by the low armchair where he always was to be found at the end of the day, and received a simple, gentle salutation, one global look, but enough to open the rusty floodgates and send one's inadequate craft swiftly back to the contradictions of life in an altogether new mixture of daring and hope."[70]

The last months of Gurdjieff's life registered on no one as last months, although his health had noticeably weakened. In the spring and summer of 1949 there was as always no end of incident, no end of silence. I asked a friend, now elderly, who helped in Gurdjieff's household in those months to say what she could of him. He was so silent, she responded. Elizabeth Bennett had the same impression. "We were often silent. I was intensely happy," she recalled of a late conversation.[71] And yet the symposium at his table continued. So, too, Movements classes; the creation of the "Thirty-Nine" advanced. There was also the occasional car trip—and to everyone's misfortune the requisite driving accident that left Gurdjieff and several companions thoroughly bruised. In the last weeks of his life, when he was already quite unwell, the caravan visited the prehistoric cave of Lascaux in central France, discovered soon after the war had begun and no doubt little visited until war's end. In 1949, one could still enter the cave itself and view the magnificent wall paintings. By all accounts Gurdjieff felt at home there, as if his largely undisclosed, multicultural lineage of seekers and initiates reached back to the shamanic origins and imagery he fluently interpreted on the wall. He turned to one of his companions, Frank and Olgivanna Lloyd Wright's daughter Iovanna, to send a message to her father: "Tell him such place exist." How touching that he thought of Wright; he must have admired him more than he let on. The poetry and feeling of the visit to Lascaux remain strong: soon to take leave, Gurdjieff looked into the abyss of time and recognized, as if a brother, the figure of a shaman dressed in animal skins and ceremonial antlers, crouched in a dance-like posture.

Gurdjieff didn't miss the pleasant side of his situation. "At the end of a meal," James Moore has written, "when Égout gave him a cigarette and Poubelle lit it for him, he said, 'See now how my life is roses, roses. And I—only a poor old dancing teacher.'"[72] But others saw what they saw. One evening when Annie Lou Staveley was there, Gurdjieff had finished playing his harmonium when "his head nodded, as is the way with old people." "All at once," she recognized, "the thought was present in the room—here is an old man!"[73] Tchekhovitch, who knew Gurdjieff far better than most, could read the signs. In the last weeks, he recalled,

[Gurdjieff's] strength declined from day to day, and he only stayed at meals for a short while. We then knew that his condition was very serious. Apart from that, his appearance was deceptive because, in spite of everything, the various activities continued under his direction as if nothing were wrong—but at what cost! I can still see him leaving his room, walking painfully down the corridor until he reached the dining room. There he would straighten himself up, smooth his moustache, and only then enter, completely transformed—he was again the master, the superb old lion. A good-natured smile would light up his face, the familiar smile that always had the effect of reassuring us and reviving our hope once again. So it was until his last days. He seemed to time the moment of his arrival at our meals carefully, in order to tire himself as little as possible and to fulfil his role most effectively. Thanks to the set progression of the "Toasts to the Idiots", he could follow it even from his bed. I noticed that he always appeared when the toast was given for "all hopeless idiots". . . [to which] Mr. Gurdjieff himself would then solemnly add, "He who works on himself also prepares for an honorable death." When it was time for the next toast, he would leave the table with a firm, determined step, which allowed no one to suspect his fatigue. "Continue, continue," he would say without looking back. . . . The atmosphere remained charged with his presence.[74]

In the last months there were enterprises. Most important, the page proofs of the American and British editions of *Beelzebub's Tales to His Grandson*, a labor of love and negotiation undertaken by Lord Pentland and others, reached him in Paris. The book begun twenty-four years earlier would at last see the light of day in the care of prominent publishers. The page proofs were both joy and portent. Gurdjieff would say at times that, upon publication, his work would be completed. "Then I can disappear . . . then I can rest."[75] Yet he was also taking steps toward the purchase of a reasonably large property one hour southeast of Paris at La Grande-Paroisse, and had commissioned an English architect among his pupils to develop a renovation plan. It would soon be known, he said, as "Coin pour reposer Auteur Belzébuth"—a comfortable place where the author of *Beelzebub's Tales* could rest.[76] With the architect Clive Entwistle he had already begun to explore the design of an elaborate new mosaic pavement. His intention was clear: to reestablish the teaching in a smaller Prieuré-like center. The demand had outgrown his apartment. In light of his state of failing health, his concern for this project cannot help but be touching. It suggested a different future than he foresaw when he told his pupils that soon he would go far away, that his apartment should become a museum.[77]

And then there were the Movements. Thirty-eight had been composed since he had started a decade earlier to work with the stunningly able French class. Elizabeth Bennett was in class, I believe in early October, when Gurdjieff began to dictate the thirty-ninth Movement.

> At 7:45 the door opened and G. came in. He was wearing his ordinary dark European clothes, with a very furry Homburg hat, which partly accounted for his appearance, but I did think he looked dreadfully ill. Very dark around his eyes, and his face quite sunken, and moving very slowly. I felt a sort of shocked clutch at my inside when I saw him. . . . We at once did No. 17, the Multiplication which he likes so much. He left after more than an hour, . . . but before he went he gave us the beginning of a truly amazing new Movement—No. 39. One sits cross-legged on the floor, and Solange came out and counted aloud, sitting at the side, "Un, deux, trois . . ." and so

on. When we had worked at it for a while, G. stopped us and made "une petite addition." Then he said we could practice this "in maison," and next time he would add to it.[78]

When he completed it some days later, and well-matched music found its way alongside, it was an inconceivably tender prayer, not at all difficult to execute, a demand and opportunity to become acquainted with purity. To this day it is given in Movements classes only on special occasions.

At the evening class on Friday, October 14, Gurdjieff collapsed. Two days later in London, Elizabeth Bennett wrote in her journal that "the news from Paris is not encouraging. Mr. G. went to the café on Friday morning and afterwards drove himself to the bath, but at the Movements in the evening he quite collapsed. Now he must be for a fortnight in bed, and they want him to stop smoking, and some sort of drug is being sent to him from America. In the circumstances I thought I had better ask permission to return to Paris."[79]

The drug was not "sent," it was hand-delivered by Dr. William Welch, who had come to know Gurdjieff as well as any in the New York circle. After the nineteen-hour flight, he went directly to the rue des Colonels Renard with whatever the wonder drug was, but more significantly with his sound medical judgment and filial love for the man who was about to become his patient. Dr. William J. Welch (1911–1997) deserves a proper introduction as he enters the difficult days ahead.[80] Born in small-town Wisconsin and educated at Yale College, where he claimed to have wasted each and every day, he had throughout his acceptably long life the style of the 1930s. Benny Goodman and Fred Astaire set the style—that, with a touch of Garrison Keillor's Midwestern, bemused self-perception and more than a little of Winston Churchill's playful interest in the long spoken sentence deftly rescued at the last moment from its own potentially strangled complexity. Elegant in speech and dress, witty and vastly humane, too well-read for a man who laid claim to negligence, he was a medical scientist and skeptical inquirer into the meaning of life who in later years left his welcome imprint on a generation of Gurdjieff students. His relation with Gurdjieff was of the simplest: he perceived him as a wise father and received without qualm Gurdjieff's multitude of offerings, from austere teachings to Rabelaisian burlesque. No one had a keener ear for Gurdjieff's turns of phrase, and so he must have known that he was home, in some large sense, when he entered the apartment at the rue des Colonels Renard, joined Gurdjieff in his bedroom, and heard Gurdjieff's greeting: "Bravo, America! Bravo, *docteur!*"[81]

"I was shocked to hear his labored breathing, to see his gray color, and the gaunt wasting of his body, except for his swollen belly and legs. The mark of death was on his face." Those were his first perceptions. He prevailed on Gurdjieff—it wasn't difficult—to be checked into the American Hospital in Neuilly, a few miles from the rue des Colonels Renard, where he could better perform procedures clearly needed. Elizabeth Bennett witnessed his departure, which "was typical," she wrote.

> The ambulance men brought the stretcher to his room, but he wouldn't have this, and walked out into the hall and got on to the stretcher there, sitting back, saying, "Oy!" as he always does. He did not dress, but wore pajamas, and his red fez on his head. He sat upright on the stretcher, and was carried away like a royal prince! All the family was clustered at the street door (the crusty old concierge was in tears!) and as they carried him across the pavement he made a little gesture, a sort of wave, with his hand and said, "Au revoir, tout le monde!" The last sight of him was as he was carried into the ambulance, sitting very upright, with his head up, his fez at a rakish angle and his cigarette between his lips.[82]

Dr. Welch had told those nearest to Gurdjieff that he was "vastly sick" with little hope of recovery.[83] "Once in the hospital," Dr. Welch has written, "it was possible to make him more comfortable, to ease his breathing and support his heart. But the more we studied him, the more the evidence emerged that no bodily system had been spared and what had seemed inevitable was indeed imminent." Two days before he died, Gurdjieff called for Madame de Salzmann and, in Dr. Welch's vigilant company, gave his final instructions. The doctor reflected years later that "much of what she has sustained and accomplished . . . since his death has followed the line laid out that Thursday afternoon."[84]

Gurdjieff died late in the morning of October 29 in the presence of Dr. Welch and Madame de Salzmann. Dr. Welch has written, "I shall not try to describe the actual moment of his death, for although I was present, and the events that occurred were unique in my experience, I do not know their significance and have no way of expressing them in a proper context."[85] From which we can gather that Gurdjieff did not die like other men. For her part, sending a message several decades later to Gurdjieff pupils and teachers in New York on the occasion of Madame Ouspensky's death, Madame de Salzmann wrote:

In the name of my relation with Madame Ouspensky, who was the nearest soul in my work, I wish to tell you this:

Once more I recognize the truth I experienced in front of Mr. Gurdjieff's body, and which has become a certitude:

There is no death. . . . Life cannot die.

The coating uses up, the form disintegrates, but life is—is always there—even if for us it is the unknown.[86]

That morning Elizabeth Bennett was housekeeping at the rue des Colonels Renard.

I felt as heavy as lead. . . . I finished cleaning the dining room and then . . . went to clean the little ornaments on the "Christmas tree" in the sitting room. While I was doing it, Emil came in, just after 11, sat down on a petit tabouret and said in a matter-of-fact voice, "Yes, Elizabeth, it's true. He did die." There was nothing to say, so I didn't say anything, but went on with my dusting. Emil went out and came back a moment later with a glass of Armagnac. He said, "I brought you this, in case you feel cold." I was so touched by this, and amused at the same time: I thanked him and made him drink some too. I finished my job and went to the kitchen. Mme Tracol arrived. . . . She came straight to me and took my hands and said, "Remember, Elizabeth, this is for all of us; French, English and American. Remember. Remember we are all together."[87]

Several of the most mature and worldly men all but refused to believe not only that he had died, but that he *could* die. "Gurdjieff dead!" Kenneth Walker recalled. "It was difficult to believe that all that vigor, that daemonic force, that keen intelligence, those unique qualities, no longer existed. . . . Perhaps he was giving us a shock for the good of our souls and then, when this had produced its effect, he, our teacher, would reappear, more vital even than before. It was impossible to connect Gurdjieff with the apathy and unresponsiveness of death."[88] Grunwald experienced the same incredulous refusal.

I thought that Mr. Gurdjieff could not die. I saw his eternal presence, and when he improvised on his little instrument, his eyes so radiant that their light like a sacred substance penetrated space and hearts, I couldn't imagine that it could end. The two last months at his apartment had extraordinary intensity, increasing with every lunch, every dinner. I could best compare it with the behavior of large, old fruit trees. In the season before their death, they carry more fruit than ever, more fruit than leaves and more beautiful than ever before. But the following spring, desolate, they display only dead branches, no budding leaves.[89]

For his part, René Zuber had glimpsed for some years that Gurdjieff was no longer only of this world. "I remember that his face," Zuber wrote, "the face of an old athlete imbued with compassion for human beings, had an air of melancholy about it, as if he belonged already to an 'elsewhere' which he would not name. This was during the last years of his life."[90]

People in the neighborhood, whom he had helped, were not doing any better than Walker and Grunwald. "It is very touching," wrote Elizabeth Bennett, "to see how his loss affects the shopkeepers of the rue des Acacias, the flower woman who said, was it true that the 'marchand de bonbons' is dead? And our own Mme Charles, who was invited years ago to drink with him once in his café, and who remembers it as an outstanding event in her life. . . . 'We never knew who he was', she said, 'but of course we knew he was very learned!' So now all that is over."[91] At the funeral on November 4 in the Russian Orthodox cathedral, rue Daru, Gurdjieff's pupils were surprised by the number of mourners whom they didn't know: the impoverished painters whom he had helped financially, the Russian exiles who found their way daily to his kitchen one flight up where he gave them food and an encouraging word, many friends of whom they knew nothing. Morning had belonged to them, afternoon and evening to the pupils.

For several days and nights there was a constant vigil in a chapel at the American Hospital. Solita Solano, who of course had reached Paris as soon as possible from her home in America, "sat by his side, near his face, for two hours."[92] She was one of many to pay

Fig. 14: Gurdjieff family gravesite, Fontainebleau-Avon. *Source*: Dr. Tony Shaw

tribute there. November 4: the funerary mass at the cathedral, then a cortege of cars making its way to the cemetery at Avon, where Gurdjieff's wife and mother—and Katherine Mansfield—had their graves. The Prieuré was nearby. Years earlier Gurdjieff had settled the character of the gravesite where his kin were buried and where he now joined them (see fig. 14). It reflects his enduring interest in Neolithic standing stones and dolmens in the Caucasus, related to the awesome art of construction at Carnac and Stonehenge. Under dangerous circumstances in the Caucasus mountains during the Russian civil war, he and his companions had come upon ancient monuments of this kind. Two uncarved standing stones of massive weight and considerable height face each other across the burial plot. There is no identifying family name, no dates and calm message. Instead, a pervasive sense of austerity, of a return to origins situated well before historical cultures and their familiar signals of peace and rest. It was here on a rainy November afternoon that Gurdjieff's coffin, accompanied by Russian Orthodox chant and prayer, was lowered into the ground. The unspoken symbol could not be missed: Gurdjieff belonged both to the rich stream of Christian tradition and to a primordial spirituality that had strength but no name.

Photographs of the mourners densely grouped around the gravesite include many men and women now unknown and others who were destined to continue the teaching in Europe and America for decades to come. Madame de Salzmann was the first to break the stillness that must have followed the conclusion of formal prayers. Only Grunwald thought to preserve an account of that moment. "Madame de Salzmann, dressed entirely in black, advanced alone, knelt in the mud and saluted the now hidden coffin, her head touching the ground in a dignified and solemn gesture which made of that moment the gravest and most arresting of the day. Then, in a last homage, she threw a few flowers and a shovelful of earth on the coffin."[93] Everyone followed suit; that is what one does.

Dorothy Phillpotts surely spoke for many when she later wrote, "He had turned me around. Pulling the string of my awkward perseverance sharply, and to the limit, he had then walked away for ever, secure in the certainty that I would indeed never give up until I had inherited at least an echo of his truth, of his impeccable inner life, and a fragment—infinitely small—of his unquenchable courage and daring."[94] Frank Lloyd Wright was far from Avon in that early

November. Receiving an award from the famed Cooper Union in New York, he asked to say a few words. "The greatest man in the world has recently died. His name was Gurdjieff."[95]

Gurdjieff had a unique way of taking leave in New York after dinner with pupils and friends in a restaurant. He would tip his hat at the door—so Dr. Welch remembered—and say, "Good night, all kinds." What better could a colleague of life say?

CHAPTER 7

The Great Prayer: 1950–1956

THE LOSS OF A REVERED TEACHER is a physical event for those who remain behind. As if one has received a heartless blow in the middle of one's chest, it takes one's breath away. It is the death of a cherished parent. For days the fact of moving is strange when the departed teacher is no longer there to move; one's body feels wooden, animated but distant, a dull miracle. Within one's mourning and the round of practical matters that need attention, the strangeness persists for some time. Excellent teachers convey worlds of meaning to their pupils, but something escapes them because it cannot be taught, it can only be discovered later: how to be, how to continue after the teacher's death. There is a new force in the field of experience: the teacher's irremediable absence. People respond differently. "Olga we must work," Jeanne de Salzmann wrote to Olgivanna Lloyd Wright in the months after Gurdjieff's death. "G. I. has given us something sacred, a germ of being that we are responsible for and we cannot let perish. We owe him that, otherwise all his efforts will have been in vain."[1]

Two days before his death, Gurdjieff did what he could to lay out for Madame de Salzmann his vision of what comes next. Who knows all that he said, but years later she published her recollection of that moment. "'The essential thing,' [he said], 'the first thing is to prepare a nucleus of people capable of responding to the demand which will arise. So long as there is no responsible nucleus, the action of the ideas will not go beyond a certain threshold. That will take time . . . a lot of time, even.'" Further, she shared how she understood what he was asking. "The task became clear to me: . . . it would be necessary to work without respite to form a nucleus capable, through its level of objectivity, devotion, and the demands it would make on itself, of sustaining the current that had been created."[2] This trinity of values and the concept of a current—of a teaching not pooled in on itself but flowing—have long echoes. Gurdjieff students still hear them, and the three linked values are anything but exclusive: every humane and challenging enterprise relies on them, however fully or thinly articulated.

In the evening after the burial at Avon, Madame de Salzmann gathered at her apartment the most senior French group and a number of English pupils to look at the future. Her thoughts had already turned to a theme that would be central for some years and never disappear from view. It followed directly from Gurdjieff's charge to her. "When a teacher like Mr. Gurdjieff goes," she said, "he cannot be replaced. Those who remain cannot create the same conditions. We have only one hope—to make something together— what no *one* of us could do, perhaps a group can. We no longer have a teacher, but we have the possibility of a group. Let us make this our chief aim for the future."[3]

That was the first conversation. The next evening there was also a first Movements class. Elizabeth Bennett recalled:

Everyone wore their costumes, and Mme de S. chose the numbers with great care. First No. 17, then 19, 5, 36, 4, 39, 38, 34, 16—I forget which others. We finished with 20 minutes of arms-out-sideways, audience included. Mme de S. went straight through the Movements without comment, although they were done unusually badly. There were many mistakes, and the whole effect, from the point of view of execution of the physical gestures, was ragged. Yet I have never known such feeling in them. At the end, she came forward from the piano and spoke to us, saying that we must work hard and come to the practices regularly, and that from next Monday we will begin to go through them all again. . . . Not in any way blaming us for our performances tonight, but saying how work must be from now on.[4]

An elderly friend, also in class, remembers back over the decades to that moment and, with scarcely any details, conveys the essential. "Madame de Salzmann had us sit on the floor and asked, '*Voulez-vous apprendre les Mouvements?*'" Do you want to learn the Movements? It was as if the Movements had not yet been learned despite years of prior work, that everything remained to be discovered. In an unpublished memoir Gurdjieff is reported to have said that "The real work will begin for you after my death." It was beginning.

Here also could begin, but will not, a second book: a chronicle of the many decades ahead. Guided by Jeanne de Salzmann, a good number of Gurdjieff's pupils—and, in turn, some of their pupils—matured into capable teachers. The nucleus appeared. Institutes under various names were established in several countries to preserve and offer the teaching, which gradually seeded other centers nearby and worldwide. The process was private, intensely so; it asked nothing of the world except peaceful circumstances to meet, work, explore, think, and act in whatever ways necessary. In those years and to this day it remains true, as one of Gurdjieff's pupils expressed it, that "this teaching isn't hidden, but it doesn't put itself forward."[5] I underscore the privacy and need for undisturbed time in the early years after Gurdjieff's death because, as the next chapter will make clear, that was not to go unchallenged. A reasonable destination in time is the year 1956, when *Beelzebub's Tales* was published in French, six years after the Anglo-American edition, and the people and structures of the teaching were well founded in France, Britain, and the United States. As well, Venezuela had become the creative center for numerous other countries on that continent.

If I could write the balance of this chapter as a tone poem, I would: a chapter to be hummed rather than read. It needs not so much detail but rather a felt sense for people and events. As a tone poem (a nearly obsolete term, I know), it would have the forte and piano of music, heroic and muted passages, moments of bright confidence and appalling doubt, spells when a single instrument playing against the silence makes silence audible. Major participants in what lies ahead would be represented by musical signatures in the manner of Wagner; you would always know when they were there. Their peace wouldn't be disturbed, history wouldn't summon them from wherever they are. There would be no names, simply a lighted sky and the sounds of a deep kind of goodness at work. But that won't be possible.

Why "The Great Prayer" as the title of this chapter? Factually speaking, it is the title of a majestic Movement in the 1923–1924 public demonstrations in Paris and North America. A ritual ceremony of utmost intensity yet collectedness, implacable and deliberate with slowly evolving music set in the bass register, it incarnates aspects of the nature of prayer as Gurdjieff taught: prayer as a kind of remembering, an act of sustained attention in body, mind, and feeling, and, specifically in this Movement, an expression of worship entwined with remorse for what one is—what one still is. "I must experience remorse for what was wrong yesterday," we have heard Gurdjieff say, "and stay with that material. Only there will I find the strength necessary to act differently." There are other prayers of very different character in the repertory. This one darkly, with intense beauty, "stays with that material." There is nothing like it.

Those few words, the Great Prayer, capture the feeling that prevailed through these years, particularly in the beginning. Scarcely anything was sure. Much help was needed from wherever help comes. There were subtle and coarse risks on every side, so to speak, and in true Gurdjieffian fashion those risks had to be recognized and understood if they were not to enter the situation unseen. Everything depended on the responsiveness, understanding, and perseverance of groups of pupils facing an entirely new circumstance. Everything depended on the depth of understanding, astuteness, and sincerity of those who met those groups to bring a renewed sense of direction. Of course, there were casualties: some pupils distanced themselves because they saw no further hope or need, others because they felt, realistically or not, that they had received enough to continue on their own. Some few migrated to other teachings. Most participants recognized that the teaching was to be taken up and explored anew in a circle of like-minded men and women for whom the adventure had only begun. From the beginning it was obvious that Madame de Salzmann represented a steady, inspiring center in relation to whom everything could begin again. Many looked to her—but she couldn't be everywhere at once, couldn't reason with every fear and untangle every confusion. She needed colleagues and, as we'll see, they were ready. She didn't assert herself as Gurdjieff's successor in those early years, and a few contested her leadership: "You are exhausted, Jeanne—shouldn't you take a rest in the country?" Though many recognized her without hesitation, oral sources report that she allowed things to take their course. In the end, even authentically great and moving teachers of the next generation, in whom the Gurdjieff teaching was intact and radiant, acknowledged her with good reason.

We encountered in that striking conversation with Luc Dietrich Madame de Salzmann's willingness years earlier to be severe when circumstances require. That served her well as she traveled the world of the teaching after Gurdjieff's death and assessed its possibilities and needs, an itinerary that took her in a very few months as far as Olgivanna in Arizona, to New York and London, and the first of what would become annual visits to Caracas during the Christmas holiday. We can only look at a few examples of her meetings with experienced groups, but those examples are telling. In mid-March 1950, she was in London, where the group had hoped to see Gurdjieff soon among them. Groups that had not previously met together had assembled as one. This was what she wished—the unification of groups that had been separate in the past. She said on the point of departure from the London group:

I didn't want to leave before speaking with you about your situation. You need to realize your situation and, after having spoken with several people, it doesn't strike me that you see it for what it is.

I don't know if you see where your efforts have led you. Today they have led you to one thing only—outer activity. You are numerous, the scale has grown, but the raison d'être of your work, your purpose, is absent. You have forgotten it.

Perhaps life conditions have brought you to this state of affairs but, to be able to move on, you absolutely must recognize it.

It was Mr. Gurdjieff who advised you to meet all together. He sent you his books, he sent you the Movements, so that you could prepare yourselves to understand him when he came to work with you. But books and Movements can never replace a master. Books and Movements cannot give you real and direct work on yourselves, they cannot allow you to change. What Mr. Gurdjieff would have brought you is the possibility of approaching a higher level of being. Through his words, through the relations he would have established with you, through his presence alone, he would have made you feel certain human qualities which would have awakened in you the wish to go further in that direction. He would have drawn you toward him, toward his level, and at the same time would have made you suffer terribly by making you see the reality of your state. . . .

Of course, we no longer have that possibility for work since we have lost our master. But his teaching remains. If our aim is inner growth, we must submit to the principles of the teaching. And that you cannot do alone. You can achieve nothing alone, and that is your situation. You have remained alone. If you look sincerely, you will see that you serve nothing, you respect nothing, you have no aim in common, you carry nothing together, you carry nothing whose life depends on you. You are not responsible for one another, not dependent on one another. And so your relations have no meaning. You have exactly the same relations as in ordinary life, you are lost, without direction.

And yet each of you was brought to the teaching by someone who took it upon himself or herself to help you understand the ideas, to work on yourself. . . . Someone who helped you! Today you have no help. You must ask for help. The relation with those who brought you to the teaching is your only hope. You must understand this and turn toward them to ask to be helped. This is how I understand your situation, and if you truly suffer from it, no one could wish you anything better.[6]

Though what Jeanne de Salzmann said that day must have been hard to bear—a "shock," in the lexicon of the teaching, and not a small one—it marked the birth moment of a large and creative group still intact today, the hub of affiliated groups from Ireland to Poland. She knew how to go on from there toward sufficient reconciliation: she had brought from Paris the transcript of a meeting with Gurdjieff at rue des Colonels Renard. "I thought you would be happy to hear his voice." And Thomas de Hartmann was at her side; he and his wife, Olga, had returned. He would be of immense and loyal help to her until his death in 1956, and Olga for many more years. "Fama Alexandrovich," she recalled of that occasion, "played the prayer of the institute, marvelously." She had kept the Russian version of his name; it echoed back over decades to their first encounter in Tiflis, when everyone was young.[7] And so that difficult meeting in London ended with the goodness of music. There would be equally difficult meetings and unsettled stretches of time there and elsewhere over the next few years. Madame de Salzmann and the nucleus with which she had begun to work were laying the foundation for a school.

The first anniversary of Gurdjieff's death found her in the pleasant country mansion at Mendham, New Jersey, acquired by the Ouspenskys in the early 1940s as a home for the teaching. "It was as if time hadn't passed," she recorded in her journal.

> He is just as alive and present for me as a year ago. What has truly existed death cannot take away. What has not existed death takes, and takes away even the possibility. It is more than hard. This inexorable law gives the need to make use of immediate possibilities, and the strength to do so. The cruelty of G. I.'s absence and his presence in me and in the others—Sophia Grigorievna, Olga and Fama—has created a need to come together in him, in his spirit. We are united by his memory and what he gave each of us.

There was a commemoration that day of a kind that would become traditional in later years, though not on the anniversary of Gurdjieff's death, rather on January 13, his birthday: Movements, readings, music, special food, a toast to Gurdjieff. Madame de Salzmann had mixed feelings as the day unfolded: "The day was at the same time grand and miserable. Grand because it brought everyone together around material left by G. I.—Movements, the reading, music. And hard because it is all only a possibility. Later it is our material that must create bonds among us—our understanding, our efforts, our achievements. We must stay together consciously, and push one another forward."[8]

I have the impression that Madame de Salzmann knew she could rely on the French groups; that was her stability, while in

Britain and America it would take several years to unify and set-tle separate groups insofar as possible, with the help of men and women in both countries who understood the good sense of what she wished to accomplish. Not everything worked out as hoped. Friends have asked me to provide some measure of detail about the difficulties she faced. It's true that there was nothing abstract in her encounters with established groups and their leaders in the years after Gurdjieff's death. In some instances fate and character were almost visibly at work, as if a larger hand arranged outcomes. In front of all this, I hesitate: the documentation available to me is somewhat thin, and, well beyond that, I have no wish or right to judge the wisdom of key participants. Nonetheless, why not look at one relationship, which began in confidence and trust, changed utterly for years, and by the mid-1970s had created a structure still standing today that poses legitimate challenges for all concerned.

MADAME DE SALZMANN AND J. G. BENNETT

J. G. Bennett (1897–1974) is familiar to us in this book as an invalu-able witness to life and teachings at the rue des Colonels Renard, and we have drawn on his insight into the pace of life at the Prieuré. He has written that he spent three months at the Prieuré in 1923, then perforce returned to England to resume earning his livelihood and caring for his family.[9] He did not see Gurdjieff again until 1948, when for eighteen months he was a frequent visitor to Paris and earned the regard of Gurdjieff, who named him his future repre-sentative for Britain—in a limited capacity, it is true, as collector of subscriptions toward the publication of *Beelzebub's Tales*, but the assignment implied something more. For many of the years between 1923 and 1948, Bennett had participated in the Ouspensky groups in London and its region, but relations became increasingly uneasy with P. D. Ouspensky, who severed relations with him in 1945. Bennett's formidable intelligence and appeal as a speaker and interpreter of ideas had led naturally to the formation of Gurdjieff groups around him, eventually centered at an independent country house, Coombe Springs, and given formal identity as an institute. He and Madame Ouspensky had, I suppose discreetly, remained in touch. Bennett heard from her after World War II that Gurdjieff was alive and well in Paris.

In Gurdjieff's late years and for some years after, Bennett unreservedly recognized Madame de Salzmann. At a moment of difficulty, for example, while driving her home from Colonels Renard, he sought her advice. "The work changes," she said to him as they moved through the city. "Up to one point, one gets fairly clear guidance. Then comes a time when it is made so confusing that you can easily do exactly the wrong thing in the conviction that it is right." Bennett adds that "she was to me, and to many others, a wise counselor and friend in our stumbling efforts to discover what Gurdjieff wanted of us."[10] In 1950, Bennett encouraged members of his group to participate in the London meetings and Movements classes sponsored by Madame de Salzmann, and he himself met with her periodically in one city or the other. With some of his pupils, Bennett participated in rehearsals for the May 1952 public Movements demonstrations at the Fortune Theatre in London, though he fell ill at the last moment and couldn't continue. It is a sign of Madame de Salzmann's confidence in him that she asked him to give a series of four lectures on the Gurdjieff teaching later that year in New York, and a sign of his regard for her that he accepted the challenging assignment.

Nonetheless, there was a countercurrent, perhaps unexpressed at the time but forthrightly registered in Bennett's autobiography. The small English group of experienced participants in which he was a peer and member struck him as stagnant, not really moving on. Similarly, the groups for which he was responsible at Coombe Springs seemed to be moving "at an even pace"—which struck Bennett as insufficient.[11] For years, and still at that time, he had been writing a genuinely vast synthesis of the Gurdjieff teaching, spirituality, and science, *The Dramatic Universe*, which reflected his willingness and need to put the Gurdjieff teaching in a broad cultural context. In 1953, he was drawn again to travel in the Islamic world, where he was preternaturally at home and had fluent command of the Turkish *lingua franca*. Perhaps the remedy for stagnation and an all-too-even pace lay somewhere there. It was not in his nature, he wrote years later, "scrupulously to adhere to the letter of the teaching. I was ready to experiment with new ideas and new methods, providing they conformed to the fundamental principles of Gurdjieff's work."[12]

Distance and misunderstanding between J. G. Bennett and Madame de Salzmann slowly became evident. She seemed to mistrust what Coombe Springs was becoming at the same time that he recognized the need to support that large community of some four hundred participants through public lectures in London. And then, looking back at the publication of *Beelzebub's Tales* in 1950 through well-known commercial publishers, he felt that Gurdjieff's intention for the book had been "betrayed"—a strong word. Bennett felt that it would have been preferable to publish on the basis of generous subscriptions received and to distribute the book free of charge.[13] He recognized the impracticality of that approach but still felt that the book was "being treated as a disreputable elderly relative, best kept in the background."

These seem to me causes on the surface; there were deeper causes, differences in vision and destiny. Madame de Salzmann knew the Gurdjieff teaching to be complete. From her perspective, what was needed was to work with it, rediscover it again and again through direct experience, treasure it, deepen into it, sustain its purity, pass it on with care to the next generation and the next. For his part, Bennett immensely valued the teaching and what he had gained through his participation in it. But it was his nature to look past it, to discover what he felt to be missing—missing methods, missing attitudes. She was building a school in three countries, and soon four with the addition of Venezuela, with walls and welcoming doors. He wasn't ready for even that much enclosure. Until his late years he was by nature a purposeful wanderer, and he dearly wished to wander toward a brighter light that could in time be shared with others—the light in the East that Gurdjieff in his own early *Wanderjahre* had discovered and drawn upon.

In 1955, Bennett reports, Madame de Salzmann separated Gurdjieff groups under her purview from groups for which he was responsible. He expressed to her the hope that the separation would not be longer than a year, but he had a private premonition that something would occur to maintain the distance.[14] Bennett's path from that point forward is, to my mind, dazzling, strange, sometimes saddening, and ultimately touching. In 1956, he became deeply involved in a new teaching from Indonesia, Subud, for which he became the key exponent in English. Coombe Springs became a center for the practice of Subud, which revolved around an "opening" process called the *latihan*, sometimes a quiet entry into heightened awareness, sometimes dramatic and hugely emotional.[15] For her part, at the height of Bennett's commitment to Subud, Madame de Salzmann wrote to an English pupil and friend, George Adie. "I heard about Coombe events. Of course, the worst thing in all that is that they continue to connect their activities with the Gurdjieff system. In fact it has nothing to do with it, it is even sometimes quite contradictory. And I don't wish my name to be associated with it."[16] For his part, though he had distanced himself, Bennett had not forgotten Madame de Salzmann. "I was only too well aware of the terrible burden she was carrying in sustaining the faith and courage of hundreds of followers of Gurdjieff's ideas, and had no wish to add to her difficulties; but I could not feel that she was wise to allow complete authority to be thrust upon her."[17]

Bennett eventually perceived shortcomings and dangers in the practice of Subud and left it behind. But there were other teachers and teachings ahead for him, two that conferred good fortune, one that stripped him—so it can't help but seem—of good fortune. His periods of quiet meditation at the Benedictine Abbey of Saint Wandrille, in Normandy, and his warm confidence in its abbot, led to his admission to the Catholic Church. And then, his travel in Asia brought him in touch with a Hindu teacher, the Shivapuri Baba, a yogi of immense age, perhaps 136 years old. A skilled and wise teacher, he helped Bennett to reorient his life.[18] And then there was Idries Shah (1924–1996), who arrived in London in the early 1960s and presented himself as a very senior Sufi teacher, representing the traditions in the history of Sufism that Bennett particularly valued. Again, Bennett gave himself to this new arrival of wisdom and, after due consultation with the members of his council at Coombe Springs, decided to give Coombe Springs to Shah as the new center for Shah's teaching activities. Within a short time after making this exceptionally generous gesture, Bennett learned that Shah had put the property on the market and sold it to a developer.

J. G. Bennett and Madame de Salzmann met in New York in 1967. The sacrifice of Coombe Springs was now in the past. "She was very curious about Idries Shah and asked me what I had gained from my contact with him," Bennett recalled. "I replied: 'Freedom!' Until then I had always looked for some support—even the realization that I had been given both hope and faith did not set me free to follow my own destiny. By setting myself to do all in my power to further Shah's mission, in which I personally had no place, I had paid the debt I owed for the help I had received from other men. I could now turn myself to pay the debt I owe my Creator."[19] It may be that this rationale put a redemptive framework around a grievous loss, but who knows?

The last act of this unique drama: J. G. Bennett "returned to what he knew," as I once heard Madame de Salzmann express it. He conceived of a residential school dedicated to the Gurdjieff teaching with additions from his knowledge of other ways, particularly Sufi thought and practice. His newly constituted International Academy for Continuous Education made its home at Sherborne House, a large manor house in the English Cotswold countryside. Opening its doors on October 15, 1971, with a plan to offer five cycles of ten months each for student residents, it proposed an intensive experience of all aspects of the Gurdjieff teaching, including Movements. The model of the Prieuré was not far off. In keeping with Bennett's personal magnetism and ability to communicate, students flocked to the Academy. And when they departed after ten months, some became founders in turn, or strong supporters, of a network of groups soon implanted in the United States and elsewhere. Bennett's death in December 1974 left Sherborne and the larger network in the care of his wife, Elizabeth, and senior pupils such as Pierre Elliot and Anthony Blake.

I visited Sherborne in May 1972 with Lord Pentland, who had in mind to go over with J. G. Bennett some publishing matters on which Bennett's views, and his warm link to Gurdjieff's heirs, would be influential. The two men, who had long known one another, spoke at length in Bennett's office. Of course we met Elizabeth, and in time we joined a silent lunch with all of the students in a space much like a refectory. As we drove away a little later, Lord Pentland looked back at the quite immense manor and said in a wondering tone, "I don't know whether there is the sun over it, or the moon."

J. G. Bennett's late initiative, his return to the Gurdjieff teaching in a version colored by his extensive knowledge of other ways, has had a lasting result. There are many Bennett groups in the United States and elsewhere. They offer Movements classes to the public and much else. They are only thinly related to the multinational school developed by Madame de Salzmann, though there are personal friendships and good reasons for respect across this somewhat broken cosmos. I am quite sure that as the two protagonists of this slow drama released one another, they had regrets. Bennett was one of Gurdjieff's three "chosen ones"—he for Britain, René

Zuber for France, Lord Pentland for America. Two would provide leadership in later years much as Gurdjieff must have wished: Zuber was centrally important to Madame de Salzmann for filmmaking and book publication, and Pentland was an altogether central and inspiring figure in the development of the teaching on the American continent. Bennett had distanced himself.

Jeanne de Salzmann was a brilliant, dedicated, resourceful woman. J. G. Bennett was a brilliant, dedicated, resourceful man. Different, of course: their shared story makes differences clear.

A GERM OF BEING FOR WHICH WE ARE RESPONSIBLE

We should return to an earlier year, 1951, to follow at least a little the consolidation of the Gurdjieff teaching under Jeanne de Salzmann's guidance. An oblique sign of her confidence in those closest to her in Paris is a series of fifteen questions, literally a written questionnaire of July 1951, to which she asked them to respond.[20] More than any document I have seen from those years, the questionnaire reflects the two directions of her thought and the thought of those around her: toward the past, toward what Gurdjieff was and taught, and toward the future of the teaching—for it clearly had a future, at that time largely in their hands. "How do you understand the current era?" she began by asking. And then, "What significance do you give to Mr. Gurdjieff as an individual? And, in your view, what did he bring?" They must have spoken of this often in times past, but the moment had come for shared clarity. And then, "To what should men and women who have worked according to his indications conform their lives?" And a related question, nearly its converse: "What causes prevent human beings from conforming their lives to an aim and bring about the situation in which humanity finds itself today?" There were still more questions. "What is our role today?" "Is there a work we must undertake? What is it?" And a key question that was already occasioning much shared thought in France, Britain, and America: "What is the meaning of a group? What can be its life? Its role? Its limits?" The questions looked back and forward and toward each participant.

It is time to meet again Henri Tracol (1909–1997), whose response to Luc Dietrich about working with Gurdjieff we have already encountered. A member of the group to which the questionnaire was addressed, in the years we are exploring he was Madame de Salzmann's nearest French colleague, often accompanying her in the English-speaking world and developing substantial groups of his own in Paris and the south of France. When I and many others knew him, from the early 1960s forward, he was a gentle, radiant man of a quality one meets rarely if ever in a lifetime. His understanding of the teaching—of the full scope of human experience inner and outer—was all his own yet permanently rooted in his work with Gurdjieff and, for decades, with Madame de Salzmann. The books now published of his writings, talks, and interviews bear witness to that understanding.[21] In his exchanges with pupils, he had a notable custom of thought and sensibility: to view all good things, all inner discoveries, as gifts. "It is granted us to experience," he would say; "we are invited to awaken." It was both a test and a privilege to speak with him. Thoreau in *Walden* would sometimes come to my American mind when I sat down with Henri Tracol: "To be awake is to be alive. I have never yet met a man who was quite awake. How could I have looked him in the face?"

In his responses to the questionnaire, Tracol gave particular attention to the direct question about Gurdjieff.

As a fully formed "individual", [Mr. Gurdjieff] was the living example of a being capable of "doing", that is, of manifesting consciously in the service of his own highest possibilities—as an "active force" influencing the whole of the forces of resistance in him and subordinating them to the higher order of reality which he represented—and this without eluding the normal exigencies of the human condition or attempting to escape the limits they impose.

This last point is one of the distinctive features of the direct way he proposes to mankind for inner transformation. This way is not outside of life, not dependent on exceptional conditions. It is in the very midst of the circumstances of daily life that we must find our equilibrium, through simultaneous work on the three elements constituting our individuality.

What is striking in the Gurdjieff teaching is its emphasis on practical meaning. If its cosmogonic system opens the immense perspectives of objective knowledge of the fundamental laws that govern the world, that is to better underpin, through transpositions and analogies based on the principle of relativity, a psychological doctrine entirely oriented toward the attainment of higher levels of consciousness and their free manifestation in the midst of ordinary existence.[22]

This is not quite Henri Tracol in his full maturity, but it will do; it is a document of its time and person. In later years he was a poet of the teaching; his words reached past words.

The intensity and seriousness of response to the 1951 questionnaire are also evident in lines written by Dr. Michel Conge several days after first reading it. A person of both exacting and passionate temperament, Dr. Conge was responsible in later years for well-concerted groups in France and overseas.[23] He exemplified the dignity and intellectual resourcefulness of the nucleus gathering around Jeanne de Salzmann. For decades his was one of the most eloquent and individual voices in the French groups. He had found his way to Gurdjieff in 1944, after wartime service as a physician and experiences of danger and exhaustion so extreme that he had been thrown on several occasions into wholly unfamiliar states of illumination, of unaccountable inner freedom and perceptiveness. Over the years I have known most of the people we'll encounter in this chapter, but to my regret I did not meet Dr. Conge or hear him speak. I saw him just once long ago in Paris at the far edge of a crowd outside a movie theater after a showing of one of Madame de Salzmann's documentary Movements films. I remember him as a very tall man, handsome, and for some reason recall that he had ears like seashells. Let us not trust the mind overmuch.

This, too, is not quite the mature voice of Conge, but it will do; it is a document of its time and person, already reflecting a lifelong concern for the religious dimensions of the Gurdjieff teaching and the light it sheds upon and receives from the Gospels. "In place of the notion of a CENTER," he reflected in response to the questionnaire, "men have only the notion of 'the manifested.' Mr. Gurdjieff insisted on the fact that man forgets himself by forgetting the seed that is in him, by turning his back on this reality, the sole reality. So doing, he increases his suffering, worsens his state, hastens his own and others' fall, and increases the Suffering of the Creator—for in a certain way He is within each of us. The only direction is to REUNITE."[24] Few, burning words.

Already in Russia Gurdjieff had described the teaching as a way of inquiry: questioning was and remains central to its life. Madame de Salzmann's questionnaire gave a degree of shape and specificity to a process of questioning that had necessarily begun at Gurdjieff's death. Questionnaires are uncommon in the Gurdjieff teaching; there is incomparably greater trust in direct exchange, in search together. In this instance, however, the exercise served as preparation for a meeting several weeks later when the issues were taken up again. There was a consensus on some obvious needs, particularly to publish Gurdjieff's writings in a number of languages and gradually to create a comprehensive record of the Movements on film. Although it would take some years more to publish French editions of *Beelzebub's Tales* and *Meetings with Remarkable Men*, an excellent French translation of Ouspensky's account of the teaching in its first Russian exposition was published in 1950. In both

English and French, and later in other languages, the book became a trusted resource.[25]

From that meeting around the questionnaire, a further point deserves its moment here: the danger and unwitting deception of imitating Gurdjieff. I don't know whether François Grunwald attended the meeting, but he understood the issue.

The example that a father, professor, master, etc., offers to a child, student, or disciple has educational value. Mr. Gurdjieff and Madame de Salzmann were in this sense living examples but not models. Woe to those, concerned with their own development, who would try . . . to imitate one or the other. Such people fall between Scylla and Charybdis in themselves. Madame de Salzmann never tried, not even remotely, to imitate Mr. Gurdjieff, neither before nor after his death. She guided the teaching in keeping with her own way of being, and if some details gradually changed, the fundamental spirit of "the work" was maintained.[26]

In these few pages we have twice heard that the teaching would necessarily move on from the years with Gurdjieff. "It is our material that must create bonds among us," said Madame de Salzmann on the first anniversary of his death; I can't help but hear *our*, as if the available notes fail to reflect an emphasis. From a close pupil's perspective, Grunwald has just told us that Madame de Salzmann was her own person with her own way of being, and that "some details" of course changed over time. Certain things were left with Gurdjieff as his property, so to speak. There was something like an edit, in part deliberate, in part guided by wise instinct. The toasts to the idiots were no longer practiced, though they were remembered and remain a pleasingly enigmatic icon of his time and mind. And then, Gurdjieff had been a magus in the full sense of this all but obsolete identity: a master capable of concentrating and projecting energy, a healer, at times an inscrutable shamanic presence. That too was his property. Yet work with the energetic potential of human being remained central in the coming decades through inner exercises, Movements, and gatherings large and small where the shared field of awareness made its characteristic demands. This was fundamental and, as Grunwald wrote, the fundamentals of the teaching were maintained.

Gurdjieff remained present through nearly endless, intricate memories—this book is in part a skein of memory. He remained present through his formal writings and transcripts of meetings, through the Movements and music, and through the example of practical forms he had established, notably the Prieuré. One could always turn toward him. But it was now time for men and women of the West to carry his teaching forward and deepen their understanding of it, and of themselves, in the absence of the founder.

This is the most important point; the rest is details. In Gurdjieff's lifetime, particularly in the 1940s, it is difficult on the basis of meeting transcripts to discern the quality of his pupils. They are questioners, often lucid and able, but somewhat generic; apart from the few who kept contemporaneous journals or published essays and novels, their individuality isn't terribly apparent until the years we're now exploring. The same is true, though much less so, of Jeanne de Salzmann: we have heard her independent voice in Gurdjieff's lifetime, but the fullness of her identity only becomes clear as she assumes responsibility for the teaching. Then something crucially important becomes evident: she herself, and the men and women in France on whom she particularly relied in these earliest years, were immensely thoughtful, deeply cultured, capable of careful eloquence as they faced the new shared circumstance. All that time they had been listening with minds and hearts shaped by their local quotient of Western culture—by the inquiring spirit of Montaigne, the formidable lucidity of Pascal, the often-criticized but classic capacity for reasoned inquiry in Descartes. Even Rabelais counts: his overflowing vitality had prepared the way for Gurdjieff's overflowing vitality, his fearlessness and humor. Introduced by Gurdjieff with such intensity and Diogenes-like disregard for convention, the teaching now needed to bond more thoroughly with Western culture, to find a new voice unlike Gurdjieff's—he was inimitable—but moving, true, and persuasive. With few exceptions, the most gifted and experienced representatives of the teaching were not from the Caucasus, Central Asia, or even Russia. It was not a disadvantage.

There was nonetheless a risk, an inevitable one. Madame de Salzmann and those closest to her in several countries needed to live for themselves and share with others what Gurdjieff had brought. The challenge was to do so through their own being, in their own languages—without denaturing the teaching. The current he had initiated needed to flow on, to enrich in thought, experience, and practical forms, and reach a new generation of seekers of truth. This was the challenge, and this was the accomplishment.

"Do you want to learn the Movements?" she had asked. The collective answer must have been unison yes. Thoroughly willing to dare, despite her cool and observant demeanor, Madame de Salzmann set in motion two major enterprises: the first professionally produced film of the Movements (1951) and the first large-scale public demonstration of Movements since 1924 (Fortune Theatre, London, 1952). The films created under her direction, eight in all and requiring decades to complete, have remained a private archive for teachers and students, so that "what was found will not be lost again," to quote the introduction to the first film. Our trusted witness, Dorothy Phillpotts, may have been a participant in the Fortune Theatre demonstrations, two days in May, but however that may be, she offers in her book an account of the event.[27] That Madame de Salzmann acted quickly and decisively, where the Movements are concerned, speaks to her overall attitude toward the continuation of the teaching.

In early spring 1953, she told those closest to her in London that the American groups, centered in New York but soon reaching well beyond, had overcome the divisions that had earlier caused difficulty. In point of fact, the New York pupils were about to purchase a spacious carriage house in midtown Manhattan as the home, to this day, of the teaching. "An understanding of what work on oneself can be has brought people together," she said of New York. "A truly shared search is taking shape."[28] She went on to evoke the demand facing the next generation of teachers.

> Mr. Gurdjieff brought ideas, but living ideas, that is to say, truths, realities, potentialities, and we must try first to live them in order to transmit them without completely altering them, and without fear of modifying forms whenever a surer understanding indicates the need to do so. Our way is to live these ideas in order to understand them, and to pass on the teaching to others if and to the extent we are able to live it with them. Sowing ideas without living them is sowing ideas that are empty. Mr. Gurdjieff left us not only words and ideas to be transmitted, but a certain life to be lived, a drama to be passed through with others around us, without which the work will remain imaginary.
>
> The ideas are there. What is missing is people capable of living the drama, of making these truths of another order the basis for life on earth.

"To live the drama." None of this was meant to be easy, but it *was* meant to be life-giving and transformative, as it had been in Gurdjieff's time. So it was, in the care of Jeanne de Salzmann and her colleagues in France and elsewhere. So it remains, when and wherever people are careful with it.

CHAPTER 8

Derision

I was sitting years ago in the welcoming home of Dr. Rama Coomaraswamy, son of the polymathic scholar Ananda K. Coomaraswamy
(1877–1947) to whom I dedicated nearly a decade of research and
publication. Rama and I were friends, intellectual collaborators
as I pursued my work. We joked that we were changelings: I had
been expected by my family to be the surgeon he was, and he had
been expected to be the scholar I was. That particular day we were
speaking of Gurdjieff and his teaching, which was a target for derision among members of the spiritual circle around the Swiss mystic
Frithjof Schuon, to which he belonged. "If the Gurdjieff teaching is
so marvelous," he said to me, "why aren't there bodhisattvas flying
around? Why is its influence slight and hidden?" We soon dropped
the subject; there were many others between us. As far as I was concerned, there *were* in effect bodhisattvas, not overhead but walking
firmly enough on the ground and available for conversation when
courteously approached. Gurdjieff had remapped and renewed the
possibilities of awakening and conscience, and had passed on a
coherent body of ideas, practices, attitudes, and even memorable
music to the next generation. His closest pupils were remarkable,
and they in turn taught further generations. Wings unnecessary.

You would think that derision would be out of the question, that
the merit of Gurdjieff's accomplishment would shelter his reputation
and teaching from assaultive extremes of criticism. That was not to
be. Soon after his death in autumn 1949, and from time to time since,
he has been personally savaged and the teaching ridiculed, notably

by two celebrated French authors who had also directed widely read periodicals. We will need to engage with the writings and careers of Louis Pauwels (1920–1997) and Jean-François Revel (1924–2006)— particularly with Pauwels, who reached a large public in France and in translation in the English-speaking world. Aggressive critics, they had both participated for a few years after World War II in the Gurdjieff teaching before going on to what would prove to be their destined lives as public intellectuals of considerable though widely differing influence. A third prominent author, the British psychiatrist Anthony Storr (1920–2001), described by the *Guardian* as "Britain's most literate psychiatrist," had no direct experience of Gurdjieff or the teaching but included a chapter on him in his last book, *Feet of Clay: Saints, Sinners, and Madmen; A Study of Gurus*.[1] Storr did not like gurus, and did not like what he knew of Gurdjieff. We'll consider his perspective. As well, we shouldn't disregard the views of Whitall Perry (1920–2005), an American member of the Schuon circle who descended like a humorless, enraged angel upon what he knew of Gurdjieff and the teaching. From time to time we will need to rely on the reflections of pupils we have met—Walker, Zuber, Grunwald, Hands, Bennett—who directly experienced the two ends of the stick, the radiance and goodness, the rough lessons and disregard for convention.

Some of Gurdjieff's critics in the years after 1949 unknowingly or deliberately misunderstood. Absent a reasonable grasp of fact and context, absent good will or a measure of objectivity, nothing is easier than to read in whatever one wishes to read in. Professor Peter Washington has edited a substantial and attractive series of editions of classic poetry; I have no idea why he was moved to publish in 1993 a dismissive critique of Western occult tradition, including but not limited to Gurdjieff and his teaching. In *Madame Blavatsky's Baboon: A History of the Mystics, Mediums, and Misfits Who Brought Spiritualism to America*, Washington sourly misinterprets a poignant moment in summer 1944.[2] Dramatis personae: Luc Dietrich and Gurdjieff. We have already met Dietrich, the superbly gifted young writer whom Gurdjieff called "mon collègue." In late May of that year Dietrich joined his friend Dr. Hubert Benoît in Saint-Lô, a small city in Normandy that came under Allied bombardment in June as German forces retreated across France.[3] Dietrich shadowed the doctor on his medical rounds through Saint-Lô and neighboring villages, where there were many wounded. During yet another bombardment, Benoît was pinned under debris from a fallen chimney and Dietrich was flung into the air but sustained seemingly minor injuries. Benoît survived despite grave injuries that left a hand paralyzed, while some days after the bombardment Dietrich showed signs of infection that gradually became systemic. In the absence of antibiotics, his condition was life-threatening; he was transported to a hospital in Paris.

Alerted by Madame de Salzmann, Gurdjieff paid him a visit during what proved to be the last days of the young writer's life. He brought the rarest of things—two oranges obtained at who knows what price on the black market—and placed them in Dietrich's hands. Gurdjieff knew Dietrich's devotion to Earth, to its beauty and wonders, and knew his sensuality. Bright fruit carried the consolation of all good earthly things. A photographer as well as writer, Dietrich had published in the previous decade a youthful book of photographs entitled *Terre*, his homage to farms and fields and placid livestock.[4] The gift of oranges brought him some measure of peace. Gurdjieff said to him, "All your life has been a preparation for this moment."[5] It is among the oldest of wisdom, Socratic if not earlier.

I dwell on this incident because Professor Washington distorts the meaning of Gurdjieff's words, as if Gurdjieff were saying that Dietrich's life hadn't mattered. How far from the truth. Dietrich had been if anything a preferred pupil, a young man whose searching questions and hard early life touched Gurdjieff.

A further example from Washington, describing the rue des

Colonels Renard: "His tiny apartment, crudely decorated with mirrors, dolls and glittering pseudo-orientalia."[6] This is hearsay scholarship; it is inconceivable that he visited. Nearly everything Washington touches darkens. The Prieuré "had the atmosphere of a savage boarding-school run by a demented if genial head-master, and most of the pupils loved it—for a while."[7] Nearly everything Washington notices in the literature is disfigured. Again focusing largely on the Prieuré years: "Gurdjieff is part of the . . . fascination with barbarism and primitivism which colors the politics of Fascism and works of art from Lawrence's novels to Stravinsky's early ballets. Gurdjieff's doctrine was war and his method of teaching was to stir up productive strife with all the means at his disposal."[8] Few in twentieth-century litera-ture have written more wisely and forcefully—and with sorrowing wit—than Gurdjieff in *Beelzebub's Tales* against what he called the "mass psychosis" of war. His portrait of powerful men briefly conscience-stricken by the ravages of World War I, then forget-ting what they had felt, is altogether striking.[9] War was not his doctrine.

Washington mocks what he doesn't understand. Not to under-stand isn't blameworthy, but to write as if one understands and to mislead others is another matter. "In October 1948," he writes, "Gurdjieff set out on his final trip to America. It is hard not to feel that by this time he simply enjoyed acting the fool for the hell of it. Seen off from the railway station in Paris by a group of devout pupils, his parting words to them as he leant out of the carriage window were: 'Before I return I hope with all my being that every-one here will have learned the difference between sensation and feeling'—an absurd request over which they nevertheless puzzled."[10] In 1993, when Washington published, many sources were available in which he could have teased out what Gurdjieff meant—Ouspen-sky's *Fragments*, Gurdjieff's transcribed talks in *Views from the Real World*, and many others. Gurdjieff wasn't acting the fool for the hell of it, he was touching on a fundamental aspect of his teaching, the distinction between the life of the body and the life of the emotions. Sorting them out by direct perception can lead to a more vivid sense of reality and finer emotional intelligence. But in pages intended to denigrate and dismiss, why would that matter?

Enough of Washington, although there will be other Washingtons. There is a need for critical thinking about Gurdjieff, particularly his writings, but Washington and those like him offer next to nothing of the kind. A sensible word from one of Gurdjieff's close pupils, not naïve, will restore perspective. "So many stupid stories have been written about Mr. Gurdjieff," wrote Olga de Hartmann, "and so many lies and misrepresentations have been heaped on his head. We all did 'suffer' to stay with him and to try to understand his teaching. But it was a kind of suffering through which he could challenge us to develop an understanding in ourselves."[11]

At this ragged interface between Gurdjieff and his later critics, we should acknowledge the obvious—that his teaching, and any serious teaching that asks something real and at length from participants, cannot be to everyone's taste or strike everyone as necessary. Up to a point we all wander into life, and, God willing, find what we need to engage and flourish. Many cannot imagine participating in a teaching—why would one do that? Others, fewer but not lesser, detect something in a teaching, religious way, or psychological discipline that intimately speaks to them. Hence a natural and growing kinship. Some will "join the history," as we were saying many pages ago; others will acknowledge and perhaps even help from a distance. However this works out over time, the point is not to shout at one another, not to devalue the choices others make. The decisive test of the value of any teaching or way is not so much its ideas and practices as it is the quality of the men and women who participate: how they are, how they relate, how they act, what they care for, what they strive to further. The literature critical of Gurdjieff and his teaching would be smaller and wiser if authors lacking a sense of kinship, or at least a bridge of some kind from here to there, passed by in silence.

Louis Pauwels was in some respects the most interesting and certainly the most effective adversary. Entering the worlds of French literature and journalism after World War II, he found his way from point to point, success to success, as a novelist, essayist, cultural innovator, and eventually as the long-serving director of *Le Figaro Magazine*, a Sunday newspaper supplement that reached a vast readership thanks largely to his editorial creativity. The Académie française twice considered inviting him to membership in the 1980s; the larger and more diversified Académie des beaux-arts elected him to membership in 1985 as a *membre libre*—not a painter, sculptor, graphic artist, or composer but a notable contributor to French cultural life. In his middle years, as coauthor in 1960 of a best-selling book, *Le Matin des magiciens* (*The Morning of the Magicians*), and throughout the 1960s as founding director of a highly original bimonthly magazine, *Planète*, he was a pied piper, a more innocent Timothy Leary, leading young people not specifically to psychedelic drugs but to the expansion and enrichment of their vision of the possible. The copy of *Planète* on my desk, no. 22 from the mid-1960s, does indeed have a pair of articles on drugs and sacred mushrooms but also cybernetics, vanished civilizations, Teilhard de Chardin (proscribed at that time by the Vatican), telepathy, the search for extraterrestrial life, the labyrinth at Chartres Cathedral—and, oh well, a few more topics. Every issue was like this: a splash of ideas, of possibilities. *Le Matin des magiciens* was also of that kind. Some of its ideas at a midpoint between science and science fiction, history and fantasy, psychology and reverie, were carefully presented; others were goofy but entertaining. Concerning Gurdjieff in the few pages about him, the book was horribly wrong, among other things falsely suggesting that he had been in touch with and influenced Nazi intellectuals. But the book struck a perfect 1960s note, and when that note faded at decade's end, Pauwels went on with no less success to other public enterprises and themes for his individual writings. In later years he was a sincere convert to Catholicism and a politically conservative editorialist who commanded a wide readership. And, as in his youth, a spiritual seeker.

Pauwels was introduced into the Gurdjieff circle in 1948 by the pioneering composer of concrete music, Pierre Schaeffer. He participated for eighteen months in a group led by Jeanne de Salzmann; by his own account he saw little of Gurdjieff and only at the Salle Pleyel for Movements classes. His experience as a participant was mixed and ultimately disastrous. At the end of that period he was urgently hospitalized, emaciated, with suicidal thoughts, and a burst blood vessel in one eye—miseries for which he blamed both the Gurdjieff teaching and his own flawed approach to it. "The really anguished disciples," he has written, "approached the teaching through their anguish, and . . . the troubles and disturbances suffered by some—of whom I was one—were primarily caused by their anguished way of approaching everything."[12] His account of participating in a Movements class reflects something of this self-assessment.

> I . . . have practiced some of the movements and I know how much effort they require. They are the result of a kind of crucifixion of the self. Imagine making contradictory movements with all your limbs; this in itself is very difficult and assumes a certain mastery of the body. Imagine doing, at the same time, extremely complicated mental calculations with rules that outrage the rules of ordinary arithmetic. . . . Finally, imagine concentrating all your emotional powers on a given theme (say, for instance, "Lord, have mercy on me" and feel this from the bottom of your heart) and you will then have some idea of the "work" involved in these dances. . . . We came away from these sessions shattered, and curiously drained of our ordinary "I's," extremely receptive to "something else" and

as though invested with a divine freedom. We were, in fact, dehumanized.[13]

A crucifixion of the self? Dehumanized? Contradictory movements rather than a harmony of differences? He should have spoken with someone more experienced. During the last months with Gurdjieff at the rue des Colonels Renard, J. G. Bennett questioned Jeanne de Salzmann about trying too hard. "I felt rebellious when Mr. G. told me to make fewer efforts," Bennett later recalled.

> She said, "This is necessary; you cannot force the organism too fast. One or two people in the French group did so and would not listen to him, and had bad results." I said, "But he always drove himself without any pity. Why can I not at least try to make the same efforts?" She said, "No, you are not quite right. Mr. Gurdjieff has always relaxed from time to time. Ever since I have known him, he has had trips and other things just to relax and enjoy himself. If he tells you to relax, you must do it."[14]

I doubt that she was referring to Pauwels, who hadn't participated in a group with Gurdjieff, but her advice might have served him well. I cannot bring myself to doubt that Pauwels belonged in the Gurdjieff circle, but he collided with his own youthful vehemence and tendency to excess without grasping a point that Grunwald had clarified for himself. "I observed," writes Grunwald, "that every discovery allowed me to progress a step on condition that it had a spontaneous character. Conversely, whatever I forced became artificial and deceptive. All tension, every impatient expectation infallibly led to an impasse. . . . Those who listened without intelligence to indications [about exercises] became their victim."[15]

After publishing what must have been a brief pilot essay in 1952 in a French arts magazine—I haven't seen it—Pauwels went on to publish in 1954 his book *Monsieur Gurdjieff*, with the elaborate subtitle (I translate) *Documents, Testimonies, Texts, and Commentaries on a Contemporary Initiatic Society*. He explained in the preface that "it seemed to me urgent and necessary to gather as many clear documents and testimonies as possible, on the person, the doctrine and the influence of George Gurdjieff and on the activities of the groups that he founded in France and elsewhere; to try to put into perspective the experiences of thousands of his pupils, to give accurate information on an enterprise unprecedented in this century, so as to bring home to a wide public both its dangers and its unusual importance."[16]

Michel Random, biographer of Luc Dietrich, has written that Pauwels was "the first in France to raise *le problème Gurdjieff*—the problem of Gurdjieff—and to attract public interest in this controversial spiritual master."[17] It seems to me rather that Pauwels created *le problème Gurdjieff*, more his problem than anyone else's, and this in the years of the Great Prayer among Gurdjieff's closest pupils when they were reassessing what had been, what was to be. The last thing they needed was disturbing public scrutiny. That is precisely what Pauwels delivered in a book that reached a considerable readership. Published in English translation quite a few years later, in 1972, with the addition, for some wildly extraneous reason, of erotic surrealist illustrations by a French artist, Félix Labisse, it had little impact in the English-speaking world, though it was read. But France was another matter: literary and cultural life is concentrated in Paris and a few other cities; a shout from the Left Bank is heard everywhere else.

The book is a marvel of ambivalence tilted toward rejection and alarm. Gurdjieff was a uniquely important teacher—and harmful. The teaching began to show the Western world how to assimilate esoteric and Eastern truths—but it led some pupils to be "stricken by strange illnesses, in some cases fatal."[18] Pauwels reached back to collect and reprint articles from the 1920s by authors we have encountered—Denis Saurat, Llewelyn Powys (he of the tyrannical "riding master"), and many others. He also reached out to his own contemporaries for sometimes lurid accounts of Gurdjieff's impact. He was fair-minded enough to include eloquently positive "testimonies and commentaries," but they are much outweighed. Where Katherine Mansfield is concerned—a sensible test of Pauwels' perspective—he was unsparing and untrue. Honestly reprinting some of her letters from the Prieuré, he construed many of them in a negative light that suited his brief against Gurdjieff. For example, he argued that "the key to the whole life at the Prieuré [was the] work of 'death to oneself' that she was trying to carry on. . . . She said nothing [of this in letters to her husband] because this work gave a tragic flavor to [her] days, and her husband could not bear tragedy."[19] Have we read the same letters? Pauwels overlaps his own anguished experience onto Mansfield's very different experience. You will recall her words: "ease after rigidity." In his last paragraphs concerning Gurdjieff and Mansfield, Pauwels passes on and elaborates a dreadful thing he read somewhere without questioning it. "As for Gurdjieff," he writes, "when anyone asked him about Katherine Mansfield he always replied, with apparent sincerity, 'Me not know.' For him, she had not attained to real *existence* in his meaning of the word, she had no true 'I', no soul. On the level of ordinary human beings, however noble their ambitions, and splendid their attempts, however great their sufferings, their intelligence and their sensibility, all is worthless, completely worthless. 'Me not know' says Gurdjieff, the True Man."[20] This has nothing to do with Mansfield or Gurdjieff, everything to do with Pauwels' anguish.

René Zuber could recall a brief sighting of Pauwels in 1948 or 1949: "I remember a misadventure," he has written, "which many years ago befell a promising young writer who was interested in the teaching of Gurdjieff as a method of self-development. He had never met the master. One day, however, the encounter almost took place. The young man saw the redoubtable silhouette in the distance (it was in the corridors of the Salle Pleyel) and immediately projected onto this image his ancestral fear of the bogeyman, which was no doubt waiting for just this moment to materialize. He then undertook to write a book over five hundred pages long on Monsieur Gurdjieff."[21] In the journal where he first recorded this near encounter, Zuber reflected that "the idea of the black magician still exists in the Western, Judeo-Christian . . . collective unconscious. G. filled this empty box."

Setting out to write his own book, Grunwald took Pauwels as the model of what not to do. Grunwald was aware, he wrote, "that professional writers have seen [in Gurdjieff] only their own image in the mirror. For that reason the rascal, the scoundrel, the philanthropist, or the saint create hidden self-portraits. L. Pauwels' book, on Gurdjieff the magician, furnishes the best possible proof: the gross untruths it contains describe only its author."[22]

The book shook Madame de Salzmann and the circle around her. In April 1954, she shared her concern by letter with the English architect, George Adie.

> All the Paris events have worried me very much. But as always, something good has come out of it. People have become more united and have given more value to their work. I did not wish any reply. It is bound to happen that the force of the ideas will be rejected by a level not prepared to receive it. People like Pauwels, who have not been able to receive any profit from the ideas, feel menaced by them and wish to destroy their force. The best reply will be the publication of the books—I hope to publish very soon the *Remarkable Men*.[23]

In point of fact, it would take some years more to publish the French edition of *Meetings with Remarkable Men* (1960), but it is striking that she viewed Gurdjieff's own writings as the just response to derision.

Pauwels' book went through several editions, the most recent in 1996 with a new preface from the author. In 1979, Madame de Salzmann and her colleagues in France collaborated with a well-known television journalist, Henri de Turenne, to create a program about Gurdjieff on the basis of filmed interviews with Tracol, Zuber, Michel de Salzmann, and others. Even at that time, so many years later, it was a response to Pauwels. Zuber had the custom of debating with himself in his journal much that was currently on his mind. "Why are you creating this program?" he asked there. "A question posed by Turenne to Madame de Salzmann . . . Why are we doing it? As a response at more than twenty years' distance to Pauwels. There is a time for silence and a time to speak. While there is still time, those who knew Gurdjieff will speak so that legend does not take the place of reality."[24] And why, we in turn might inquire, had they waited so long? Zuber asked himself the same question. "What makes this program difficult, and the reason why it has been postponed for so long: as soon as we speak of G., we enter the most intimate territory."

Pauwels has many cruelties and stupidities in his book; we won't dwell much longer on them. But to be certain this is so, consider the following, an untrue obituary: "Having lost the wish to live," he wrote, "George Ivanovich Gurdjieff died very quickly in the American Hospital at Neuilly in October 1949, at the end of his eighty-third year. He had not said everything; he had not had time, or rather, amongst the thousands of men he knew, he had not been able to find the one capable of extracting his real secrets. His groups were very numerous and very active, but for some time past he had seemed indifferent to the 'work' they carried out."[25] Elsewhere in the book he wrote that "towards the end of his life Gurdjieff seemed to have given up teaching, either from fatigue or from distaste for other people."[26] I have no idea with whom he was speaking; perhaps no one at all.

Pauwels' book had two impacts that lasted for decades. When the

French group purchased a home for the teaching in Paris in 1963, the name of Gurdjieff figured neither in its legal name—the Society for Study and Research toward Knowledge of Man (I translate)—nor in the convenient name by which it was known to participants. In my view—not all may share it—Pauwels drove the Gurdjieff teaching in Paris into hiding. Some years ago, that was set right; the home of the teaching is now the Institut G. I. Gurdjieff. There was a second impact: with its mix of valid historical documents and frequently derisive or unfounded interpretation, his book became a source for subsequent critics such as Whitall Perry. It surely contributes even today at second or third hand to the casual dismissiveness of some opinion makers. A recent review of a new book critical of Freud mentions in passing "the cultish G. I. Gurdjieff."[27]

And yet . . . There was something at work in Pauwels, acknowledged by him only from time to time, clear as day to readers willing to follow him from 1954 forward. Start with a warm family scene. In the charming and affectionate biographical memoir (2003) written by his daughter, Marie Claire, she remembers the early days when her father had become director of *Le Figaro Magazine*. He would be revising on Sunday night an editorial that had to be submitted the next morning. No leisure time for him, she wrote—and he explained to her that "effort doesn't count, only super-effort counts."[28] Pure Gurdjieff, originally from the Russian exposition and the Prieuré, never forgotten.

In 1949, Pauwels published a little book, a metaphysical and religious fantasy now difficult to find.[29] Its frontispiece is interesting: a drawing, quite fine, of the young Louis Pauwels in meditation, his eyes quiet and composed, his hands folded together—a lovely illustration, although nowhere identified as an author portrait. One would think that was that, but two decades later, in a book called (I translate) *The Apprenticeship of Serenity* (1978), Pauwels published the drawing again as a frontispiece portrait with the caption: "*Du temps que j'étais à l'école de Gurdjieff*"—from the time when I was in the Gurdjieff school.[30] Much of the book draws on Gurdjieff without mentioning him. It is surprising, but evident when one looks into it, that Pauwels's troubled participation in the Gurdjieff teaching became in later years something like a credential and also a touchstone, a foundation of truth. "Gurdjieff was a barbarian Socrates," he wrote elsewhere in 1978, "but it was on that path that I learned the most."[31] Pauwels knew literature; he may have remembered that Plato called Diogenes a "mad Socrates." Michel Random was not wholly wrong, though largely wrong, to write that "despite his reservations, Pauwels remained perhaps one of Gurdjieff's best disciples."[32] To be a disciple who has turned on a teaching and blackened its reputation, to be a disciple who cites ideas and attitudes from the teaching without attribution, is to be much less than a best disciple. And yet when Pauwels published a book-length credo in 1974 (*Ce que je crois*), what he believed was by and large what he had learned in the Gurdjieff circle. "In the end," he wrote there, "I distinguished only two sorts of men. Those (most numerous) for whom reality is dual: their person and the world. And those (I am one) for whom reality is triple: their person; the world; and a presence to themselves and to the world which is more than their person and more than the world."[33] "I believe in the invisible," he wrote elsewhere in the book. "But for me the invisible is only the visible awaiting attention. Attention is the key faculty."[34] There are many such passages, pure Gurdjieff though expressed in Pauwels's way. Like J. G. Bennett, Pauwels had returned to what he knew—with his reservations intact. In the new 1996 preface to his book he wrote, "Was Gurdjieff a true master? No doubt. And a good master? Certain people say they were destroyed by him. And I? I also was somewhat destroyed. But also somewhat made."[35]

Henri Tracol was thinking about Pauwels and others in a conversation of 1962. "Among those who were with us around Mr. Gurdjieff during the 1940s," he said, "many are no longer here. Some have died, others had to move away, still others left slamming the door, sneering or spitting at us. Yet, like it or not, they all remain objectively linked to us, and we to them. They are part of the same adventure."[36]

We need a lighter topic—an entertainment, something to lift our spirits. Why not money? Anthony Storr, the psychiatrist of renown who all but reduced Gurdjieff to a bedside chart of symptoms of mental illness, must have encountered in the literature tales of Gurdjieff's fundraising activities. There were dinners, Storr wrote, "at which large quantities of alcohol were drunk, and large sums of money extracted from the diners."[37] Elsewhere in his book he added, "Gurdjieff was . . . an accomplished confidence trickster who had no hesitation in deceiving other people and extracting money from them when he needed to do so."[38] Deception and extraction—so far not very entertaining, but bear with me. In fact, and over the decades, Gurdjieff created something like a theater around the need for money, in which his showmanship roamed a wide range of scenarios and attitudes. He could deftly perform the roles of a grasping merchant or sinister confidence man—let's adopt Storr's term. That made quite a spectacle for his students. Zuber recalled that "the first time I saw him counting a bundle of notes with all the dexterity of a cashier, it was something of a shock."[39] He could play just as convincingly the roles of a generous host, heedless spendthrift, or sage with novel ideas about money. One zone was out of bounds: he was not creating theater among or for his pupils when he privately bought the cast-off paintings of poor Russian exiles or fed them in the morning from his kitchen. Those activities were exempt. Gurdjieff discussed that side of things with Fritz Peters when they met in Paris after the war.

I play many roles in life . . . this part of my destiny. You think of me as teacher, but in reality, I also your father. . . . I also "teacher of dancing", and have many businesses: you not know that I own company which make false eyelashes and also have very good business selling rugs. This way I make money for self and for family. Money I "shear" from disciples is for work. But other money I make for my family. My family very big, as you see—because this kind old people who come every day to my house, are also family. They my family because have no other family.[40]

Late in life, with children at Christmas in New York, he conjured up a particularly vivid theater around money. Louise March recalls:

Two plates are set in front of the children. On one there are shining silver dollars. On the other, paper dollars. Mr. Gurdjieff talks very slowly. "I old man. Not time have, go shopping presents. Children, I wish make you present. You can choose. Choose eight silver dollars—you know silver something real, always good—or ten paper dollars. Ten more than eight. If you wish buy something quickly, can choose ten. Think from all sides. Not quick decision. Paper money, it can happen like in France. Someday, no good as money, only as wallpaper. Think, then choose. Your choice."[41]

The Wise and Foolish Adolescents: to this day a friend of mine has her eight silver dollars, made into a necklace, while another friend can't recall where he spent the paper money.

Rina Hands was listening carefully at Gurdjieff's table when a new episode around money began to unfold.

Mr. Gurdjieff used to tell us that every morning he would go round to "my café" in the rue des Acacias, sit down and order a coffee. Although he had no money to pay for it, everyday someone came and saved him. Indeed by the end of the day, he would find his pockets, which had been empty in the morning, were cram-full of money. This he did not like to keep for himself, he said, so each night before going to bed, he would empty his pockets and throw what money he found there out of the window. One evening when I had been doing some shopping for him, I took him my purchases and some change. He took out a large roll of bank notes, added the ones I was returning and put the lot back in his pocket. Greatly daring, I said, "Oh Mr. Gurdjieff, isn't it time you threw all that out of the window?" He looked at me with an expression of utmost gravity and replied, "You know, Égout, sometimes I make joke."[42]

An incident closer to what Storr must have had in mind is again in Hands's memoir, though in the end its disarming honesty makes it a poor match. Gurdjieff started off in full sinister mode.

At dinner Mr. Gurdjieff was speaking, as he sometimes does, about how he was only interested in people who have "fat check books," his work being to shear such sheep. The only really rich member of Mr. Bennett's group present looked around and said of course he understood how it was, as "all this must cost a pretty penny." "Yes," said Mr. Gurdjieff, "each day one million francs it costs me." "Then," said this rather rich man, "perhaps I can make a contribution." Mr. Gurdjieff looked at him with an expression of complete amazement and replied, "You nothing receive—why you give?" I have seldom seen anyone looking so disconcerted as our rich friend and he protested that nevertheless he would like to help, but it was all in vain. His offers of help were all brushed ruthlessly aside at that time. He really gave a great deal later.[43]

Gurdjieff's household surely didn't cost him a million francs daily, but for purposes of theater—and a rigorous lesson—exaggeration is permitted.

There are many more stories; thus far I haven't been able to saddle Gurdjieff with Storr's chosen epithet, "confidence man." We can rely on two thoughtful pupils to bring the topic home. Kenneth Walker has written:

> He required a great deal of money for his work, and for the support of his numerous dependents. People, he said, only valued what they had paid for and he had no hesitation in extracting from his followers as much as, or often more than, they could afford. This painful process of reducing bank balances was always referred to as "shearing" and was accompanied by much badinage and mirth. Money poured out of his pocket as quickly as it entered it, for he was princely in his gifts. He would pay the expenses of people who were insufficiently well off to come to Paris to see him and support others of his followers who had fallen on bad times. He was well acquainted with poverty, and although little attempt was made to reduce the cost of his entertaining in his flat—to some of us it seemed unnecessarily extravagant—he spent comparatively little on himself. Money was of no interest to him except as a means to the carrying on of his work.[44]

Walker's characteristically thorough account is convincing. The badinage and mirth were theater; the need for money was real.

François Grunwald was aware, as he wrote in the late 1980s, that Gurdjieff's critics liked to take him to task for his allegedly rapacious ways.

> Questions about money always give rise to the same songs. Yet it was clear that the sums needed to feed so many people afternoon and evening, seven days a week, twelve months a year, and the sums he regularly offered to impoverished Russian émigrés, didn't fall from the sky. He took from the rich to

give to the poor and to delight everyone. Isn't that reasonable and praiseworthy? He often spoke of this and declared that he would again have to shear his sheep: "Only naïve people can be content to say, 'Legendary Prince Mukransky give all this money.'"[45]

The Georgian prince, a congenial myth from his Caucasian boyhood, came to Gurdjieff's mind more than once. In the last chapter of *Meetings with Remarkable Men*, concerned with the myriad ways he had earned money in earlier years, Gurdjieff assures the reader that Prince Mukransky had nothing to do with it.

I don't altogether understand why some intellectuals, typically well-credentialed, want to slay Gurdjieff. He can't be slain; there will always be enough people of good will and good mind to care for his legacy, to know its value and keep it alive. I don't altogether understand why some authors want, so to speak at all cost, to turn readers away from Gurdjieff and his teaching, to make it seem louche and hazardous. Sometimes I look with the mind's eye at the theater with which Gurdjieff surrounded himself, at the provocations, the furies, the deliberate stepping on corns, and as well the warm and understanding embrace of "all kinds," as we have heard him say. And I see, of course, the Diogenes of our time—hard to be and hard to bear, as D'Alembert tells us in the epigraph to this book. But I see something else as well: a vastly gifted teacher protecting himself, colorfully and thoroughly . . . from us.

But not from us all without exception. Grunwald recalled that during a lunch at the rue des Colonels Renard, the doorbell rang; it was the mailman delivering a package.

Mr. G. invited him to come in and, among all the guests around the table, engaged him in conversation about his work. Quite at ease, the mailman declared: "How can I put it, Mr. Gurdjieff . . . Work is a necessity for me, not only to earn money.

It is also how I learn about the world." Mr. G. rose, had him served a glass of Armagnac, clicked glasses with him, and then solemnly said to us all: "Exactly so you must speak. Work is a necessity." He went on to offer the mailman a bottle of old cognac, a precious rarity in 1949.[46]

I don't think the lesson to be drawn is that the Gurdjieff teaching is unsuited to people with well-trained minds engaged in intellectually demanding professions. But there is a lesson all the same that I hesitate to put into words: to let Gurdjieff and the teaching speak to us. It is so very easy to block. I recall, for example, a review written by a respected biologist and science writer, Jean Rostand, when Ouspensky's now classic rendering of the Russian exposition *In Search of the Miraculous: Fragments of an Unknown Teaching* was first published in French (under the subtitle) in 1949. Missing virtually everything the book has to offer in its account of the human condition and human possibility—our sample, in chapter 3, concerns knowledge and being—he raged at the alternative science and cosmology, not dominant in the book but presented with due care. "On the ramblings of a moon-struck philosopher," Rostand called the review. Subtitle: "These 'fragments of an unknown teaching' make fools of snobs and dupe the ignorant."[47] The neo-Pythagorean, somewhat Theosophical account of natural law and cosmology in *Fragments* is difficult; I'm not well-versed in it myself. I admire those, such as Christian Wertenbaker, now a retired neuro-ophthalmologist, who publish soberly and searchingly about it.[48] Whatever one's view of that part of the teaching, to be blind to the rest is quite sad. Years ago a knowing friend described Gurdjieff in a novel way, as a translator—a translator of Eastern wisdom and practice for Western minds. I don't know whether he was thinking of Marpa the Translator, a twelfth-century Tibetan sage central to the passage of Indian Buddhism to Tibet, but their roles were similar. In both instances the translation was good.

Anthony Storr, who was both admired and admirable, assembled in his book of 1996 (*Feet of Clay*) a miscellany of characters in his quest to understand and warn the public against people of their kind. There is an opening chapter on a reviled mass murderer—Jim Jones of Jonestown, Guyana; chapters on Freud and Jung, to both of whom he grants much merit though they were gurus; on two Indian teachers, one of whom (Rajneesh) was charged in the United States with grave crimes and deported; and then chapters on Rudolf Steiner and Gurdjieff. According to Storr, gurus tend to have certain traits in common.

> A person becoming a guru usually claims to have been granted a special, spiritual insight which has transformed his own life. . . . Some gurus are inclined to believe that all humanity should accept their vision. . . . Gurus . . . seldom have close friends. They are more interested in what goes on in their own minds than in personal relationships. . . . In other words, they tend to be introverted and narcissistic. . . . Gurus tend to be intolerant of any kind of criticism, believing that anything less than total agreement is equivalent to hostility. . . . The relationship which the guru has with followers is not one of friendship but of dominance. . . . Because they claim superior wisdom, gurus sometimes invent a background of mystery.[49]

Storr collects more characteristics; these give the flavor. He finds Gurdjieff interesting because, particularly through Ouspensky in London, he attracted so many distinguished followers—Orage, Mansfield, Walker, Heap, Anderson, and others we have encountered in these pages. Storr seems to have had little knowledge of the French participants and focuses his interpretations on accounts of Gurdjieff in the 1920s. He does throw a few bones of goodness Gurdjieff's way. He writes, for example, that "Gurdjieff's complete disregard for science and for the views of generally accepted experts is narcissistic in the extreme. But he did, at times, show consider-able interest in other people, and compassion for those who were suffering. He sometimes exhibited a capacity for intense concentration upon individuals, which was certainly one component of his undoubted charisma."[50] But there is little else to be said on Gurdjieff's behalf.

> Gurdjieff was a dictator. He had the capacity so completely to humiliate his disciples that grown men would burst into tears. He might then show the victim special favor. He demanded unquestioning obedience to his arbitrary commands. . . . Those less infatuated are likely to think that, like other gurus, Gurdjieff enjoyed the exercise of power for its own sake. . . . Gurdjieff also developed an elaborate cosmology. His picture of the universe and man's place in it is complex, and unsup-ported by any objective evidence. It is deliberately obscure and often incoherent. Yet, because Gurdjieff was a powerful guru whose followers included some sophisticated, intelligent people, attempts have been made by his followers to make sense out of what appears to the skeptical reader to be a psy-chotic delusional system.

At this point in his roster of charges, Storr turns specifically to *Beelzebub's Tales*, one of whose features is a wealth of neologisms—newly coined, composite words—typically assembled from Russian, Greek, Armenian, and Turkish roots. One such, a favorite of mine, is "the sacred Martfotai," glossed by Gurdjieff as "self-individuality." Gurdjieff's thought is that we must do all we can to attain at least that level of awareness, not the most advanced, and help others to do so. Friends more learned than I report that the term resolves into two source words: Armenian *mart,* or man, and a reworking of Greek *photía,* fire or light. Hence, something like "the light of man" or the proper light of humanity. For readers with linguistic experience similar to Gurdjieff's—he was fluent in the four languages mentioned—the neologisms are in part comprehensible, and for all readers they convey what another friend and close student of the *Tales* calls its "off-planet perspective." Gurdjieff wants us to perceive everything anew; this was one of his means. Storr has no patience with it: "The task [of reading *Beelzebub's Tales*] is rendered more difficult by the numerous ludicrous neologisms which Gurdjieff introduced. It is appropriate to remind the reader that chronic schizophrenics often invent words which carry a special meaning for them but which others find hard to understand. . . . I am not suggesting that Gurdjieff was schizophrenic, but his use of language resembled that employed by some psychotics."[51]

The cosmology is "a psychotic delusional system" and the word-play in the *Tales* isn't—but really is—well-nigh schizophrenic. And for that matter, the work regime at the Prieuré "was certainly a convenient way of obtaining free labor. . . . Moreover, Gurdjieff, as an experienced hypnotist, would have realized that physical exhaustion makes people more suggestible, although one of his avowed aims was to discover some means of 'destroying in people the predilection for suggestibility.'"[52] Yet Storr knows enough not to reject all and everything where Gurdjieff is concerned. At the end of his chapter he demonstrates what I take to be a good ear for Gurdjieff's psychological and ethical teachings.

It is possible to salvage a few valuable ideas from what he taught. Gurdjieff believed that man had obligations as well as rights. He did not think that the world was made for man, or that progress consisted in further technological domination of the environment. He considered that man had lost touch with the meaning of his existence, which was to fulfil a cosmic purpose rather than merely to satisfy his desires. Now that we realize that we are destroying the earth we live on, Gurdjieff's view that man should serve the world rather than exploit it seems apposite. His notion that most people are 'asleep' and are driven by their instincts to behave automatically rather than with conscious intention is probably true of the majority.[53]

In a chapter intended to turn the reader definitively away from Gurdjieff, this intelligent arc of ideas is a touching discovery. I hope that, in future, authors of Storr's essential merit will do better than he did.

Pauwels reported in 1954 that he had spoken with "two or three real alchemists in Paris," one of whom told him that the West was under spiritual attack from the East, and further that "a man such as Gurdjieff was appointed from Above to work . . . at the disintegration of the West. These plans have been maturing for centuries."[54] Silly paranoia of this kind shouldn't matter, but it does look as if Whitall Perry, in his book *Gurdjieff in the Light of Tradition* (1978), took it seriously. "The time has now come," he wrote toward the end of his book, "to ask what Gurdjieff, or the 'Power', 'Great Source' . . . or what not from whom he received his investiture, was really up to. The answer is as simple as it is devastating: *the total upheaval of the world order*. This is not to say that he was up to it, but that he intended it."[55] It is uninviting to continue thinking about Perry after such a ridiculous claim, but there is more to understand. At the time Perry published, and I believe for many years earlier and later, he was a disciple of the Swiss metaphysician and spiritual teacher Frithjof Schuon (1907–1998).

Schuon and the distinguished circle of scholars and authors with whom he was associated—including René Guénon (1886–1951), Ananda K. Coomaraswamy, and others—were dedicated to the Perennial Philosophy or Sophia Perennis. Guénon had been the pathfinder, the creator and finely intellectual exponent of what soon came to be called the Traditionalist perspective. A French convert to Islam who eventually chose to live in Cairo, he was the author of books (cited in their English translations) from the early *Introduction to the Study of the Hindu Doctrines* (1921) to remarkably intelligent and influential critiques of modern Western culture. Books of that kind, such as *The Crisis of the Modern World* (1927) and *The Reign of Quantity & the Signs of the Times* (1945), were all but "required reading" for participants in the Gurdjieff teaching; there was much to learn from them, and one encountered in their pages both the keenest of minds and a dry but real love for God and man. Guénon had little to say about practice but a very great deal to offer at what he called the "principial" level, the level of first things and the divinely ordained order in which we human beings have our place, possibilities, and duty. Before he moved definitively to Cairo, he was a familiar enough figure in Parisian intellectual circles— hence his chance meeting at a café with Alexandre de Salzmann, whom he already knew. "René Guénon does not exist," he said with ascetic chill to de Salzmann, whom you will recall as one of Gurdjieff's companions since Tiflis. De Salzmann's reply: "What a shame!" Something of the distance between Guénon's loftiness of mind and the rooted practicality of Gurdjieff and his circle is evident in this memorable exchange.[56]

In the next generation, Schuon furthered this discourse through books much like Guénon's in voice and breadth of interests—among them, *The Transcendent Unity of Religions* (1953), *Understanding Islam* (1963), and *Esoterism as Principle and as Way* (1981). Without considering the difficulties that beset Schuon and his circle in very late years, when he had settled in the United States, it must be said that he conducted for years a dignified, rigorously intellectual and learned exploration of spiritual traditions of the East and West, including Native American traditions. Guénon, Schuon, A. K. Coomaraswamy—these men of vast learning spoke and taught the language of universal spiritual tradition.

Schuon must have agreed to Whitall Perry's project if he didn't actually commission it: to impose a Traditionalist critique on

Gurdjieff and his teaching in order to invalidate them. Setting to work, Perry deployed brittle righteousness, elaborate metaphysical argument, and ceaseless contempt in lofty Guénonian and Schuonian language that had had better and wiser uses in the past. There was considerable charm and common decency in the way A. K. Coomaraswamy attacked the values of the modern, post-traditional world in polemical essays and occasional radio broadcasts in the 1930s and 1940s. One felt addressed by a fellow human, a fellow sufferer. There is no such charm or fellowship in Perry's attack; it is rehearsal for an Inquisition. The conviction of his own spiritual orthodoxy and rightness conferred the privilege of consigning "Gurdjieff and his hosts," as he once apocalyptically puts it, to Outer Darkness or whatever comes after Outer Darkness.[57]

Perry's first charge is that Gurdjieff asserted no familiar lineage, no acceptable credentials.

> Since Gurdjieff claimed to be the recipient of teachings transmitted from antiquity, all depends on being able to determine whether or not the spiritual organization(s) involved and the line(s) of transmission are authentic, valid, and orthodox; whereas the whole crux of the matter is contingent on whether he was himself a legitimate representative and faithful purveyor of any truths to which he may have been exposed. . . . It goes without saying that anyone purporting to come from the fastnesses of Central Asia with a teaching for the West about the regeneration of mankind could simplify matters enormously by presenting clear and unequivocal credentials.[58]

Simplify what matters?

Gurdjieff's pupils had also thought this question through and, not surprisingly, reached other conclusions. "Gurdjieff himself was a sufficient source for me," Margaret Anderson has written. "All that he said was so vast that it left me no time to inquire about the original source. The knowledge he knew, wherever it came from, was far more important to me than any inquiries about its historical beginnings. In Gurdjieff's own words, this knowledge traces back to 'initiate people.'"[59] If this seems intellectually lazy—though I don't think it is, it is simply loyal to her experience—the same cannot be said of René Zuber, who had made documentary films about traditional peoples and spent summers in rural Morocco.

> Was Gurdjieff a traditionalist? It would be much more correct to say that everything about him was traditional: he was himself the tradition. Many a time on the journeys some of us have made to Morocco, Afghanistan, Tibet and India, we have imagined ourselves coming across him on a street corner or in a bar at the heart of some bazaar! . . . There is no doubt that Gurdjieff wanted to cover the tracks of his past, to conceal the name of the chain of tradition, or initiation of which he was the culmination. This has always made him suspect in the eyes of the traditionalists; I mean those who did not possess, besides other necessary qualities, the sense of humor indispensable for "scenting", even from afar, his allegiance to tradition.[60]

Perry's assessment of Gurdjieff's vision of a cosmos of many levels, material throughout but ineffably refined in the upper reaches, is couched in Schuonian language that draws on traditional Hindu and Gnostic concepts. It isn't pleasant language, but we should hear it.

> The Absolute for [Gurdjieff] is the primordial All or Whole, from the differentiation of which arises the diversity of phenomena. But his teachings fall within the *guna* of *tamas*, since everything is interpreted from a quantitative, materialistic, and non-transcendent perspective. The Emerald Tablet in his case is a matter of: "As below, so beneath," seeing that he never

gets off the ground save to descend into the subconscious. In other words, the only "worlds" open to his consciousness are the corporeal domain and the lower reaches of the psychic realm. The supraformal, noumenal, or archetypal spheres of reality—namely, everything spiritual—are completely sealed off from his "common presence"—not to speak of principial Existence itself, and above all the Absolute.[61]

In other words, there is no spirituality in Gurdjieff; there is only from here down. Everything spiritual is sealed off.

Once he had chosen Beelzebub as the hero and narrator of his major work, *Beelzebub's Tales to His Grandson,* Gurdjieff couldn't hope for many sympathetic readers among literal thinkers, Christian or other. "He identified himself unequivocally," writes Perry, "with the 'Devil', only, having this identification, he naturally did not envisage the 'Devil' as 'evil', but simply as 'realistic'."[62] In the next chapter we'll explore the *Tales* and, among other things, think about Gurdjieff's choice of hero. Meanwhile, Perry draws on a testimony in Pauwels's book, written by a physician, to reiterate utter nonsense. "With a cold medical eye he reached the studied conviction that whatever the appearances, Gurdjieff's real motivation was the obscure and Luciferian quest for powers (*siddhis*) as taught through brutal methods in certain Mongolian monasteries where he probably received initiation—powers acquired with a view to ruling our planet."[63]

We have spent enough time with Perry. The book is self-assured zealotry throughout. It lacks gentleness even toward the spirituality it prefers.[64] Someday, in what Perry describes as the "Celestial Pantheon with its supraformal domains and deities, Divine Qualities and Attributes, Archetypes, Angelic Intelligences, and hierarchy of Powers as revealed by all traditions,"[65] he might be surprised to find the soul of George Ivanovich Gurdjieff in trusting conversation with an Intelligence or Power. Such things were not in the least alien to Gurdjieff. He had taken it upon himself to show men and women how to work on themselves and, through conscious labor and intentional suffering, to find their way on while bringing a little more peace and wisdom into the life around them. This he accomplished with great force, a wealth of means, and inimitable flair.

I regret the relentless derision heaped on Gurdjieff and the teaching by a representative of the community of thinkers that once included A. K. Coomaraswamy, who was one of my principal mentors—a word that means, at root, the maker of a mind. Though I never met him, I spent nine years with his writings and other papers, published a great deal by and about him, and since then have periodically written and lectured about him.[66] Coomaraswamy would have dismissed Gurdjieff. But I dismiss neither Coomaraswamy nor Gurdjieff.

Jean-François Revel is almost certainly best remembered now in the United States, if not in France, as the father of an outstanding son, Matthieu Ricard, with whom he published a fascinating book, *The Monk and the Philosopher: A Father and Son Discuss the Meaning of Life* (1998).[67] The gap between them, and cause for extended dialogue, was unique. The father was a prominent author and journalist, a member since 1997 of the Académie française, a forceful voice on political and social issues—and, as well, a rigorously trained philosopher, graduate of the elite École normale supérieure. The son trained initially as a molecular biologist, launched a promising career in the field—and converted to Tibetan Buddhism. He became an honest and eloquent spokesman in the West after many years in the Himalayas as the disciple of outstanding lamas known in the West through their writings, and not least through Matthieu's accounts, both in books and on film, of their persons and teachings. The dialogue between father and son is memorable, stern, and affectionate: a debate between equals.

In 1997, an annus mirabilis for Revel, he published a lengthy autobiography that remains untranslated into English: *Mémoires: Le voleur dans la maison vide*[68] (The Thief in the Empty House, recalling a tenth-century Zen teaching tale about an experience so comically futile—attempted theft in an empty house—that one relaxes and awakens). The book is not about Gurdjieff; it reflects a long life richly lived at the center of national and international issues about which Revel had much insight to contribute. Nonetheless, there are two chapters on Gurdjieff, the teaching, and life at rue des Colonels Renard after the war.[69] In 1947, Revel was just twenty-three years old, already married for two years to Yahne Le Toumelin and the father of Matthieu, soon joined by a sister. Though Yahne came from a sea-going Breton family, she had an innate impulse toward the search for truth and self-development that brought her quite early into Gurdjieff's circle, where I have the impression that she was treated like a daughter. It was principally Yahne who persuaded her philosopher husband to meet Gurdjieff and join his circle for several years, evoked in a section of the memoirs called "Harmful Influences." It seems likely to me that from the beginning his heart wasn't in it, although he participated fully alongside his wife.

Revel's recollection in much later life equals Perry in its ceaseless contempt. Nothing and no one escapes censure; it is as if the act of writing was an exorcism, a condemnation somehow needed. Taking his points roughly in the order he presents them: Jeanne de Salzmann is portrayed as a kind of Mother Superior and apologist for Gurdjieff. Gurdjieff's writings are mocked. The coherence of the group is mocked. The toasts to the idiots are misunderstood and mocked. The meals are mocked as fundraising events; those who gave more received preferential treatment. The teaching itself is a "trivial potpourri."[70] Revel failed to understand why the company of pupils around Gurdjieff included eminent men and women—future presidents of major businesses, high government officials, respected doctors and journalists: What were they doing there? What was he doing there, listening to a teacher whom he describes as "an impostor and crook whose smooth talk should not have concealed from me his intellectual poverty."[71] And then, Gurdjieff's sexual invitations to younger women among his pupils . . .

We need a steadying hand here, and it is offered by a recent interview in French media with Matthieu Ricard. Asked about his father's participation in the Gurdjieff teaching, he replies: "If I'm to believe my mother, . . . the *Memoirs* are not totally objective. For a certain time he was undeniably interested in Gurdjieff, about whom I don't know a great deal and don't know his writings. My father spoke of his 'black years,' including his life with my mother. That is surely an exaggeration—at the beginning they loved each other."[72] There is a second helping hand from Yahne Le Toumelin herself—in later life a Tibetan nun, a person of quicksilver mind and enduring charm into her nineties, who never forgot the years with Gurdjieff that prefaced her decades of life on the Tibetan Buddhist path.[73] She includes her friend and mentor Luc Dietrich in her thoughts here, which touch on the question of sexuality. "There is quite a lot of talk of immoral happenings where Gurdjieff is concerned. Now, what struck me in the teaching is an apprenticeship of respect, of honesty. Gurdjieff and Luc called me back to respect, not a bourgeois respect, not moralistic, but one that drew its nobility from a quality of being."[74]

Zuber had much the same impression.

If I had to sum up in a word everything I understood about Mr. Gurdjieff, I would say that, compared with the behavior of any of us, or of my family, or of anyone I came across in public, he was a monster of modesty. People have said that he was cynical, coarse, and that he told jokes which would make a regiment blush. There is a host of anecdotes to support this view, some of them extremely spicy, and on the basis of these he could be described as a monster of immorality. In reality, however, everyone who approached him saw only one side of him.[75]

Revel had missed or forgotten the side seen by his older colleague René Zuber and by his wife of those years.

It is true that Gurdjieff had several children with women of the Prieuré in the years when it had become clear that there was no chance of children with his wife. True also that during the 1930s, when he typically had little money, he could do little or nothing for those children. A son lived with him for a time and helped in the household.[76] It is true that after the war and Occupation, he assembled many of his children—one had not survived the war—and gave them all he could. The best account of that moment and those relations is from a daughter, Dushka Howarth, whom we knew well for many years in New York.[77] There is a further element of eyewitness, expressed by J. G. Bennett as well as any.

The story was always going about that Gurdjieff was seducing almost every woman who came to him, and he himself lent color to this. He used to say to a young girl, for example, coming to visit him for the first or second time, that she should stay behind after everyone had gone or come back and knock at his door; he conveyed that this was the promise of a very special kind of experience. Sometimes girls were frightened and did not go. Others went but with some kind of wrong attitude, in which case they usually received a handful of sweets and were told to go away, Gurdjieff putting on an air of not understanding what it was they had come for. It seems that those who were discreet, and who understood that by going to visit Gurdjieff they were not receiving any high spiritual benefit but simply a sexual occasion, were able to stay with him and have a relationship.[78]

Bennett's conclusion is disingenuous: it doesn't typically work that way between powerful older men and young women.[79] Even after allowance is somewhat blindly made for differences between Caucasian and French sexual mores in Gurdjieff's lifetime and sexual mores today, there is something to face here.

What are we to say? Perhaps nothing more than what Solita Solano said in 1935: "If he could have a weakness, I'd say it was for women."[80] This she said without derision. It was a part of the man. An insightful friend, a psychoanalyst and the wife of a close colleague, once offered the trial view that Gurdjieff found it worthwhile to work with the women of the Rope in the 1930s, nearly all lesbian, in part because it gave him the opportunity to relate closely to women without the pull of sexuality. What an interesting thought. I have no idea how true it is.

We need to ask the women in Gurdjieff's circle at rue des Colonels Renard for their thoughts; thus far we have heard from Yahne Le Toumelin. Solange Claustres, strikingly beautiful and already helping with Movements, leaves no doubt of the probity of their teacher-pupil relation. "He alone," she has written, "gave me a deep feeling of confidence, which I had never received from anyone else. Through the quality of his listening, I could be myself and express myself. He called forth and tested my possibilities, made me aware of them and gave me confidence in them, which is what I most needed."[81] Elsewhere in her memoir, she writes that "he was for me an extraordinary support through his attitude, which was so present, calm, without any reaction, with a profound understanding and love for the other, for others."[82]

Dorothy Caruso (1893–1955), widow of the great tenor, was of middle years when Margaret Anderson introduced her to Gurdjieff. "Gurdjieff was gentle with my soul," she recalled. "It was a soul that had not grown up, as I grew up. It had been timid, but trusting. Often it had been betrayed, but it had not been murdered. . . . Enrico had loved, molded, sustained and protected it. Gurdjieff gave it courage.

From his mysterious and conscious world he guided it with the kind of understanding he called 'objective love'—the 'love of everything that breathes'; and 'it' responded with unlimited trust—the highest type of love there is, I think, in this immediate and unconscious world."[83]

One further voice, that of Rina Hands reporting an uncanny, surely unique conversation with Gurdjieff.

> All the time he was talking to me, I felt very strangely that a quite different conversation was taking place between us. He was really telling me what I wanted to know about objective love. I began to understand how the greater does not preclude the lesser, but includes it and, in fact, the greater could not exist without the lesser. I saw how his love was not at all a personal love, but love for all humanity, for all living beings, perhaps even for all creation. Although this was something quite beyond anything I could aspire to or attempt to understand, when I came into contact with it, as I did now, it could only appear to me as personal love, answering the personal love that was the best I had to offer.[84]

As we have encountered in nearly every chapter of this book, words were not the only teacher in Gurdjieff's world; words were one thing, intelligent energy was another. Hands's experience was richly in two modes of knowing.

What are we to say? The evidence points to two levels, two different sensibilities. At one level, Gurdjieff the incomparable teacher of Being. As he lived and animated life around him, his circle came in touch with a quality of transcendent love they struggled to describe—"impersonal," "objective," "for all creation." As well, he conducted relations with women from that level with delicacy of feeling. At another level was Gurdjieff the man with sexual needs like other men, more than most, who created colorful theater around sex much as he did where money was concerned. The two levels coexisted in him; he must have made his peace with that situation, though others to this day might wish it had been otherwise.

When she first met Gurdjieff, Elizabeth Bennett saw first one, then the other. When she was a newcomer listening to a reading in the salon, he had returned from a car trip quite badly injured. He opened the door and entered.

> As he came [in], he looked directly at me, and all my former ideas and expectations fell away and never returned. How could anyone be afraid of this being? His grave, rather sad face was dark complexioned, and darker now with extensive bruises, but his eyes, large, dark and sparkling beneath his massive brow and the great dome of his shaven head, expressed nothing but compassion. I have never seen a creature more beautiful, more radiant of love and understanding. He could not, I thought, be of this world. From that moment I loved him. When he recovered from his injuries, he was once more the enigmatic, ironic, contradictory Gurdjieff of whom I had heard so many anecdotes, but in those first days of my meeting him he had need of all his powers to keep his body in action: he could not also play a role or wear a mask. But his later extravagant and occasionally outrageous behavior could never eradicate my first impression.[85]

It must be time for forgiveness. Gurdjieff's adversaries in the decades after his death have occasioned a strenuous interpretive journey, now completed. For this they can be thanked. Washington, Rostand, Pauwels, Storr, Perry, Revel—there has been much to learn from them, not that Gurdjieff or the teaching were anything like what they said, but that reputation is amazingly fragile:

knock it a few times, and down it comes. There has been something more to learn: the workings of the mind when it toys with an unfamiliar reality and recoils. The obscuring dust shed by what they wrote—particularly by what Pauwels wrote—continues to reach some opinion makers who simply don't take the time needed to know whereof they speak and write. That is a shame, and it needn't continue. But consider: do we need to forgive Gurdjieff? I think so. He was an utterly remarkable, resourceful teacher for our time, and remains so. But he was also one of us, human, not without error. Incomparable, not without error. For his share in what we are, he too must be forgiven.

CHAPTER 9

Beelzebub's Tales

Beelzebub was sitting alone in a café in Montmartre—as Gurdjieff did from time to time—when he was overwhelmed with sad
thoughts. Looking about him, he saw that humanity had not
changed for the better through the thousands of years he had
taken interest in us, hoped for us, even accepted missions to us
from Sacred Individuals highly placed in the celestial hierarchy.
"How many centuries have passed since that time when I began
to observe the existence of the three-brained beings of this ill-
fated planet!" he thought with considerable passion and pain. He
was usually something of a scientist and buoyant storyteller, an
explorer of the human condition and teacher of universal law and
process. He was usually detached, probing, ironic, humorous. But
not now. "Are not the beings sitting here the same, and do they
not behave as unbecomingly as the beings of the city Samlios on
the continent Atlantis . . . where I also sat among the beings there
in their, as they then called similar restaurants, 'Sakroopiaks'?" We
are encountering Beelzebub's characteristic language and cast of
mind; we'll return to those topics, but for the moment we should
share his thoughts. Everyone he notices in the café is precisely like
everyone he noticed centuries earlier and elsewhere.

Over there, on the left, . . . a contemporary young man is sitting, who in a squeaky voice convincingly holds forth to his
bottle-companion about the causes of disorders which proceed
in some community. . . . Dress his head in a "chambardakh"

and would he not be exactly like a real, as they were then called, "Klian-of-the-mountains"? And that tall man pretending to be an important gentleman, sitting alone in the corner, making eyes at a lady who sits with her husband among the neighboring company . . . is he not a real "Veroonk"? . . . And in their majestic city Babylon where I also happened to be . . . was it not the same there? Were not the three-brained beings of the city Babylon those same . . . Veroonks, Klians, and so on? . . . I saw their center Babylon; what has remained of this truly great Babylon? A few stones of the city itself and a few remnants of peoples formerly great.[1]

Who knows what a Veroonk or Klian is, but presumably Beelzebub knew, and that suffices: his vocabulary suggests times and places unknown, though once as real as what surrounds us today.[2] Gurdjieff is not the only author to offer a powerful lament of this kind; we know this sound. Ecclesiastes the Preacher spoke long before: "A generation goes, and a generation comes, but the earth remains forever. . . . All things are full of weariness; a man cannot utter it. . . . Is there a thing of which it is said, 'See, this is new'? It has been already, in the ages before us" (1:4–10). Marcus Aurelius in his *Meditations* also spoke long before, when his thoughts turned to the reigns of previous emperors. "Think . . . of the times of Vespasian," he wrote, "and what do you see? Men and women busy marrying, bringing up children, sickening, dying, fighting, feasting, chaffering, farming, flattering, bragging, envying, scheming, calling down curses, grumbling at fate, loving, hoarding, coveting thrones and dignities. Of all that life, not a trace survives today."[3] I cite these moving parallels to Beelzebub's threnody in part because the reputation of the *Tales* is of a book apart, something like a land mass that rose in the ocean with no neighbors.

Without question, it is unique. It speaks a highly styled language unlike any other, it draws us into a religious universe unlike any other, it offers an alternative history of Earth and mankind unlike any other, and it delivers an unrelenting critique of what we are, again unlike any other—a critique accompanied nearly on every page by a vision of true values that endow life with dignity and larger purpose. Yet it has literary kinships. In part a science fiction of space travel and planetary visits, it owes something to the founders of science fiction, Jules Verne—whose books were translated and devoured by the Russian public when Gurdjieff was young—and in a later generation H. G. Wells. That Gurdjieff cared for Verne is evident through a Christmas gift he offered Fritz Peters at the Prieuré: a copy of *Twenty Thousand Leagues Under the Sea*.[4] The Russian edition (first published in 1870, reprinted innumerable times) was known as *Eighty Thousand Versts Under the Sea*, the modified title a sign of naturalization into Russian literature.[5] I have sometimes perversely enjoyed telling friends that Beelzebub *is* Captain Nemo, and that the *Occasion*, Beelzebub's superb spaceship, *is* Captain Nemo's technically advanced submarine, the *Nautilus*. It's not literally true, but the influence is unquestionably there. Like Verne's hero, Beelzebub is an exile who takes an interest in human affairs from a distance without disclosing himself. And again like him, Beelzebub is critical of what humanity has allowed itself to become. They both roam, they study and advance knowledge, on occasion they intervene helpfully, and with rare exceptions they maintain distance.

There is another literary kinship, by far more difficult to account for, although a look in that direction provides additional context, a better sense for where the *Tales* fit in the continuum of literature. While some in Gurdjieff's circle were aware of the kinship with François Rabelais, author, priest, and physician, no one was more keenly aware of it than François Grunwald, who married into a family with commercial apple orchards near Chinon in the Loire Valley, where Rabelais was born and where his memory is kept fresh. What could Gurdjieff have known of Rabelais's

URDJIEFF RECONSIDERED

writings in the late nineteenth century, when by his own account he was a voracious reader? Perhaps nothing directly—the only edition available in Russian was an 1896 selection, no doubt bowdlerized, purified of its glorious impurities. Though cosmopolitan Russians before the Revolution typically knew French well, Gurdjieff learned French only in his middle years and only enough to suit himself. Yet *Beelzebub's Tales* in purpose, style, and flooding abundance of novel language, original thought, and blended irony and humor is spookily akin to Rabelais's masterworks. "The two authors," writes Grunwald, "reach for the same goal by the same means: an impartial criticism of the life of men for the sake of their genuine education. Both take as their hero a being of another dimension, superior to ours. . . . Don't deny yourself the pleasure of these two books, *Pantagruel and Gargantua* and *Beelzebub*. Both are sound."[6]

Most important in this kinship is the sheer force of the two authors. Rabelais had in mind to shake his contemporaries out of habit and sleep, out of religious and social prejudice—to set them free. His torrent of words and ideas was dizzying, his laughter and verbal inventiveness were a solvent. With identical force in the *Tales*, and not wholly dissimilar means, Gurdjieff pursues a similar purpose: "To destroy, mercilessly, without any compromises whatsoever, in the mentation and feelings of the reader, the beliefs and views, by centuries rooted in him, about everything existing in the world."[7] *Meetings with Remarkable Men*, the second book in Gurdjieff's trilogy, is a response to the first; it is intended "to acquaint the reader with the material required for a new creation and to prove the soundness and good quality of it."[8] But our focus here is the *Tales*, the more difficult book to approach and appreciate. There are other obvious kinships—notably with *The Arabian Nights* and with Madame Blavatsky's alternative history of the world and mankind in *The Secret Doctrine*—but one further kinship is more difficult to uncover: the *ashokh* tradition to which Gurdjieff's father belonged. His father was a bard, a repository and exponent of a vast

294 ·

tradition of oral poetry, typically recited while playing a stringed instrument. In the provincial city of Kars, now part of Turkey, where the young Gurdjieff grew up, there is even today said to be an unusually strong bardic tradition. I would know nothing of this tradition, apart from what Gurdjieff wrote in *Meetings*, without a welcome book of 1995, *The Song Contests of Turkish Minstrels: Improvised Poetry Sung to Traditional Music*.[9] The practices described there don't resemble his father's ancient, memorized repertory—at least not the little we know of it through Gurdjieff. At a particular café in Kars, there were (and doubtless still are) hours-long competitions between rival bards, known in Turkish as *ashiks*—who among other things deftly and often comically insult one another as they improvise on established themes and musical structures. It will need a scholar of this overall tradition to assess its influence on Gurdjieff's literary style, but of this much we can be sure: the declamatory quality of the language of the *Tales*, its aptness for oral reading and its deliberate repetition of certain phrases, such as "this ill-fated planet" and "the abnormal conditions of being-existence established by them themselves," must owe something to bardic tradition, in which repetition is a memory aid and component of stately speech.

Gurdjieff's Beelzebub is not the biblical Beelzebub, not the enemy of mankind and no part of the hierarchy of Hell. Gurdjieff recounts that, owing to his brilliance, Beelzebub was called while still a "fiery and splendid" youth from his home planet Karatas to the "Sun Absolute," Heaven itself, where he served His Endlessness—Gurdjieff's recurrent term for God—until an unfortunate episode resulted in his exile to our solar system for long, long ages. With the meticulousness characteristic of the *Tales*, Gurdjieff specifies that "owing to the as yet unformed Reason due to his youth, and owing to his callow and therefore still impetuous mentation with unequally flowing associations—that is, owing to a mentation based, as is natural to beings who have not yet become definitely responsible, on a limited understanding—Beelzebub once saw in the government of the World something which seemed to him 'illogical', and having found support among his comrades, beings like himself not yet formed, interfered in what was none of his business. . . . The effect was to bring the central kingdom of the Megalocosmos almost to the edge of revolution. Having learned of this, His Endlessness, notwithstanding his All-lovingness and All-forgiveness, was constrained to banish Beelzebub with his comrades to one of the remote corners of the Universe"[10]—specifically, to our solar system and to the planet Mars, where he and those close to him made their home in exile. When we as readers first meet Beelzebub, eons have passed since his banishment, he has been pardoned, and he is again able to move freely in the universe and to return to the Center.

In appearance Beelzebub looks much like us, though he has a tail that he carefully conceals when he visits Earth, and he has antlers—removed as part of his punishment in exile but restored at the end of the *Tales* in a remarkably poignant chapter. Gurdjieff offers an exuberant explanation for his choice of "the Great Beelzebub Himself" as his hero and narrator, comically focused on Beelzebub's vanity, which would prompt him to help any author who flatters him.[11] But there is surely more to it than that. Beelzebub's impetuous youth, the errors, long penance, and remorse, the exile, his willing engagement on beneficial missions, the emergence of wisdom and knowing compassion: it all bears some resemblance to Gurdjieff himself. This did not go unnoticed by his pupils. "When I express my admiration," Irmis Popoff has written, "of the Mr. Gurdjieff who had become what he was by the time I met him when he last visited New York, there are persons who exclaim with indignation, 'But you did not know him when he was young. He was a devil.' Perhaps he was a devil. But the point is that he had redeemed himself. And no doubt 'the errors of his fiery youth,' as Beelzebub says . . . 'had to be atoned for.'"[12] I believe this to be one of the good lessons underlying Gurdjieff's choice of hero: redemption, not only for the fictive Beelzebub but for us all or nearly all. The possibility of passing from fiery youth with its missteps to maturity and old age graced with knowledge and kindness is central to the *Tales*. Gurdjieff's Beelzebub embodies a strong ideal.

Gurdjieff often spoke of the light and dark energies in us, and of the need to reconcile them again and again, to draw on both with a certain acquired self-mastery. It was a thought that belonged to the twentieth century: C. G. Jung framed it in terms of the shadow and the anima or animus we neglect at our peril; Freud summoned us to explore and understand the unconscious rather than let its drives drive us where they will. Twentieth-century thinkers by and large stopped asking us to be "perfect, as your Father in Heaven is perfect" (Matthew 5:48), and instead called on us to confront all that we are—and to make that movement toward self-knowledge the basis for integrity. Already in Russia Gurdjieff had framed this thought as both a cosmic and a psychological law, the Law of Three: affirmation, denial or resistance, and their reconciliation. During the Prieuré years the emblem of the Institute visualized this thought as angel, devil, and the integration of their energies in the contained presence of the central human figure. As the years went by, Gurdjieff had many different ways of reminding those around him of the need to know and integrate the denying force, which is either passive and indifferent or energized and aggressive. It is a virtually inevitable challenge to whatever good we set out to accomplish. "God has three faces," he said in a meeting of 1943. "Your religion says that also. One face is not the whole, neither are two. God is one and has three faces—think of that. One face represents the angel, the other represents the devil. The angel without the devil can do nothing. The angel alone is a nullity. The devil, too, if he is alone, is a nullity. It is only together that they can do something. If you do everything like an angel, you will not get very far."[13] He was wary of angels. "'*Diable* will help you,'" Dorothy Phillpotts recalls him saying. "*'Ange* too busy—will not listen; he makes so,' and waving his arms above his head he gave his inimitable representation of an angel praising God."[14]

"Angel no good, devil no good in this world. Must be both."[15] So he said in Solita Solano's hearing. Hence Beelzebub, who was both devil and angel: an archdevil in his youth, an archangel of understanding and wisdom in his old age.

I have no idea how the concept for *Beelzebub's Tales to His Grandson* came to birth at the Prieuré. It was a place of practice, everything was close to the bone or bone itself. The Movements encompassed all levels from high to low, from the peace that passeth understanding to the sweat of rehearsal; the music was heaven-sent, truly beautiful. But in other respects, life there, for all participants and presumably for Gurdjieff also, was a lot of hard work: to meet the needs of the community, to practice in all sincerity the inner exercises as given from time to time, the unending discipline of return to oneself, to one's own mind, heart, and body. Yet this was the matrix in which Gurdjieff's vast myth of "world creation and world maintenance," as he put it, and his utterly meticulous examination of the human condition, its forlornness and hope, came to birth. Though Beelzebub has visited Earth at length in the past, throughout the narrative he is elsewhere, traveling in a spaceship with leisure to share knowledge with his grandson Hassein, far from Earth to which he will presumably never return. I have the oddest impression: as if a huge prehistoric bird, a dinosaur or the storied Persian *simurgh*, flew out of the past to deposit an egg, its best treasure, somewhere on the property. And Gurdjieff noticed. I know that this is hardly a convincing explanation, but it has at least the merit of capturing something of the disjuncture between daily life at the Prieuré and the *Tales*. In one of the most memorable passages, Beelzebub describes the symbolic emblem of an ancient society he admires: a sphinx, one of whose traits is the wings of an eagle, "the strongest and the highest soaring of all birds, [which] constantly remind us [that] it is necessary to meditate continually on questions not related to the direct manifestations required for ordinary being-existence."[16]

As must already be evident, Beelzebub's language and his form of "mentation"—Gurdjieff often used this weighty Latinate word— are only sometimes like ours. He does enjoy conversation with earthlings—for example, with a young Persian living in Paris who represents an uneasy blend between the traditional ways of his native culture and the corrupting influences he has absorbed in the West.[17] On such occasions his speech and manner of speech can be direct, forceful but simple, as with the priest Abdil who became one of his few trusted friends on Earth.[18] When he wishes to tell a tale—for example, his breathtakingly comical campaign to establish a chemical laboratory in pre-revolutionary St. Petersburg—he can be a master storyteller who throws nothing in the way of sheer enjoyment. Layered into pleasant tales may well be messages of another kind; it is often so. But symbolic or "esoteric" content doesn't interfere with *story*, to which Gurdjieff gave great value, as if more can be understood through story than by many other means. Late in life, rather enigmatically, he said as much to the young Paul Beekman Taylor, who had lived in his household for a time. "All is story," he said. "Man pay for story. Story is like soap, it cleans off smell of work. You know how to play role of story-teller and role of story. After, you clean of body and mind. In story you make yourself known to others."[19]

Beelzebub's many stories are often described as myth or allegory. No one has put this more vividly than P. L. Travers, author of the Mary Poppins books and a direct pupil of Gurdjieff. "Into this vast allegory," she has written, ". . . top-heavy from its sheer weight of argument and at the same time soaring off into space, like a great, lumbering flying cathedral, Gurdjieff gathered the fundamentals of his teaching."[20] I suppose that it is all allegory, if not always myth: there is *all and everything* in the book, just as the title of the trilogy promises, from tales possessing the spare intensity of Noh drama to a hilarious, purportedly German recipe for chicken soup in times of economic distress, quite exhausting for the chicken, which eventually "goes on strike."[21]

This brief chapter, no more than an invitation to read the *Tales*, cannot hope to encompass all and everything in its pages, but I want to call attention to two extended episodes bearing on the genesis of spiritual community—or, to use words close to Gurdjieff's, the genesis of communities of seekers of truth. The first episode is set in Atlantis, of course long ago, where a man named Belcultassi "was once contemplating, according to the practice of every normal being, and his thoughts were by association concentrated on himself, that is to say, on the sense and aim of his existence, [when] he suddenly sensed and cognized that the process of the functioning of the whole of him had until then proceeded not as it should have proceeded according to sane logic. This unexpected constatation shocked him so profoundly that thereafter he devoted the whole of himself exclusively to be able at any cost to unravel this and understand."[22]

Belcultassi's responses to his discovery move through stages, first of intensified, sincere self-examination, which leads him to see clearly the impulses of "'self-love,' 'pride,' 'vanity,' and so on," that disrupt his inner life. He enters into systematic self-study "to recall just which impulses evoked which reactions in him . . . in his body, in his feelings, and in his thoughts, and the state of his essence when he reacted to anything more or less attentively, and . . . when . . . he had manifested consciously with his 'I' or had acted automatically under the direction of his instinct alone." This prolonged inner work accomplished, but doubting the correctness of his observations, Belcultassi turns to friends and acquaintances to share his inquiry: could they confirm in their own inner lives what he has encountered in himself? "All of them sensed and saw in themselves everything just the same as he did," and several "earnest beings" among them, "having penetrated to the gist of the matter," begin to meet with Belcultassi from time to time to share observations and insights. Others soon join their circle, enough to found the "Society of Akhaldans," dedicated to "the striving to become aware of the sense and aim of the Being of beings."[23] The society evolves rather quickly from that point into a center for work on oneself and for research across many fields of knowledge needed to support the society's aim.

There is much more detail to explore and appreciate in this grand story, but we have seen enough to know what it is: a tale of the genesis of shared inner work among serious, dedicated people, in turn generating a culture of search and research. It begins with one alarmed individual, one partial awakening. It progresses toward the efforts and shared concern of a group of people who hold one another to the standard they recognize as necessary. They are the friends of one another's aspiration, the adversaries of one another's forgetfulness. We are no longer speaking of Atlantis; we are speaking of the development of the Gurdjieff teaching.

The tale of Belcultassi and the Society of Akhaldans represents a movement from grassroots up: Belcultassi is simply a serious human being who found his way and shared insights with others consequentially. There is another tale, requiring three chapters to recount, of a "Messenger Sent from Above," Ashiata Shiemash by name, who in contrast represents an initiative from above to help humanity.[24] Again, there is too much story to encompass. Suffice it to say that, once arrived on our planet with an urgent mission to accomplish and no clear path forward, Ashiata Shiemash imposes long ascetic isolation on himself in order to reflect with utmost clarity. He realizes that faith, hope, and love—the human impulses upon which former Messengers from Above had relied—had been worn thin, corrupted. They could no longer serve. But he comes to recognize that one promising factor remains intact, long buried in human nature and out of harm's way: conscience. This is what he would teach: Objective Conscience, the resurrection of conscience from nearly mute darkness to a guiding role in individual and social life. All else could follow from that; faith, hope, and love would also find their places and integrity. The divine impulse of Objective Conscience, as Ashiata Shiemash understands it, is not merely a restored, heightened sense of right and wrong. It is a light with the potential to suffuse all things with a new awareness.

Ashiata Shiemash begins by teaching a very small circle of initiates; they in turn teach others. A widening circle eventually influences the whole of society in that place and time—not that everyone understands or practices what he teaches, but nearly everyone can feel respect both for the teaching and for those who ably transmit what Beelzebub describes as "Ashiata's renewals." It was not an entirely new teaching; there was no need for it to be entirely new— the elements of tradition were sound and needed only to be reconceived, reweighted, set in motion. "At that time all the principles of Being of the initiated beings there were renewed by the Very Saintly Ashiata Shiemash and later came to be called 'Ashiata's renewals.'" Many pages ago I mentioned the emphasis Gurdjieff gave to the notion of renewal as true teachings move through time and changing circumstance. I believe that he wished his teaching to be understood in that light: not a departure but a return to what has always been true—reconceived, reordered, tied firmly to practice, supported by the timeless means of conversation, meditation, dance, music, and crafts of daily life from cooking to wood carving. Gurdjieff's renewals resemble Ashiata's renewals.

In the third chapter dedicated to Ashiata Shiemash, Gurdjieff painstakingly chronicles "the destruction of all the very saintly labors of Ashiata Shiemash" by an eloquent demagogue, Lentrohamsanin—a name likely recalling Lenin and Trotsky. Some readers who know the *Tales* well have difficulty settling on a single understanding of the majestic and ultimately tragic chronicle of Ashiata Shiemash. Is it an instructive fiction, or perhaps a prophecy of what might be—complete with a warning about the need for protection from adversaries? Is it a true history that Gurdjieff somehow plucked from the world's latent memory? Does it reflect, without insisting, how Gurdjieff viewed his own teaching? This much is clear: like the tale of Belcultassi and the Society of Akhaldans, it concerns the genesis of shared inner work, first in a small circle, then in an ever-widening one, and the gradual transformation of society toward a condition more sound and sane, more sustainable.

Much of the knowledge Beelzebub offers his grandson—a wealth of tales and matters more difficult, including the history of God—is conveyed in strikingly long sentences and a vocabulary his alone. Long sentences allow him to detail the multitude of features of a human characteristic or cosmic circumstance without leaving anything out. It is as if Beelzebub is constantly telling us to look more closely, to look perseveringly under the surface for the intricacies that govern the human psyche, society, and the larger world—telling us that we won't grasp anything fully without exercising attention much as he does. Language structured in this way becomes an exercise in attention for both readers in their privacy and for oral readings, which remain a tradition in Gurdjieff houses since the Prieuré, when the *Tales* were a work in progress.

Beelzebub's vocabulary is another matter. He uses many words and phrases never heard before. We have already encountered his unique adjectival use of the word *being*: being-existence, being-duty, being-mentation, being-Reason—and there are others. Gurdjieff makes clear that he wishes to speak not just to his reader's day-to-day mind but also to a layer much further down, which he calls the subconscious: closer to real feeling and recognitions, closer to what one really is. His adjectival use of the word *being* is a recurrent reminder of the two lives within us: surface consciousness, the realm of information and patterned response, and authentic depth where genuine Reason can grow and refine over a lifetime, where duty and also love are recognized without compromise and acted upon. *Being* refers us back again and again to the whole of human nature, to the possible anchoring of thought, feeling, and action at depth in ourselves. A related term in Beelzebub's lexicon: *common presence*. Used throughout the book, it is another reminder of our possible unity and coherence, of the dignity of the human presence when more fully developed: aware, sensitive, inquiring, guided by sound values, capable of gentle or decisive action, free but not remote. *Beelzebub's Tales* is a twelve-hundred-page argument for decency and dedication.

Add to these usages based on familiar words a wealth of unfamiliar terms around which Beelzebub builds his account of cosmogenesis, cosmos, the local history of planet Earth, and human nature and society. The term *Solioonensius* refers to a periodic tension in the solar system to which human beings can respond in two radically different ways: by agitation and violence or by turning toward themselves with longing for a more awakened state of being. Is there really such a phenomenon? I don't know—but Beelzebub knows and, no surprise, our responses to it don't compare well to those of three-brained beings in other solar systems. Best for Beelzebub to explain; note that he refers to us earthlings as "your favorites" because his grandson Hassein has taken keen interest in learning about us.

> ". . . the cosmic law of Solioonensius. First of all you must be told that all the three-brained beings, on whatever planet they arise and whatever exterior coating they receive, always await the manifestations of the action of this law with impatience and joy, somewhat as your favorites look forward to their feasts of 'Easter,' 'Bairam,' 'Zadik,' 'Ramadan,' 'Kaialana,' and others. The only difference is that your favorites look forward to these feasts of theirs with impatience because on these 'holydays' it has become customary among them to

allow themselves to be more 'jolly' and to 'booze' freely, while the beings of other planets await the action of Solioonensius with impatience because, thanks to it, the need for evolving, in the sense of acquiring Objective-Reason by them, increases in them by itself. . . .

"The 'tension' in all the planets acts . . . on the common presence of all beings arising and breeding on them, always engendering in the beings, besides desires and intentions of which they are not aware, the feeling called 'sacred Iabolioonosar', or as your favorites would say, the feeling of religiousness, namely, that 'being-feeling' which at times appears in the desire and striving for . . . more rapid self-perfecting in the sense of Objective-Reason."[25]

This is Beelzebub. To however slight a degree, we can now consider ourselves initiates; we have encountered his world and voice. Somewhat difficult, different, unfamiliar—and enlarging, vastly enlarging. Actually, we have little right to complain about difficult literature in the era of Heidegger, Wittgenstein, and James Joyce's *Finnegans Wake*, the era when the exquisitely complex text of the Chinese *Book of Changes*, the *I Ching*, reached us, and of repeated attempts to translate into Western languages Dogen's astoundingly difficult thirteenth-century Zen masterpiece, *Shobogenzo*. A spiritual tradition is fortunate to have a seriously long, occasionally difficult, and vastly insightful book as a point of departure and return. Such works don't leave one in peace: there is always more to understand, more to reflect on and match to one's life experience, however awkwardly or vividly. *Beelzebub's Tales* belongs in that small company; it is an ocean of story and thought, inexhaustible—and it is a taste acquired through attentive reading over time, through gradually settling into Beelzebub's universe and finding it altogether acceptable, full of brightness and sorrow.

CHAPTER 10

Coda

When my daughter and her cousins were young, they shared gala winter holidays. Year in and year out they were all stacked in one bedroom—I have a crowded memory of children and beds—and with childhood's unyielding will they expected a glorious entertainment before day's end. That suited me, there was a book I wanted them to know: Arthur Waley's *Monkey*, his spectacular version of the sixteenth-century Chinese masterpiece, Wu Cheng-en's *Journey to the West*.[1] I read it aloud, of course, and the silence of listening, punctuated with laughter, enveloped us all. The book is literature as elixir. Its imaginativeness left us nightly breathless and entranced.

One of the leading characters in the book's little troupe of pilgrims seeking holy scripture "in the West"—in India—is Monkey, a born troublemaker with a mischievous mind and awesome powers. A refrain is heard throughout the book: "Bad, bad monkey!" With iron logic, the children freely applied it to themselves. They acknowledged their inability to stay out of mischief and—"Bad, bad monkey!"—forgave themselves.

Monkey has a cudgel, sometimes enormous—a terrifying weapon against any who impede the pilgrims' progress—and sometimes as small as a toothpick, conveniently stored behind an ear. Large or small, a fact in the world or invisible, Monkey's cudgel is unaccountably memorable, surely a symbol: it tumbles into one's deeper place where matters are actually worked out and meanings assigned. Whatever Wu Cheng-en may have intended, the cudgel says more than a little about teachings as they make contact with the world.

Teachings are a small thing in our large world with its crushing burden of seemingly insoluble problems and crises. Participation in a teaching is the participant's secret—what business is it of anyone else that he or she feels it worthwhile to "remember oneself" in the course of daily life, to reassemble oneself as a thinking, feeling, sensing human being, to examine one's motives on the model of Belcultassi's search for self-knowledge? It need concern no one else that a participant in a teaching loves the mind—loves its capacity for clarity and penetration, its capacity to create good things from slight clues—and knows all too well how easily it wanders off into its own little worlds, how easily it distorts what it encounters. Hence the teaching about vigilance: dreamers, awaken. Why should anyone else care if the participant in a teaching has an organic need to be present, to be aware here and now, and this for strong reasons: it feels right, it delivers oneself to the world and the world to oneself, it is the basis for authentic relations. In all of these respects and more, a teaching is a small thing, no matter for notice, private.

Yet when circumstances require, a teaching can be a cudgel, a large thing—larger than the world when the world is confused, violent, idiotic. Then a teaching needs to appear and speak its word with a force and originality that command attention. We have seen something like this often, though never often enough, in men and women who have left the mark of life in recent history. Martin Luther King, Sakharov, Mandela, Havel, Ayaan Hirsi Ali, young Malala Yousafzai, and, reaching back, Hammarskjöld, Gandhi, and still others. Some of these might disbelieve that they were rooted in a teaching when they spoke their word; Sakharov might have said that he was rooted in the obvious. But each was moved by precise ideals—of nonviolence, of resistance to evil, of social justice, of religious reform, of universal education, of politics as a service and moral exercise. However great their personal sacrifice, each understood the need to call us back to ourselves, to simple decency, mutual respect, and at least the minimum of policies and attitudes needed for survival as a species among other species on a generous planet.

I have no idea whether the Gurdjieff teaching or any other will in future exercise that degree of humane influence. Perhaps they will remain secret. Perhaps they should remain secret. The well-being and even wisdom they generate in individuals will surely influence the geographical and professional communities in which those individuals make their lives. That would be enough, and already a great deal. When I look into your eyes and listen to you, I have no need to know if you are a Gurdjieff pupil or a Buddhist meditator, a Sufi or Vedantist, an engaged Christian or Jew, a secular humanist; I perceive you, not your path to maturity. This is as it should be. At some point, when we're better acquainted, we may compare notes. We'll take out our journals, so to speak, and show one another what we've written there over the years. And for the most part it will be the same.

Afterword

I am aware that this book provides scarcely any acquaintance with the distinguished leaders of the North American and British groups, and as well of the South American groups. It would be convenient to write that this is a topic for another day, but that day is unlikely to come for me personally; others will find their way to it. As there are too many men and women to note by name, I limit myself here to those who were generous enough to allow me, and many others of my generation, to learn from them at length. All of these direct pupils of Gurdjieff, with one blessed exception, have passed on.

Lord Pentland, the vastly creative president of the Gurdjieff Foundation of New York from its first day, should have a book of the kind this is. He was the embodiment of the teaching, forceful, wise, and—truth be known—a man of benevolent shamanic energy: he had assimilated that aspect of the teaching, although as far as I know it wasn't taught. There are several books based on meetings with Lord Pentland in New York and San Francisco. William Segal in New York is well represented in books available today and in videos created by his friend, the documentary filmmaker Ken Burns. Margaret Flinsch, also in New York, wrote little but exercised a strong and welcome influence. Her work with children, brilliantly recorded in Lillian Firestone's book, *The Forgotten Language of Children*, gives her a lasting place in the field of early education. Mrs. Flinsch's sister, Dorothea Dooling, founder of *Parabola*, the quarterly magazine, is well represented in the literature and in the pages of *Parabola* in its earlier years. Christopher Fremantle, British but living in New York with responsibility also for groups in Mexico, is represented by a book, though no book can capture his refinement. Dr. William Welch has his place in this book; his gifted wife, Louise, who founded groups in New York, Toronto, and Halifax, must be remembered. Martin Benson also has a book, a riotous late homage from some of his pupils to a riotous and faithful teacher. Louise March, founder of the Rochester Folk Art Guild and familiar in New York, has her place in this book, but something more should be said. It was as if she had come directly from the early Bauhaus, with its strong ideals, to our vicinity—not factually true, but symbolically exact. Paul Reynard, teaching Movements with immense skill and leading groups in New York, San Francisco, and elsewhere, was among the youngest pupils to have heard Gurdjieff at rue des Colonels Renard. There are others also to be remembered; I am thinking of them all.

Henriette Lannes carried in her lifetime the large responsibility for the groups in London and Lyon; she is well represented by two books of writings and edited transcripts. After Madame Lannes's passing in 1980, Dr. Bernard Courtenay-Mayers was for years in London the center of gravity, the true voice—a man who almost didn't wish to speak, or so it seemed, but when he spoke the teaching was reborn.

I have not had occasion to mention several outstanding men and women in Paris, among them Jeanne de Salzmann's son, Michel, a psychiatrist by profession, and his wife, Josée. Many of us, from many countries, looked to them. Dr. de Salzmann somehow combined originality of insight, human understanding, and a festive spirit. Around him no one's question was idiotic; every question, however halting, fit somewhere in the pattern of the teaching and the pattern of useful truth. I wish also to remember here Pauline de Dampierre, a leader in Paris whom we saw from time to time in New York. Her understanding was extraordinarily exact and inspiring; in her care the teaching became a science. And, at the last, a friend in Paris, Lise Etiévan, who would not tolerate here an excess of kind words; she deserves them all.

I trust that these few words express some part of the gratitude owed to the generation of teachers who were the nucleus that Gurdjieff knew to be necessary.

Notes

CHAPTER 1: DISPARU! ÉTEINT!

1. Georgette Leblanc, *The Courage Machine: A New Life in a New World*, trans. Margaret Anderson and Solita Solano (London: Book Studio, 2012), 105.
2. François Grunwald, *Un chemin hors de l'exil: De Freud à Gurdjieff* (Paris: L'Originel, 2017), 557 (trans. from the French by the author).
3. Grunwald, *Un chemin hors de l'exil*, 462 (trans. from the French by the author).
4. Robin Lane Fox, "Russell Page's Garden at Villar Perosa and a Tale of Two Masters," *Financial Times*, 13 (May 2016), accessed October 2, 2017, https://www.ft.com/content/ff53792c-1208-11e6-91da-096d89bd2173.
5. John G. Bennett and Elizabeth Bennett, *Idiots in Paris: Diaries of J. G. Bennett and Elizabeth Bennett*, 1949 (Daglingworth Manor, Gloucestershire, UK: Coombe Springs Press, 1980), 17.
6. The main text of the Institute's prospectus, dated 1922, is available at http://www.gurdjieff-bibliography.com/Current/10_institute-prospectus_2004-07-02.pdf, accessed February 12, 2018.
7. See Paul Beekman Taylor, *Gurdjieff in the Public Eye: Newspaper Articles, Magazines and Books 1914–1949* (Utrecht: Eureka Editions, 2011), passim.
8. Katherine Mansfield, entry for 17 December 1919, *The Diaries of Katherine Mansfield, including Miscellaneous Works*, ed. Gerri Kimber and Claire Davison (Edinburgh: Edinburgh University Press, 2016), 289.
9. Katherine Mansfield, *The Collected Letters of Katherine Mansfield*, ed. Vincent O'Sullivan and Margaret Scott (Oxford: Oxford University Press, 2008), 296, letter dated 13 October 1922.
10. Tcheslaw Tchekhovitch, *Gurdjieff: A Master in Life; Recollections of Tcheslaw Tchekhovitch* (Toronto: Dolmen Meadow Editions, 2006), 80.
11. Paul Beekman Taylor, *Gurdjieff and Orage: Brothers in Elysium* (York Beach, ME: Weiser Books, 2001), 26.
12. See James Moore, *Gurdjieff and Mansfield* (London: Routledge and Kegan Paul, 1980), 201; Taylor, *Gurdjieff and Orage*, 26.
13. The groundbreaking biography is Antony Alpers, *The Life of Katherine Mansfield* (New York: Knopf, 1953).
14. Gerri Kimber, *Katherine Mansfield: The View from France* (Bern, Switzerland: Peter Lang AG, 2008).

15. It will come as a surprise to readers familiar with the Gurdjieff legacy that both of his parents were Greek; the assumption has long been that his mother, Evdokia, was Armenian. For further information, see Paul Beekman Taylor, *Gurdjieff's World of Words: A Methodological Reading* (Utrecht: Eureka Editions, 2014), 15–16. On Gurdjieff's early exposure to Armenian culture and his great regard for the language, see David Stephen Calonne, "G. I. Gurdjieff's Spiritual Quest for Kars and Ani," in *Armenian Kars and Ani,* ed. Richard G. Hovannisian, (Costa Mesa, CA: Mazda Publishers, 2011), 349–65.

16. Taylor, *Gurdjieff in the Public Eye*, 30.

17. Taylor, *Gurdjieff in the Public Eye*, 60–61.

18. Gorham Munson, cited in James Moore, *Gurdjieff: A Biography; The Anatomy of a Myth* (Shaftesbury, Dorset, UK: Element Books, 1991), 201.

19. Henri Tracol, *The Real Question Remains: Gurdjieff; A Living Call*, trans. Jenny Koralek (Sandpoint, ID: Morning Light Press, 2009), 74–75 (trans. from the French, slightly revised by the author from an archival version).

20. Grunwald, *Un chemin hors de l'exil*, 567.

21. Jeanne de Salzmann, *The Reality of Being: The Fourth Way of Gurdjieff* (Boston: Shambhala, 2010).

22. Margaret Anderson (unpublished document, 1949), private archive.

23. Kathryn Hulme, notes, 22 April 1939, box 55, folder 768, Kathryn Hulme Papers (1846–1981), Beinecke Rare Book and Manuscript Library, Yale University, New Haven. Published with permission. A virtually identical text is in Margaret Anderson, *The Unknowable Gurdjieff* (New York: Samuel Weiser, 1962), 34.

24. Diogenes Laertius, *Lives of Eminent Philosophers*, trans. Robert D. Hicks, vol. 2, Loeb Classical Library, 185 (Cambridge, MA: Harvard University Press, 1925), 22–85.

25. Anderson, *The Unknowable Gurdjieff*, 161.

26. Annie Lou Staveley, *Memories of Gurdjieff* (Aurora, OR: Two Rivers Press, 1978), 70.

27. G. I. Gurdjieff, *The Herald of Coming Good: First Appeal to Contemporary Humanity* (Paris, 1933), 12. Reprints show slight differences in pagination.

28. Annabeth McCorkle, *The Gurdjieff Years 1929–1949: Recollections of Louise Goepfert March* (Utrecht: Eureka Editions, 2012), 66.

29. C. S. Nott, *Teachings of Gurdjieff: The Journal of a Pupil* (New York: Samuel Weiser, 1961), 22.

30. Kathryn Hulme, May 1948, in Solita Solano, "My Gurdjieff Notes—Daily in Paris (1935–1940)," box 6, folder 6, Janet Flanner and Solita Solano Papers (1870–1976), Library of Congress, Washington, DC.

31. Gurdjieff, *The Herald*, 66.

32. Gurdjieff, *The Herald*, 63.

33. Gurdjieff, *The Herald*, 64–65.

34. Gurdjieff, *The Herald*, 68.

35. Gurdjieff, *The Herald*, 67.
36. De Salzmann, *The Reality of Being*, 3–4.

PROLOGUE TO CHAPTERS 2–6:
THE DECADES OF A TEACHER

1. See Roger Lipsey, "Signore: Parabola Visits the Monastero di Bose in the Foothills of the Italian Alps," *Parabola Magazine*, October 28 2015, accessed March 18, 2018, www.parabola.org.
2. Hulme, 25 March 1939, in Solano, Gurdjieff notes, and in Hulme, Notes, box 55, folder 768, "Addenda," p. 6.

CHAPTER 2: TIBETAN TEA VERY WISE CREATION

1. Solita Solano, Gurdjieff notes, 21 March 1937, p. 33.
2. Joseph Azize, *George Adie: A Gurdjieff Pupil in Australia* (Waukee, IN: By the Way Books, 2015), 245.
3. Solano, Gurdjieff notes, 8 July 1937, p. 42.
4. Solano, Gurdjieff notes, 25 July 1936, p. 19.
5. Parish registers, 1879–1917, Russian Orthodox Church, Voyennoga sobora (Kars). (Salt Lake City, UT: Genealogical Society of Utah, 1996), microfilm 2/2, accessed October 17, 2017, https://www.familysearch.org/search/catalog/682432?availability=Family%20History%20Library. Discovered by Thomas Daly, Jr.
6. Taylor, *Gurdjieff and Orage*, 30.
7. See Basarab Nicolescu, ed., "Alexandre de Salzmann, un continent inexploré," in *René Daumal et l'enseignement de Gurdjieff* (Paris: Le Bois d'Orion, 2015), esp. 81 ff. See also Carla Di Donato, *L'invisibile reso visibile: Alexandre de Salzmann (1874–1934). Vita, opera e ricerca tra teatro, luce e movimento* (Rome: Aracne Editrice, 2013).
8. James Webb, *The Harmonious Circle: The Lives and Work of G. I. Gurdjieff, P. D. Ouspensky, and Their Followers* (New York: G. P. Putnam's Sons, 1980); reference to repainting the Monks' Corridor unfortunately mislaid. Olga de Hartmann also refers to the project in *What For?*, unpublished manuscript, *terminus ante quem* 1979, private archive, chap. 12, p. 2.
9. Solano, Gurdjieff notes, 20 April, 1937, p. 36.
10. Ezra Pound, *Guide to Kulchur* (London: Faber & Faber, 1938), 112, where Pound writes that Gurdjieff prepared "Persian soup, bright yellow in color, . . . delicate—you might say Pier della Francesca in tone." See Noel Stock, *The Life of Ezra Pound* (London: Routledge, Kegan Paul, 1970), 254, and also Paul Beekman Taylor, *Gurdjieff's Invention of America* (Utrecht: Eureka Editions, 2007), 49, for Gurdjieff's discussion with Lincoln Kirstein about meeting Ezra Pound.

11. Kathryn Hulme, diary, 22 April 1937, folder 96, Kathryn Hulme Papers, box 55, folders 760–766, Beinecke Rare Book and Manuscript Library, Yale University, New Haven. Published with permission.

12. Hulme, diary, 26 March 1937, folders 86–87.

13. G. I. Gurdjieff, *Life Is Real Only Then, When "I Am," All and Everything*, Third Series. (New York: E.P. Dutton & Company, 1981), 9.

14. Grunwald, *Un chemin hors de l'exil*, 543.

15. G. I. Gurdjieff, *An Objectively Impartial Criticism of the Life of Man or Beelzebub's Tales to his Grandson, All and Everything*, First Series. (New York: Harcourt, Brace & Company, 1950), with many subsequent editions. Note that pagination consistently refers to the 1950 edition; pagination for the 1992 edition differs. For Gurdjieff's Tibet, see chaps. 22 and 38.

16. Hulme, diary, 21 June 1936, folder 31.

CHAPTER 3: THE FIRST EXPOSITION: RUSSIA 1912–1917

1. Among Ouspensky's biographers, James Webb, *The Harmonious Circle*, offers an extended, sympathetic portrait. Among quite a few other sources, consider William Patrick Patterson, *Struggle of the Magicians: Why Uspenskii Left Gurdjieff; Exploring the Teacher-Student Relationship* (Fairfax, CA: Arete, 1996); Gary Lachman, *In Search of P. D. Ouspensky: The Genius in the Shadow of Gurdjieff* (New York: Quest Books, 2006); and Colin Wilson, *The Strange Life of P. D. Ouspensky* (London: Aeon Books, 2005).

2. P. D. Ouspensky, *In Search of the Miraculous: Fragments of an Unknown Teaching* (New York: Harcourt, Brace and Company, 1949), 8.

3. Ouspensky, *Fragments*, 242–44.

4. See Ouspensky, *Fragments*, 21, 68, and from many years later, Rina Hands, *Diary of Madame Egout Pour Sweet: With Mr. Gurdjieff in Paris 1948–1949* (Aurora, OR: Two Rivers Press, 1991), 36.

5. Gurdjieff, *Beelzebub's Tales*, 1064.

6. Gurdjieff, *Beelzebub's Tales*, 1096–97.

7. Ouspensky, *Fragments*, 14.

8. Ouspensky, *Fragments*, 64–67.

9. See Christian Wertenbaker, *Man in the Cosmos: G. I Gurdjieff and Modern Science* (New Paltz, NY: Codhill Press, 2012) and *The Enneagram of G. I. Gurdjieff: Mathematics, Metaphysics, Music, and Meaning* (New Paltz, NY: Codhill Press, 2017).

10. Quoting here the title of P. D. Ouspensky's classic study, *The Psychology of Man's Possible Evolution* (New York: Hedgehog Press, 1950), with many subsequent editions.

11. Gurdjieff, *Beelzebub's Tales*, 386.

12. Gurdjieff, *Views from the Real World: Early Talks of G. I. Gurdjieff* (New York: E. P. Dutton, 1973), 274, with many subsequent editions.

13. See Johanna Petsche, "Gurdjieff and Blavatsky: Western Esoteric Teachers in Parallel," *Literature & Aesthetics* 21 (2011): 98–115.

CHAPTER 4: SONNEZ FORT: THE PRIEURÉ 1922–1932

1. Solano, Gurdjieff notes, 30 October, 1937, p. 45.
2. See Maxine Fawcett-Yeske and Bruce Brooks Pfeiffer, eds., *The Life of Ol-givanna Lloyd Wright: From Crna Gora to Taliesin, Black Mountain to Shining Brow* (Novato, CA: ORO Editions, 2017).
3. The foremost book for the years of migration is Thomas and Olga de Hart-mann, *Our Life with Mr. Gurdjieff*, ed. T. C. Daly and T. A. G. Daly (Sandpoint, ID: Sandpoint Press, 2008) (best read if available in this definitive edition); other essential works include Ouspensky's *Fragments*, Tchekhovitch's *A Master in Life*, and Fawcett-Yeske and Pfeiffer's *The Life of Olgivanna Lloyd Wright*.
4. De Hartmann, *What For?*, 5.
5. See the bibliography for details on the four-volume publication of the Gurdjieff/de Hartmann scores. The fragments composed for *The Struggle of the Magicians* appear in G. I. Gurdjieff and Thomas de Hartmann, *Music for the Piano, Volume IV: Hymns from a Great Temple and Other Selected Works* (Mainz, Germany: Schott Musik International, 2005), 49–66.
6. Taylor, *Gurdjieff in the Public Eye*, 53.
7. Mansfield, *Diaries*, 435–36.
8. Taylor, *Gurdjieff and Orage*, 75.
9. Margaret Anderson, *The Fiery Fountains: The Autobiography; Continuation and Crisis to 1950* (New York: Hermitage House, 1951), 114, recalling Matthew 4:18–20.
10. Nott, *Teachings of Gurdjieff*, 60.
11. Solano, Gurdjieff notes, 1 January 1937, p. 30.
12. Llewelyn Powys, cited in Taylor, *Gurdjieff in the Public Eye*, 167.
13. McCorkle, *The Gurdjieff Years*, 37.
14. Hartmann, *What For?*, 23.
15. Gurdjieff and Hartmann, *Music for the Piano, Volume IV*, 72–79. Though the music survives, the Movement is now lost.
16. See Roger Lipsey, "Chez Monsieur Gurdjieff," in *Katherine Mansfield and Russia*, ed. Galya Diment, Gerri Kimber, and Todd Martin (Edinburgh: Edinburgh University Press, 2017), 163–72.
17. Mansfield, *Letters*, 305. Mansfield's spelling and punctuation retained.
18. Mansfield, *Letters*, 306.
19. Mansfield, *Letters*, 308.
20. Mansfield, *Letters*, 310.
21. Mansfield, *Letters*, 310.
22. See Olgivanna, "The Last Days of Katherine Mansfield," *The Bookman: A Review of Books and Life* 73 (1931): 6–13, accessed September 26, 2017, www.gurdjieff-bibliography.com/Current/KM_042006_02_OLGIVANNA Last Days of KM.pdf; and Adele Kafian, "Looking Back to the Last Days of Katherine Mansfield," *Adelphi* 23 (1946–1947): 36–39, accessed September 26, 2017, gurdjieff-bibliography.com/Current/KM_05_2006_02 _KAFIAN_Last_Days_KM.pdf.

23. Mansfield, *Letters*, 331.
24. Mansfield, *Letters*, 336–37.
25. Mansfield, *Letters*, 322.
26. Mansfield, *Letters*, 331.
27. Mansfield, *Letters*, 341.
28. Mansfield, *Letters*, 346.
29. Bennett and Bennett, *Idiots in Paris*, 43.
30. For the Institute program, see www.gurdjieff-bibliography.com /Current/10_institute-prospectus_2004-07-02.pdf, accessed September 27, 2017.
31. For Orage on duliotherapy, see C. S. Nott, *Teachings of Gurdjieff*, 27.
32. De Hartmann, *What For?*, chap. 9, pp. 5–6.
33. Nott, *Teachings of Gurdjieff*, 27.
34. Nott, *Teachings of Gurdjieff*, 49.
35. Roger Friedland and Harold Zellman, *The Fellowship: The Untold Story of Frank Lloyd Wright and the Taliesin Fellowship* (New York: HarperCollins, 2009), 65; see also Fawcett-Yeske and Pfeiffer, *The Life of Olgivanna Lloyd Wright*, 65.
36. Taylor, *Gurdjieff in the Public Eye*, 35.
37. See "Questions and Answers, Prieuré, October 1922," in *Gurdjieff's Early Talks 1914–1931 in Moscow, St. Petersburg, Essentuki, Tiflis, Constantinople, Berlin, Paris, London, Fontainebleau, New York, and Chicago*, ed. Joseph Azize (London: Book Studio, 2014), 170–71.
38. For Orage teaming with another man to pull a heavy roller, see Taylor, *Gurdjieff in the Public Eye*, 25, lower right illustration, man on far right, at too small a scale to identify clearly, though the original news clip in the collection of the Institut G. I. Gurdjieff leaves no doubt.
39. Gurdjieff's own account of the difficulty between himself and Orage is in Gurdjieff, *Life Is Real*, 73–101. See also the eyewitness account in Louise Welch, *Orage with Gurdjieff in America* (Boston: Routledge & Kegan Paul, 1982), 81 ff., and Paul Beekman Taylor, "What Happened between Orage and Gurdjieff," in *Real Worlds of G. I. Gurdjieff: Chapters in the Life of a Master* (Utrecht: Eureka Editions, 2012), 91–115.
40. Welch, *Orage with Gurdjieff*, 137.
41. Philip Mairet, *A. R. Orage: A Memoir* (New York: University Books, 1966), 115.
42. Taylor, *Real Worlds*, 112.
43. Mansfield, *Letters*, 347–48 (Early January 1923).
44. Peter Washington, *Madame Blavatsky's Baboon: A History of the Mystics, Mediums, and Misfits Who Brought Spiritualism to America* (New York: Schocken Books, 1996), 3.
45. Taylor, *Gurdjieff in the Public Eye*, 100.
46. Tchekhovitch, *A Master in Life*, 121.
47. J. G. Bennett, *Gurdjieff: Making a New World* (London: Turnstone Books, 1973), 117.

48. See *Views from the Real World*, 273–76.

49. Tchekhovitch, *A Master in Life*, 114.

50. René Zuber, unpublished journal, private archive.

51. G. I. Gurdjieff, *Paris Meetings 1943* (Toronto: Dolmen Meadow Editions, 2017), 278.

52. G. I. Gurdjieff, *Meetings with Remarkable Men, All and Everything*, Second Series. (New York: E. P. Dutton & Company, Inc., 1963), 31.

53. Anderson, *The Unknowable Gurdjieff*, 90.

54. Tchekhovitch, *A Master in Life*, 46.

55. Grunwald, *Un chemin hors de l'exil*, 568–69; Margaret Anderson, unpublished correspondence, 1 August 1949, private archive.

56. Gurdjieff, *Meetings*, 239.

57. Tchekhovitch, *A Master in Life*, 142.

58. Texts will be found in *Views from the Real World* and in *Gurdjieff's Early Talks*.

59. Dr. Nicoll is best known for his multivolume *Psychological Commentaries on the Teachings of Gurdjieff and Ouspensky* and for several books interpreting the gospels in light of the Gurdjieff teaching. See bibliography for details.

60. Webb, *The Harmonious Circle*, 236.

61. Gurdjieff, *Views from the Real World*, 104–5.

62. Tchekhovitch, *A Master in Life*, 120.

63. Gurdjieff, *Views from the Real World*, 222–23.

64. Gurdjieff, *Views from the Real World*, 228–35.

65. Gurdjieff, *Views from the Real World*, 268.

66. Gurdjieff, *Views from the Real World*, 268.

67. Gurdjieff, *Views from the Real World*, 269–70.

68. Gurdjieff, *Views from the Real World*, 270.

69. Gurdjieff, *Views from the Real World*, 161.

70. Fritz Peters, *Boyhood with Gurdjieff* (New York: E. P. Dutton, 1964), 163.

71. Peters, *Boyhood*, 41.

72. Solano, Gurdjieff notes, 11–12 June 1937, p. 41.

73. Solano, Gurdjieff notes, End of August, 1936, p. 23.

74. Luba Gurdjieff Everitt with Marina C. Bear, *Luba Gurdjieff: A Memoir with Recipes* (Berkeley, CA: Ten Speed Press, 1993), 29.

75. Gurdjieff Everitt, *Luba Gurdjieff*, 30.

76. Gurdjieff, *Beelzebub's Tales*, 678–81.

77. See Frank Martin, Tibor Dénes et al., *Émile Jaques-Dalcroze: L'homme, le compositeur, le créateur de la Rythmique* (Neuchâtel, Switzerland: Editions de la Baconnière, 1965).

78. Martin, *Émile Jaques-Dalcroze*, 317 (trans. from the French by author).

79. Martin, *Émile Jaques-Dalcroze*, 332 (trans. from the French by author).

80. Jessmin and Dushka Howarth, *"It's Up to Ourselves": A Mother, a Daughter, and Gurdjieff* (New York: Gurdjieff Heritage Society, 1998), 33.

81. New scholarship is emerging about dance as a transformative discipline in the first decades of the twentieth century. See esp. Carole M. Cusack, "The

Contemporary Context of Gurdjieff's Movements," in *Religion and the Arts*, 21, no. 1–2 (2017): 96–102.

82. René Daumal, "Jaques-Dalcroze, Éducateur," in *L'Évidence absurde: Essais et notes I (1926–1934)* (Paris: Gallimard, 1972), 270–71 (trans. from the French by author).

83. Daumal, "Jaques-Dalcroze," 272 (trans. from the French by author).

84. Daumal, "Jaques-Dalcroze," 274 (trans. from the French by author).

85. René Daumal, "Le Mouvement dans l'éducation intégrale de l'homme," in *L'Évidence absurde,* 276–280.

86. The Gurdjieff/de Hartmann music for Movements is not publicly available in score; however, some of the most striking and beautiful music for Movements, including music for the "Thirty-Nine," is commercially available in recordings by Wim van Dullemen, including *Thomas de Hartmann—Music for Gurdjieff's 39 Series*, Channel Crossings, 2001, and *Gurdjieff's Music for the Movements*, Channel Crossings, date uncertain. As well, the earliest Movements music, for the 1923–1924 public demonstrations, is available on CD in de Hartmann's orchestrations in Gert-Jan Blom's unique book, *Gurdjieff /de Hartmann: Oriental Suite; The Complete Orchestral Music 1923–1924* (Aalsmeer, Netherlands: Basta, 2006).

87. See Elan Sicroff, pianist, *The Thomas de Hartmann Project—Music for Piano, Voice and Chamber Ensemble,* (Aalsmeer, Netherlands: Basta, 2016). A seven-disc boxed set.

88. See Gert-Jan Blom, ed., *G. I. Gurdjieff: Harmonic Development; The Complete Harmonium Recordings 1948–1949* (Aalsmeer, Netherlands: Basta, 2004).

89. Anderson, *The Fiery Fountains*, 126.

90. Nott, *Teachings of Gurdjieff*, 62.

91. Nott, *Teachings of Gurdjieff*, 61.

92. Diana Faidy, "Reminiscences of My Work with Georges Gurdjieff," (unpublished typescript, n.d.) 58–59, archive of the Gurdjieff Foundation of New York.

93. There is a passing mention of Diaghilev's expression of interest in Moore, *The Anatomy of a Myth*, 352, but no source reference.

94. Joseph Azize, *Gurdjieff's Early Talks*, 277.

95. Gorham Munson, *The Awakening Twenties: A Memoir-History of a Literary Period* (Baton Rouge, LA: Louisiana State University Press, 1985), 254.

96. In Gurdjieff, *Beelzebub's Tales*, see for example, 134, 637.

97. Gurdjieff, *Meetings*, 162–63.

98. Gurdjieff, *Meetings*, 162.

99. French newspaper clipping, archive, Institut G. I. Gurdjieff, Paris (trans. from the French by author).

100. British newspaper clipping, 31 March 1923, archive, Institut G. I. Gurdjieff, Paris.

101. British newspaper clipping, archive, Institut G. I. Gurdjieff, Paris.

102. British newspaper clipping, 17 June 1923, archive, Institut G. I. Gurdjieff, Paris.

103. *Time and Tide*, 2 March 1923, archive, Institut G. I. Gurdjieff, Paris.

104. Album of newspaper clippings, archive, Institut G. I. Gurdjieff, Paris.

105. Tchekhovitch, *A Master in Life,* 116.

106. Taylor, *Gurdjieff in the Public Eye*, 38.

107. See n. 86.

108. This and later quotations are from the 1923–1924 program, archive, Institut G. I. Gurdjieff, Paris.

109. Howarth and Howarth, *"It's Up to Ourselves,"* 101; *Gurdjieff's Early Talks*, pp. 278–79.

110. Dr. Mary Bell, unpublished notes, archive of the Gurdjieff Foundation of New York.

111. Taylor, *Gurdjieff in the Public Eye*, 42.

112. Taylor, *Gurdjieff in the Public Eye*, 43–44.

113. Album of newspaper clippings, archive, Institut G. I. Gurdjieff, Paris.

114. Munson, *The Awakening Twenties*, 257.

115. Welch, *Orage with Gurdjieff in America*, 7.

116. De Hartmann, *What For?*, chap. 9, pp. 25–26.

117. *Views from the Real World,* 236–42.

118. Tchekhovitch, *A Master in Life,* 164.

119. De Hartmann and de Hartmann, *Our Life*, 221–22.

120. Welch, *Orage with Gurdjieff in America*, 41, recording a recollection of Carol Robinson's.

121. De Hartmann and de Hartmann, *Our Life*, 228.

122. De Hartmann and de Hartmann, *Our life*, 229–31.

123. G. I. Gurdjieff and Thomas de Hartmann, *Music for the Piano, Volume III: Hymns, Prayers and Rituals* (Mainz, Germany: Schott Musik International, 2002), 66.

124. Taylor, *Gurdjieff and Orage*, 122.

125. See Lincoln Kirstein, *Mosaic: Memoirs* (New York: Farrar Straus and Giroux, 1994).

126. McCorkle, *The Gurdjieff Years,* 42.

127. See Nikolai de Stjernvall, *My Dear Father Gurdjieff*, trans. Paul Beekman Taylor (Dublin: Bardic Press, 2013), 27.

128. Tchekhovitch, *A Master in Life,* 176.

129. Paul Beekman Taylor noted in conversation (March 2018) that many of the American men at the Prieuré referred to Gurdjieff as "the Old Man."

130. Carl Lehmann-Haupt, ed., *Martin Benson Speaks* (New Paltz, NY: Codhill Press, 2011), 192.

131. Gorham Munson, in Taylor, *Gurdjieff in the Public Eye*, 210.

132. Tchekhovitch, *A Master in Life,* 167.

133. Gurdjieff, *Life Is Real*, 38–39.

134. Fawcett-Yeske and Pfeiffer, *The Life of Olgivanna Lloyd Wright*, 57.

135. Fawcett-Yeske and Pfeiffer, *The Life of Olgivanna Lloyd Wright*, 63.

136. De Hartmann and de Hartmann, *Our Life*, 244.

137. De Hartmann and de Hartmann, *Our Life*, 244.

138. Gurdjieff, *Life Is Real*, 38.

139. Gurdjieff, *Life Is Real*, 38.

140. Peters, *Boyhood*, 78.

141. Peters, *Boyhood*, 76.

142. De Hartmann, *What For?*, chap. 10, pp. 32–33.

143. Nott, *Teachings of Gurdjieff*, 63. Gurdjieff went to some length to explain the healing power of "magnetism" within Nott's hearing. Tchekhovitch once questioned Gurdjieff about healing water, who responded: "The ability of laboratories to identify substances dissolved in water is limited to finding gases, and then only if they look for particular ones. But when it comes to detecting special energy—which can be transferred to water and preserved—chemists are at a loss." Tchekhovitch, *A Master in Life,* 217.

144. G. I. Gurdjieff, *The Struggle of the Magicians: Scenario of the Ballet.* (London: Book Studio, 2014).

145. Gurdjieff, *Life Is Real*, 40–44.

146. Gurdjieff, *Life Is Real*, 45.

147. DeHartmann, *What For?*, chap. 12, pp. 2–5.

148. Author in conversation with Lord Pentland.

149. Lehmann-Haupt, *Martin Benson Speaks*, 194–95.

150. Taylor, *Gurdjieff and Orage*, 80.

151. Bennett, *Gurdjieff: Making a New World*, 118.

152. McCorkle, *The Gurdjieff Years*, 83.

153. Lehmann-Haupt, *Martin Benson Speaks*, 184–85.

154. Now the concluding chapter of Gurdjieff, *Meetings*, 247 ff.

155. Unpublished manuscript, private archive.

156. Bennett, *Gurdjieff: Making a New World*, 119.

157. Solano, Gurdjieff notes, 7–11 July 1936, p. 16.

158. Solano, Gurdjieff notes, 17 January 1938, p. 46.

159. Edwin Wolfe, *Episodes with Gurdjieff* (San Francisco: Far West Press, 1974), 22.

160. Taylor, *Gurdjieff in the Public Eye*, 35.

161. Paul Beekman Taylor, *Shadows of Heaven* (York Beach, ME: S. Weiser, 1998), 70.

CHAPTER 5: LUX IN TENEBRIS: THE 1930S

1. Gospel of John 1:5.

2. McCorkle, *The Gurdjieff Years*, 53. Louise March was probably reading a passage in Gurdjieff, *Meetings*.

3. See René Daumal, "Le mouvement dans l'éducation," 276–80. Something of the search and cast of characters at the community house in Sèvres is

reflected in Daumal's unfinished masterpiece, *Mount Analogue: A Novel of Symbolically Authentic Non-Euclidean Adventures in Mountain Climbing*, trans. Roger Shattuck (New York: Pantheon, 1960, for the first American edition). See also Basarab Nicolescu and Jean-Philippe de Tonnac, eds., *René Daumal ou le perpétuel incandescent* (L'Isle-sur-la-Sorgue: Le bois d'Orion, 2008).

4. Solita Solano, unedited notes, 19 January 1938, private archive. There are two "editions" of these papers: the unedited version now in a private archive and the edited version deposited in the Library of Congress, referenced here as "Gurdjieff notes." In this chapter, I place considerable reliance on the unedited version.

5. Solano, Gurdjieff notes, 4 February 1936, p. 9; also Dorothy Phillpotts, *Discovering Gurdjieff* (n.p., AuthorHouse, 2008), 200.

6. Solano, unedited notes, 9 December 1935, p. 42.

7. G. I. Gurdjieff, *The 1931 Manuscript of Beelzebub's Tales to His Grandson*, ed. Robin Bloor (Spicewood, TX: Little Crow Press, 2015).

8. For the tenor of the Gurdjieff–Frank Loyd. Wright relation, consider Moore, *The Anatomy of a Myth*, 364–65; Patterson, *Georgi Ivanovitch Gurdjieff: The Man, the Teaching, His Mission* (Fairfax, CA: Arete Communications, 2014), 366–67; and Friedland and Zellman, *The Fellowship*, 239–42 passim.

9. Taylor, *Gurdjieff in the Public Eye*, 197.

10. See again Friedland and Zellman, *The Fellowship*, and the interesting account in Kamal Amin, *Reflections from the Shining Brow: My Years with Frank Lloyd Wright and Olgivanna Lazovich* (Santa Barbara, CA: Fithian Press, 2004), passim.

11. William Patrick Patterson and Barbara C. Allen, *Ladies of the Rope: Gurdjieff's Special Left Bank Women's Group* (Fairfax, CA: Arete Editions, 1999); William Patrick Patterson, *Voices in the Dark: Esoteric, Occult & Secular Voices in Nazi-Occupied Paris, 1940–44* (Fairfax, CA: Arete Communications, 2001).

12. Solano, unedited notes, 23 October 1935, p.3.

13. Solano, unedited notes, 6 November 1935, p. 23.

14. Solano, unedited notes, 6 December 1935, p. 41.

15. Solano, unedited notes, 1 November 1935, pp. 10–11.

16. Solano, Gurdjieff notes, 6 November 1935, p. 3.

17. Solano, unedited notes, 5 November 1935, p. 12.

18. Solano, Gurdjieff notes, 26 October, 1935, p. 1.

19. Solano, Gurdjieff notes, 23 October 1935, p. 1.

20. Solano, unedited notes, 2 December 1935, p. 41.

21. Solano, unedited notes, 22 January 1936, p. 51.

22. Solano, Gurdjieff notes, 10 February 1936, p. 10.

23. Solano, Gurdjieff notes, Paris, Easter lunch, 1937 [Orthodox Easter, 2 May], p. 37.

24. Solano, Gurdjieff notes, 7 January 1936, p. 5.

25. Hulme, diary, 24 January 1936, folder 11.

26. Solano, Gurdjieff notes, 1 January 1937, p. 30.

27. Solano, unedited notes, 28 October 1935, p. 7.

28. Solano, unedited notes, 31 October 1935, p. 9.

29. Solano, unedited notes, 22 July [1936], p. 16.

30. Webb, *The Harmonious Circle*, 421.

31. Solano, unedited notes, 26 January 1936, p. 53.

32. Solano, Gurdjieff notes, 13 January 1936, p. 5.

33. Solano, unedited notes, 24 October 1935, p. 3.

34. Solano, Gurdjieff notes, 19 May 1937, p. 39.

35. Solano, unedited notes, 30 December 1935, p. 44.

36. Hulme, diary, 7 May 1936, fol. 16.

37. Hulme, diary, 15 June 1936, fol. 29.

38. Solano, unedited notes, June 11 [1936], p. 12 [p. 2 of letter].

39. Solano, Gurdjieff notes, 2 August 1936, p. 26.

40. Solano, unedited notes, lunch 12 June 12 [1936], p. 14 [p. 2 of letter].

41. Solano, Gurdjieff notes, 18 June 1936, pp. 15–16.

42. Hulme, diary, 2 February 1936, folder 14.

43. Solano, Gurdjieff notes, lunch, 11 July 1936, p. 18.

44. Solano, Gurdjieff notes, 31 July 1936, p. 21.

45. Hulme, diary, 5 May 1936, folder 15.

46. Solano, unedited notes, 2, November, 1935, p. 11.

47. Solano, unedited notes, 24 October, 1935, p. 4.

48. See Grunwald, *Un chemin hors de l'exil*, 531.

49. Solano, Gurdjieff notes, 16 August 1937, p. 44.

50. Hulme, 25 March 1939, "Notes by Kanari" p. 4, box 55, folder 768, Kathryn Hulme Papers (1846–1981), Beinecke Rare Book and Manuscript Library, Yale University, New Haven. Published with permission.

51. Solano, unedited notes, 28 October 1935, p. 8.

52. Solano, unedited notes, 28 October 1935, p. 6.

53. Solano, unedited notes, 16 January 1936, p. 50.

54. Solano, unedited notes, 2 December 1935, p. 41.

55. Solano, Gurdjieff notes, 7 May 1938, p. 51.

56. Hulme, diary, lunch, Monday, 8 June 1936, folder 22.

57. Solano, unedited notes, "Notes from Labie," 9 October 1936, p. 2.

58. Hulme, diary, 22 April 1937, fol. 95.

59. Gurdjieff, "The Two Rivers," is published in two places in slightly different versions: *Views from the Real World*, 236–42, and *Tales*, 1227–31.

60. Cecil Lewis, *All My Yesterdays* (Shaftesbury, Dorset, UK: Element Books, Ltd, 1993), 148.

61. Solano, unedited notes, Friday, 5 June 1936, "Paris—the strike."

62. Hulme, diary, 25 July 1936, fol. 47.

63. Anderson, *The Unknowable Gurdjieff*, 150 text by G. Leblanc.
64. Tchekhovitch, *A Master in Life*, 198.
65. Solano, Gurdjieff notes, 8 April 1937, p. 34.

CHAPTER 6: LÀ-BAS, RUE DES COLONELS RENARD

1. Hulme, diary, address book, n.p.
2. Solano, 19 July 194? (postwar), letter to Margaret C. Anderson, private archive.
3. Grunwald, *Un chemin hors de l'exil*, 566.
4. Reference mislaid, in Howarth and Howarth, "*It's Up to Ourselves*."
5. René Zuber, in conversation with the author.
6. Michel Random, *Les puissances du dedans: Luc Dietrich, Lanza del Vasto, René Daumal, Gurdjieff* (Denoël: Paris, 1966), 173–75.
7. Blaise Pascal, *Pensées and Other Writings*, trans. Honor Levi (Oxford: Oxford University Press, 1995), 178.
8. Grunwald, *Un chemin hors de l'exil*, 469.
9. Tchekhovitch, *A Master in Life*, 246.
10. Fritz Peters, *Gurdjieff Remembered* (London: V. Gollancz, 1965), 107.
11. Bennett and Bennett, *Idiots in Paris*, 32.
12. Staveley, *Memories*, 72.
13. Kenneth Walker, *Venture with Ideas: Meetings with Gurdjieff and Ouspensky* (New York: Pellegrini and Cudahy, 1952), 168.
14. Walker, *Venture with Ideas*, 170.
15. Anderson, *The Unknowable Gurdjieff*, 181.
16. Solano, unedited notes, 24 January, 1936.
17. Hands, *Diary,* 50.
18. Wolfe, *Episode*s, 23.
19. Walker, *Venture with Ideas*, 155.
20. Grunwald, *Un chemin hors de l'exil*, 500.
21. Solano, unedited notes, Friday, 5 June 1936, "Paris—the strike."
22. Grunwald, *Un chemin hors de l'exil*, 500.
23. Peters, *Gurdjieff Remembered*, 93.
24. Grunwald, *Un chemin hors de l'exil*, 460.
25. Taylor, *Gurdjieff's Invention of America*, esp. 264–68.
26. About Mme. Franck, see Grunwald, *Un chemin hors de l'exil*, 519.
27. Bennett and Bennett, *Idiots in Paris*, 27.
28. René Zuber, *Who Are You, Monsieur Gurdjieff?* (London: Routledge & Kegan Paul, 1980), 3.
29. Grunwald, *Un chemin hors de l'exil*, 558.
30. Elizabeth Bennett, *My Life*, 87.
31. Staveley, *Memories*, 62.
32. Staveley, *Memories*, 72.
33. Transcribed from an unpublished document, private archive (trans. from

the French by the author).

34. Grunwald, *Un chemin hors de l'exil*, 476.

35. Zuber, *Who Are You, Monsieur Gurdjieff?*, 9.

36. Yahne le Toumelin, "Le regard de Luc Dietrich," in *Luc Dietrich, Cahier*, ed. Frédéric Richaud (Cognac: Le temps qu'il fait, 1998), 150–51.

37. Gurdjieff, *Paris Meetings*; see also *Transcripts of Gurdjieff's Wartime Meetings 1941–46*, Second ed. (London: Book Studio, 2009).

38. Random, *Les puissances du dedans*, 238.

39. Gurdjieff, *Paris Meetings*, 37.

40. Gurdjieff, *Paris Meetings*, 76–77.

41. This wording of the second striving is from the 1992 revised edition of *Tales*, p. 352, where it more accurately translates the Russian original.

42. Solano, unedited notes, letter to Anderson, p. 1.

43. Staveley, *Memories*, 6.

44. Moore, *The Anatomy of a Myth*, 300.

45. Staveley, *Memories*, 32.

46. Hands, *Diary*, 59.

47. Bennett and Bennett, *Idiots in Paris*, 75.

48. Grunwald, *Un chemin hors de l'exil*, 489.

49. Le Toumelin, "Le regard de Luc Dietrich," 152.

50. Irmis B. Popoff, *Gurdjieff: His Work on Myself, with Others, for the Work* (New York: Vantage Press Inc., 1969), 118.

51. Tchekhovitch, *A Master in Life*, 200.

52. Bennett and Bennett, *Idiots in Paris*, vi.

53. Elizabeth Bennett, *My Life: J. G. Bennett and G. I. Gurdjieff; The Memoirs of Elizabeth Bennett* (Petersham, England: J. G. Bennett Foundation, 2016), 74–75.

54. Bennett and Bennett, *Idiots in Paris*, viii.

55. Bennett and Bennett, *Idiots in Paris*, 26.

56. Zuber, *Who Are You, Monsieur Gurdjieff?*, 26.

57. Grunwald, *Un chemin hors de l'exil*, 474.

58. Bennett and Bennett, *Idiots in Paris*, 37.

59. Phillpotts, *Discovering Gurdjieff*, 187.

60. Zuber, *Who Are You, Monsieur Gurdjieff?*, 17.

61. Hands, *Diary*, 38.

62. Hands, *Diary*, 36

63. Bennett and Bennett, *Idiots in Paris*, 28.

64. Walker, *Venture with Ideas*, 196–97.

65. Bennett and Bennett, *Idiots in Paris*, 7.

66. Bennett, *My Life*, 105–06.

67. Phillpotts, *Discovering Gurdjieff*, 202.

68. Phillpotts, *Discovering Gurdjieff*, 190.

69. René Zuber, unpublished document, private archive.

70. Phillpotts, *Discovering Gurdjieff*, 228.

71. Bennett and Bennett, *Idiots in Paris*, 79.

72. Moore, *The Anatomy of a Myth*, 310.

73. Staveley, *Memories of Gurdjieff*, 60.

74. Tchekhovitch, *A Master in Life*, 251.

75. Bennett and Bennett, *Idiots in Paris*, 106.

76. Bennett and Bennett, *Idiots in Paris*, 82.

77. Bennett and Bennett, *Idiots in Paris*, 106.

78. Bennett and Bennett, *Idiots in Paris*, 89.

79. Bennett and Bennett, *Idiots in Paris*, 92.

80. See Roger Lipsey, "For Dr. William J. Welch, Eulogy," *Gurdjieff International Review* 3, no. 2 (2000), accessed October 30, 2017, https://www.gurdjieff.org/lipsey2.htm.

81. William J. Welch, *What Happened in Between: A Doctor's Story* (New York: George Braziller, 1972), 137.

82. Bennett and Bennett, *Idiots in Paris*, 100.

83. Bennett and Bennett, *Idiots in Paris*, 101.

84. Welch, *What Happened in Between*, 140

85. Welch, *What Happened in Between*, 140.

86. Jeanne de Salzmann, 30 December 1961, on the occasion of the death of Mme Ouspensky, in Howarth and Howarth, "*It's Up to Ourselves*," 432.

87. Bennett and Bennett, *Idiots in Paris*, 103.

88. Walker, *Venture with Ideas*, 191.

89. Grunwald, *Un chemin hors de l'exil*, 564.

90. Zuber, *Who Are You, Monsieur Gurdjieff?*, 43.

91. Bennett and Bennett, *Idiots in Paris*, 110.

92. Solano, Gurdjieff notes, 1 November 1949, "An account of his death, 1949, American Hospital, Paris."

93. Grunwald, *Un chemin hors de l'exil*, 581.

94. Phillpotts, *Discovering Gurdjieff*, 239.

95. Taylor, *Gurdjieff in the Public Eye*, 239.

Chapter 7: The Great Prayer: 1950–1956

1. Friedland and Zellman, *The Fellowship*, 457.

2. Gurdjieff, *Life Is Real*, xi–xii.

3. Phillpotts, *Discovering Gurdjieff*, 232.

4. Bennett and Bennett, *Idiots in Paris*, 106.

5. Solange Claustres, *La prise de conscience et G. I. Gurdjieff* (Utrecht: Eureka Editions, 2002), 113 (trans. from the French by the author).

6. Jeanne de Salzmann, *The Reality of Being* (Boston: Shambhala, 2010), 3–4, with additions from a private archive.

7. Mme de Salzmann writes "Fama," which captures the normal Russian pronunciation, though the standard spelling, "Foma," differs slightly.

8. Sourced from a private archive (trans. from the French by the author).

9. J. G. Bennett, *Witness: The Autobiography of John G. Bennett* (Tucson, AZ: Omen Press, 1974), 122.

10. J. G. Bennett, *Witness*, 267.

11. Bennett, *Witness*, 285.

12. Bennett, *Witness*, 285.

13. Bennett, *Witness*, 306.

14. Bennett, *Witness*, 315.

15. See for example, J. G. Bennett, *Our Experiences in Subud* (New York: Dharma Book Co., 1959); J. G. Bennett, *Christian Mysticism and Subud* (London: Institute for the Comparative Study of History, Philosophy and the Sciences, 1961); J. G. Bennett, *Approaching Subud: Ten Talks* (New York: Dharma Publishing, 1962).

16. Jeanne de Salzmann, Letter to George Adie, 16 July 1957, private archives.

17. Bennett, *Witness*, 322.

18. J. G. Bennett and Thakur Lal Manandhar, Long Pilgrimage: *The Life and Teaching of Sri Govindanda Bharati, Known as the Shivapuri Baba* (London: Hodder & Stoughton, 1965).

19. Bennett, *Witness*, 362.

20. Published with permission (trans. from the French by the author).

21. See Henri Tracol, *The Real Question Remains; Further Talks, Essays and Interviews* (Bray, UK: Guild Press, 2003); and *The Taste for Things That Are True: Essays and Talks by a Pupil of G. I. Gurdjieff* (Shaftesbury, Dorset, UK: Element Books Ltd., 1994).

22. Private archive.

23. Michel Conge, *Inner Octaves* (Toronto: Dolmen Meadow Editions, 2007).

24. Michel Conge, personal notes, 5 July 1951, private archive. Published with permission (trans. from the French by the author).

25. P. D. Ouspensky, *Fragments d'un enseignement inconnu,* trans. Philippe Lavastine (Paris: Stock, 1949).

26. Grunwald, *Un chemin hors de l'exil*, 487.

27. Phillpotts, *Discovering Gurdjieff*, 246.

28. De Salzmann, *The Reality of Being*, 4, with addition from a private archive.

CHAPTER 8: DERISION

1. Anthony Storr, *Feet of Clay: Saints, Sinners, and Madmen; A Study of Gurus* (New York: Free Press, 1996). See also "Anthony Storr, the Face of Psychiatry, Dies," *Guardian*, obituary dated 20 March 2001, accessed December 2017, theguardian.com/society/2001/mar/20/health.mentalhealth.

2. Washington, *Madame Blavatsky's Baboon*.

3. Associated with the Gurdjieff teaching during the war years, Hubert Benoît went on to write remarkable books inspired by Zen Buddhism, notably *The Supreme Doctrine: Psychological Studies in Zen Thought* and *Let Go! Theory and Practice of Detachment According to Zen*, both available in various editions in English translation. *The Supreme Doctrine* is, paradoxically, one of the most keenly intelligent and rigorous introductions to the Gurdjieff ideas, which persist below the surface.

4. Luc Dietrich, *Terre: Vingt textes illustrés de trente photographies de l'auteur* (Paris: Denoël et Steele, 1936).

5. Washington, *Madame Blavatsky's Baboon*, 309.

6. Washington, 348.

7. Washington, 341.

8. Washington, *Madame Blavatsky's Baboon*, 170.

9. See Gurdjieff, *Tales*, chap. 43, "Beelzebub's Survey of the Process of the Periodic Reciprocal Destruction of Men, or Beelzebub's Opinion of War."

10. Washington, *Madame Blavatsky's Baboon*, 350.

11. De Hartmann, *What For?* chap. 8, p. 14, private archive, published with permission.

12. Louis Pauwels, *Monsieur Gurdjieff: Documents, témoignages, textes et commentaires sur une société initiatique contemporaine* (Paris: Editions du Seuil, 1954). All citations from the English-language edition: *Gurdjieff* (New York: Samuel Weiser, 1972), 323. See also Pauwels's biography: Gabriel Veraldi, *Pauwels ou le malentendu* (Paris: Grasset, 1989).

13. Pauwels, *Gurdjieff*, 140–41.

14. Bennett and Bennett, *Idiots in Paris*, 31.

15. Grunwald, *Un chemin hors de l'exil*, 464.

16. Pauwels, *Gurdjieff*, 6.

17. Michel Random, *Les puissances du dedans*, 403.

18. Pauwels, *Gurdjieff*, 319.

19. Pauwels, *Gurdjieff*, 307.

20. Pauwels, *Gurdjieff*, 314–15.

21. Zuber, *Who Are You, Monsieur Gurdjieff?*, 59.

22. Grunwald, *Un chemin hors de l'exil*, 557.

23. Jeanne de Salzmann, letter to George Adie, 18 April 1954, private archive.

24. Zuber, journal entry for 18 October 1979, private archive.

25. Pauwels, *Gurdjieff*, 35.

26. Pauwels, *Gurdjieff*, 102.

27. Lisa Appignanesi, "Freud's Clay Feet," review of Frederick Crews, *Freud: The Making of an Illusion*, in *The New York Review of Books*, October 26, 2017.

28. Marie Claire Pauwels, *Fille à Papa* (Paris: Albin Michel, 2003), 135.

29. Louis Pauwels, *Les voies de petite communication*, with drawings by Robert Lapoujade (Paris: Editions du Seuil, 1949).

30. Louis Pauwels, *L'apprentissage de la sérénité* (Paris: Retz – C.E.P.L., 1978).

31. Louis Pauwels, *Comment devient-on ce que l'on est?* (Paris: Retz – C.E.P.L., 1978), 45.

32. Random, *Les puissances du dedans*, 403.

33. Louis Pauwels, *Ce que je crois* (Paris: Grasset, 1974), 14.

34. Pauwels, *Ce que je crois*, 50.

35. Pauwels, *Monsieur Gurdjieff*, with a new preface (Paris: Albin Michel, 1996), 17 (trans. from the French by the author). Pauwels' last book, *Les dernières chaînes* (Paris: Editions du Rocher, 1997), 58ff., offers his concluding assessment of Gurdjieff and the teaching. "Though Gurdjieff is dead, his

midwifery operates as effectively as in his lifetime" (p. 71, trans. from the French by the author).

36. Henri Tracol, private archive (trans. from the French by the author).

37. Storr, *Feet of Clay*, 28.

38. Storr, 43.

39. Zuber, *Who Are You, Monsieur Gurdjieff?*, 13.

40. Fritz Peters, *Gurdjieff Remembered*, 92.

41. McCorkle, *The Gurdjieff Years*, 108.

42. Hands, *Diary*, 62.

43. Hands, *Diary*, 59–60.

44. Kenneth Walker, *Venture with Ideas*, 193.

45. Grunwald, *Un chemin hors de l'exil*, 565.

46. Grunwald, *Un chemin hors de l'exil*, 542.

47. Jean Rostand, in *Le Franc-Tireur Littéraire*, 1950 (further data lacking), archive of the Institut G. I. Gurdjieff, Paris.

48. See Christian Wertenbaker, *Man in the Cosmos* and *The Enneagram of G. I. Gurdjieff*.

49. Storr, *Feet of Clay*, xii–xv.

50. Storr, *Feet of Clay*, 36.

51. Storr, *Feet of Clay*, 28.

52. Storr, *Feet of Clay*, 38.

53. Storr, *Feet of Clay*, 42.

54. Pauwels, *Gurdjieff*, 190.

55. Whitall Perry, *Gurdjieff in the Light of Tradition* (Ghent, New York: Sophia Perennis, 2001), 89. All citations from this second edition; the first edition was published by Perennial Books Ltd, Bedfont (UK), 1978.

56. Xavier Accart, *Guénon ou le renversement des clartés: Influence d'un métaphysicien sur la vie littéraire et intellectuelle française (1920–1970)* (Paris: Edidit Archè, 2005), 83.

57. Perry, *Gurdjieff in the Light of Tradition*, 96.

58. Perry, *Gurdjieff in the Light of Tradition*, 3.

59. Anderson, *The Unknowable Gurdjieff*, 42.

60. Zuber, *Who Are You, Monsieur Gurdjieff?*, 56.

61. Perry, *Gurdjieff in the Light of Tradition*, 50.

62. Perry, *Gurdjieff in the Light of Tradition*, 84.

63. Perry, *Gurdjieff in the Light of Tradition*, 74n.

64. Guénon also rejected Gurdjieff and the teaching, but he was much less shrill than Perry. See his letter of 1950 in Accart, *Guénon*, 49–50.

65. Perry, *Gurdjieff in the Light of Tradition*, 96.

66. See Ananda K. Coomaraswamy, *Coomaraswamy: Selected Papers*, in two volumes (1: *Traditional Art and Symbolism*; 2: *Metaphysics*), edited with an introduction by Roger Lipsey, Bollingen Series (Princeton, NJ: Princeton University Press, 1977), and Roger Lipsey, *Coomaraswamy: Life and Writings,* Bollingen Series (Princeton, NJ: Bollingen Series, Princeton, Univer-

sity Press, 1977).

67. Jean-François Revel and Matthieu Ricard, *The Monk and the Philosopher: A Father and Son Discuss the Meaning of Life* (New York: Schocken Books, 1998), a translation of the original French edition, 1997.

68. Jean-François Revel, *Mémoires: Le voleur dans la maison vide* (Paris: Plon, 1997). (All translations from the French by the author.)

69. Revel, *Mémoires*, 149 ff. for the Gurdjieff material.

70. Revel, *Mémoires*, 151.

71. Revel, *Mémoires*, 152.

72. Bernard Chevilliat, "Rencontre avec Matthieu Ricard," *Ultreia*, 7 (printemps 2016), 60–75 (trans. from the French by the author).

73. About the life and art of Yahne Le Toumelin, see Matthieu Ricard, *Lumière: rire du ciel: Yahne Le Toumelin* (Paris: La Martinière, 2016).

74. Le Toumelin, "Le Regard de Luc Dietrich," 150, (trans. from the French by the author).

75. Zuber, *Who Are You, Bollingen Series. Gurdjieff?*, 16.

76. Nikolai de Stjernvall, *My Dear Father Gurdjieff*.

77. See Howarth and Howarth, "*It's Up to Ourselves.*"

78. Bennett, *Gurdjieff: Making a New World*, 180.

79. Some readers may want to explore the Revel material in greater depth. His attack on Gurdjieff began obliquely without mentioning Gurdjieff's name many years before the *Mémoires*, with a roman à clef written in 1953, published a few years later: *Histoire de Flore* (Paris: Julliard, 1957). Toward the end of the novel, an older male teacher loosely modeled on Gurdjieff sexually entraps the young woman, Flore. Another estranged participant, Paul Sérant, published a somewhat similar roman à clef: *Le Meutre rituel* (Paris: La Table Ronde, 1950). Soon after, Sérant published a well-informed study of the writings of René Guénon: *René Guénon* (Paris: La Colombe, 1953), and in later years explored and championed the regional cultures and languages of France.

80. Solano, unedited notes, 17 November 1935.

81. Solange Claustres, *La prise de conscience*, 167 (trans. from the French by the author).

82. Claustres, 54.

83. Dorothy Caruso, quoted in Anderson, *The Unknowable Gurdjieff*, 192.

84. Hands, *Diary*, 78.

85. Bennett, *My Life*, 73.

Chapter 9: Beelzebub's Tales

1. Gurdjieff, *Tales*, 674–76 (all citations from the 1950 edition).

2. In point of fact, linguists report to me privately that *Veroonk* and *Klian* denote members of upper classes in Armenian, though few readers would

know this.

3. Marcus Aurelius, *Meditations*, trans. with an introduction by Maxwell Staniforth (Harmondsworth, UK: Penguin Books, 1964), Book 4:32, 70–71.

4. Peters, *Boyhood with Gurdjieff*, 100.

5. I must thank my friend and colleague, the Russian-American linguist Galina Natenzon, for exploring Russian-language sources for this book.

6. Grunwald, *Un chemin hors de l'exil*, 531.

7. Gurdjieff, *Tales*, front matter.

8. The third member of the trilogy, *Life Is Real Only Then, When "I Am,"* although unfinished, is an essential element of the Gurdjieff heritage.

9. Yildiray Edener, *The Song Contests of Turkish Minstrels: Improvised Poetry Sung to Traditional Music* (New York: Garland, 1995).

10. Gurdjieff, *Tales*, 52.

11. Gurdjieff, *Tales*, 41–45.

12. Popoff, *Gurdjieff*, 137.

13. Gurdjieff, *Paris Meetings*, 157.

14. Phillpotts, *Discovering Gurdjieff*, 205.

15. Solano, unedited notes, 24 July.

16. Gurdjieff, *Tales*, 310.

17. Gurdjieff, *Tales*, 978ff.

18. Gurdjieff, *Tales*, 187ff.

19. Taylor, *Real Worlds*, 139.

20. P. L. Travers, *George Ivanovitch Gurdjieff (1877–1949)* (Toronto: Traditional Studies Press, 1973). Most conveniently found at the reliable website of *Gurdjieff International Review*, accessed 2 February 2018, www.gurdjieff.org/travers1.htm.

21. Gurdjieff, *Tales*, 924–25.

22. Gurdjieff, *Tales*, 294–95.

23. Gurdjieff, *Tales*, 296–97. The word *akhal* resolves easily, in Farsi and Urdu among other regional languages, to English "good sense" or "wisdom," while *dan* is likely to root in a Persian suffix used in Turkish, meaning "receptacle."

24. Gurdjieff, *Tales*, chapters 26–28.

25. Gurdjieff, *Tales*, 622–23.

CHAPTER 10: CODA

1. Wu Cheng-en, *Monkey*, trans. Arthur Waley (London: George Allen & Unwin, 1942), an abridgment of the complete text, now available in the three-volume translation by Anthony C. Yu.

Bibliography

UNPUBLISHED SOURCES

Album of newspaper clippings. Archive, Institut G. I. Gurdjieff, Paris.

Anderson, Margaret. Unpublished correspondence. Private archive.

Bell, Mary. Unpublished notes. Archive of the Gurdjieff Foundation of New York.

Faidy, Diana. *Reminiscences of My Work with Georges Gurdjieff.* Unpublished typescript. Archive of the Gurdjieff Foundation of New York.

Hartmann, Olga de. *What For?* Unpublished manuscript. Private archive.

Hulme, Kathryn. Kathryn Hulme Papers, Beinecke Rare Book and Manuscript Library, Yale University.

Solano, Solita. Janet Flanner and Solita Solano Papers. Library of Congress, Washington, DC.

Solano, Solita. Unedited notes. Private archive.

Zuber, René. Unpublished journal. Private archive.

And other private archives.

PUBLISHED WORKS BY GURDJIEFF

Gurdjieff, George Ivanovich. *The 1931 Manuscript of Beelzebub's Tales to His Grandson.* Edited by Robin Bloor. Spicewood, TX: Little Crow Press, 2015.

———. *Gurdjieff's Early Talks 1914–1931 in Moscow, St. Petersburg, Essentuki, Tiflis, Constantinople, Berlin, Paris, London, Fontainebleau, New York, and Chicago.* Edited by Joseph Azize. London: Book Studio, 2014.

———. *The Herald of Coming Good: First Appeal to Contemporary Humanity.* Paris, 1933.

———. *Life Is Real Only Then, When "I Am." All and Everything,* Third Series. New York: E. P. Dutton & Company, 1981.

———. *Meetings with Remarkable Men. All and Everything,* Second Series. New York: E. P. Dutton & Company, 1963.

———. *An Objectively Impartial Criticism of the Life of Man or Beelzebub's Tales to*

His Grandson. All and Everything, First Series. New York: Harcourt, Brace & Company, 1950.

——. *The Struggle of the Magicians: Scenario of the Ballet*. London: Book Studio, 2014.

——. *Transcripts of Gurdjieff's Wartime Meetings 1941–46*. Second revised and enlarged edition. London: Book Studio, 2009.

——. *Views from the Real World: Early Talks of Gurdjieff as Recollected by His Pupils*. New York: E. P. Dutton & Company, 1973.

——. *Paris Meetings 1943*. Toronto: Dolmen Meadow Editions, 2017.

Printed Music

Gurdjieff, George Ivanovich and Thomas de Hartmann. *Music for the Piano, Volume I: Asian Songs and Rhythms*. Mainz, Germany: Schott Musik International, 1996.

——. *Music for the Piano, Volume II: Music of the Sayyids and the Dervishes*. Mainz, Germany: Schott Musik International, 1996.

——. *Music for the Piano, Volume III: Hymns, Prayers and Rituals*. Mainz, Germany: Schott Musik International, 2002.

——. *Music for the Piano, Volume IV: Hymns from a Great Temple and Other Selected Works*. Mainz, Germany: Schott Musik International, 2005.

Recordings

Recordings of the Gurdjieff/de Hartmann music have become in the past decade too numerous to list. There are outstanding performances by Laurence Rosenthal, Alain Kremski, Frederic Chiu, Charles Ketcham, Yleana Bautista, and others.

Wim van Dullemen. *Thomas de Hartmann—Music for Gurdjieff's 39 Series*. Channel Crossings, 2001, 2 compact discs.

Sicroff, Elan. *The Thomas de Hartmann Project—Music for Piano, Voice and Chamber Ensemble*. Aalsmeer Netherlands: Basta, 2016, compact disk. A 7 compact disc boxed set of de Hartmann's independently written music.

Online Resources

Gurdjieff International Review (www.gurdjieff.org), a meticulously reliable, large, and thematically diverse resource.

Gurdjieff: A Reading Guide (www.gurdjieff-bibliography.com), an excellent resource.

Published Works on Gurdjieff

Anderson, Margaret C. *The Fiery Fountains: The Autobiography; Continuation and Crisis to 1950*. New York: Hermitage House, 1951.

———. *The Unknowable Gurdjieff*. New York: Samuel Weiser, 1962.

Azize, Joseph. *George Adie: A Gurdjieff Pupil in Australia*. 2nd ed.rev., and exp. Waukee, IN: By the Way Books, 2015.

Bennett, Elizabeth. *My Life: J. G. Bennett and G. I. Gurdjieff; The Memoirs of Elizabeth Bennett*. Petersham, England: J. G. Bennett Foundation, 2016.

Bennett, John Godolphin. *Gurdjieff: Making a New World*. London: Turnstone Books, 1973.

———. *Witness: The Autobiography of John G. Bennett*. Tucson, AZ: Omen Press, 1974.

Bennett, John Godolphin and Elizabeth Bennett. *Idiots in Paris: Diaries of J. G. Bennett and Elizabeth Bennett, 1949*. Daglingworth Manor, Gloucestershire, UK: Coombe Springs Press, 1980.

Conge, Michel. *Inner Octaves*. Toronto: Dolmen Meadow Editions, 2007.

———. *Life: Real Life Behind Appearances*. Paris: SET, 2017.

Blom, Gert-Jan, ed. *G. I. Gurdjieff: Harmonic Development; The Complete Harmonium Recordings 1948–1949*. Aalsmeer, Netherlands: Basta, 2004 (a well-illustrated book accompanied by CDs).

———. *Gurdjieff/de Hartmann: Oriental Suite; The Complete Orchestral Music 1923–1924*. Aalsmeer, Netherlands: Basta, 2006 (a well-illustrated book accompanied by CDs).

Claustres, Solange. *La prise de conscience et G. I. Gurdjieff*. Utrecht: Eureka Editions, 2002.

Defouw, Richard J. *The Enneagram in the Writings of Gurdjieff*. Indianapolis, IN: Dog Ear, 2011.

De Hartmann, Thomas and Olga. *Our Life with Mr. Gurdjieff*. Edited by Thomas C. Daly and Thomas A. G. Daly. Sandpoint, ID: Sandpoint Press, 2008.

Driscoll, J. Walter, and the Gurdjieff Foundation of California. *Gurdjieff: An Annotated Bibliography*. New York: Garland Publishing, 1985.

Everitt, Luba Gurdjieff, with Marina C. Bear. *Luba Gurdjieff: A Memoir with Recipes*. Berkeley, CA: Ten Speed Press, 1993.

Fox, Robin Lane. "Russell Page's Garden at Villar Perosa and a Tale of Two Masters." *Financial Times*, May 13, 2016. Accessed October 2, 2017. https://www.ft.com/content/ff53792c-1208-11e6-91da-096d89bd2173.

Grunwald, François. *Un chemin hors de l'exil: De Freud à Gurdjieff*. Paris: L'Originel, 2017.

Hands, Rina. *Diary of Madame Egout Pour Sweet: With Mr. Gurdjieff in Paris 1948–1949*. Aurora, OR: Two Rivers Press, 1991.

Hovannisian, Richard G., ed. *Armenian Kars and Ani*. Costa Mesa, CA: Mazda Publishers, 2011.

Howarth, Jessmin and Dushka. *"It's Up to Ourselves": A Mother, a Daughter, and Gurdjieff*. New York: Gurdjieff Heritage Society, 1998.

Kafian, Adele. "Looking Back to the Last Days of Katherine Mansfield." *The Adelphi* 23 (1946–1947): 36–39. Accessed September 26, 2017. www.gurdjieff-bibliography.com/Current/KM_05_2006_02_KAFIAN_Last_Days_KM.pdf.

Lachman, Gary. *In Search of P. D. Ouspensky: The Genius in the Shadow of Gurdjieff.* New York: Quest Books, 2006.

Laer, Lee van. *Novel, Myth, & Cosmos: On the Nature of All & Everything.* Self-published, 2017.

Leblanc, Georgette. *The Courage Machine: A New Life in a New World.* Translated by Margaret Anderson and Solita Solano. London: Book Studio, 2012.

Lehmann-Haupt, Carl, ed. *Martin Benson Speaks.* New Paltz, NY: Codhill Press, 2011.

Lewis, Cecil. *All My Yesterdays.* Shaftesbury, Dorset, UK: Element Books, Ltd., 1993.

Lipsey, Roger. "Chez Monsieur Gurdjieff." In *Katherine Mansfield and Russia*, edited by Galya Diment, Gerri Kimber, and Todd Martin, 163–72. Edinburgh: Edinburgh University Press, 2017.

———. "For Dr. William J. Welch, Eulogy." *Gurdjieff International Review* 3 (2000). Accessed October 30, 2017. https://www.gurdjieff.org/lipsey2 .htm.

———. "Gurdjieff Observed." In *Gurdjieff: Essays and Reflections on the Man and His Teaching,* edited by Jacob Needleman and George Baker, 324–50. New York: Continuum, 1996.

Mairet, Philip. *A. R. Orage: A Memoir.* New York: University Books, 1966.

Mansfield, Katherine. ———. *The Collected Letters of Katherine Mansfield.* Edited by Vincent O'Sullivan and Margaret Scott. Oxford: Oxford University Press, 2008.

The Diaries of Katherine Mansfield, including Miscellaneous Works. Edited by Gerri Kimber and Claire Davison. Edinburgh: Edinburgh University Press, 2016.

McCorkle, Annabeth. *The Gurdjieff Years 1929–1949: Recollections of Louise Goepfert March.* Exp. ed. Utrecht: Eureka Editions, 2012.

Moore, James. *Gurdjieff: A Biography; The Anatomy of a Myth.* Shaftesbury, Dorset, UK: Element, 1991.

———. *Gurdjieff and Mansfield.* London: Routledge and Kegan Paul, 1980.

Munson, Gorham. *The Awakening Twenties: A Memoir-History of a Literary Period.* Baton Rouge, LA: Louisiana State University Press, 1985.

Needleman, Jacob. "G. I. Gurdjieff and His School." *Gurdjieff International Review.* Accessed October 12, 2018. www.gurdjieff.org/needleman2.htm.

———, ed. *The Inner Journey: Views from the Gurdjieff Work* (Parabola Anthology Series). Sandpoint (Idaho): Morning Light Press, 2008.

———. *Introduction to the Gurdjieff Work.* Sandpoint (Idaho): Sandpoint Press, 2009.

———. *A Sense of the Cosmos: Scientific Knowledge and Spiritual Truth.* New York: Dutton, 1976.

———. *What is God?* New York: TarcherPerigree, 2010.

Needleman, Jacob, George Baker, and Mary Stein, eds. *Gurdjieff: Essays and Reflections on the Man and His Teaching.* New York: Continuum, 1996.

Nicolescu, Basarab, ed. *René Daumal et l'enseignement de Gurdjieff.* Paris: Le Bois d'Orion, 2015.

Nicoll, Maurice. *Psychological Commentaries on the Teaching of G. I. Gurdjieff and P. D. Ouspensky.* 4 vols. London: V. Stuart, 1952–1955.

Nott, Charles Stanley, *Teachings of Gurdjieff: The Journal of a Pupil.* New York: Samuel Weiser, 1961.

Olgivanna (Mrs. Frank Lloyd Wright). "The Last Days of Katherine Mansfield." *The Bookman: A Review of Books and Life* 73, no. 1 (1931): 6–13. Accessed September 26, 2017. http://www.gurdjieff-bibliography.com/Current /KM_04__2006_02_OLGIVANNA__Last_Days_of_KM.pdf.

Ouspensky, Petr Demianovich. *In Search of the Miraculous: Fragments of an Unknown Teaching.* New York: Harcourt, Brace and Company, 1949.

———. *Fragments d'un enseignement inconnu.* Translated by Philippe Lavastine. Paris: Stock, 1949.

———. *The Psychology of Man's Possible Evolution.* New York: Hedgehog Press, 1950 (with subsequent editions).

Patterson, William Patrick. *Struggle of the Magicians: Why Uspenskii Left Gurdjieff; Exploring the Teacher-Student Relationship.* Fairfax, CA: Arete, 1996

———. *Voices in the Dark: Esoteric, Occult & Secular Voices in Nazi-Occupied Paris, 1940–44.* Fairfax, CA: Arete Communications, 2001.

Patterson, William Patrick and Barbara Allen Patterson. *Georgi Ivanovitch Gurdjieff: The Man, the Teaching, His Mission.* Fairfax, CA: Arete Communications, 2014.

Patterson, William Patrick and Barbara C. Allen. *Ladies of the Rope: Gurdjieff's Special Left Bank Women's Group.* Fairfax, CA: Arete Editions, 1999.

Pentland, John. *Exchanges Within: Questions from Everyday Life Selected from Gurdjieff Group Meetings with John Pentland in California, 1955–1984.* New York: Continuum, 1997.

Peters, Fritz. *Boyhood with Gurdjieff.* New York: E. P. Dutton, Inc.,1964.

———. *Gurdjieff Remembered.* London: V. Gollancz, 1965.

Petsche, Johanna. "Gurdjieff and Blavatsky: Western Esoteric Teachers in Parallel." *Literature & Aesthetics* 21 (2011): 98–115.

Phillpotts, Dorothy. *Discovering Gurdjieff.* N.p. Authorhouse, 2008.

Popoff, Irmis B. *Gurdjieff: His Work on Myself, with Others, for the Work.* New York: Vantage Press Inc., 1969.

Random, Michel. *Les puissances du dedans: Luc Dietrich, Lanza del Vasto, René Daumal, Gurdjieff.* Denoël: Paris, 1966.

Ravindra, Ravi. *Heart without Measure: Gurdjieff Work with Madame de Salzmann.* Rev. ed. Sandpoint, ID: Morning Light Press, 2004.

Revel, Jean-François. *Mémoires: Le voleur dans la maison vide.* Paris: Plon, 1997.

Richaud, Frédéric, ed. *Luc Dietrich: Cahier.* Cognac: Le temps qu'il fait, 1998.

Staveley, Annie Lou. *Memories of Gurdjieff.* Aurora, OR: Two Rivers Press, 1978.

Stjernvall, Nikolai de. *My Dear Father Gurdjieff.* Translated by Paul Beekman Taylor. Dublin: Bardic Press, 2013.

Storr, Anthony. *Feet of Clay: Saints, Sinners, and Madmen; A Study of Gurus.* New York: Free Press, 1996.

Taylor, Paul Beekman. *Gurdjieff and Orage: Brothers in Elysium.* York Beach, ME: Weiser Books, 2001.

———. *Gurdjieff in the Public Eye: Newspaper Articles, Magazines and Books 1914–1949.* Utrecht: Eureka Editions, 2011.

———. *Gurdjieff's Invention of America.* Utrecht: Eureka Editions, 2007.

———. *Gurdjieff's World of Words: A Methodological Reading.* Utrecht: Eureka Editions, 2014.

———. *Real Worlds of G. I. Gurdjieff: Chapters in the Life of a Master.* Utrecht: Eureka Editions, 2012.

———. *Shadows of Heaven: Gurdjieff and Toomer.* York Beach, ME: S. Weiser, 1998.

Tchekhovitch, Tcheslaw. *Gurdjieff: A Master in Life. Recollections of Tcheslaw Tchekhovitch.* Toronto: Dolmen Meadow Editions, 2006.

Tracol, Henri. *Further Talks, Essays and Interviews.* Bray, UK: Guild Press, 2003.

———. *George Ivanovich Gurdjieff: Man's Awakening and the Practice of Remembering Oneself.* Bray, UK: Guild Press, 1968.

———. *The Real Question Remains: Gurdjieff; A Living Call.* Translated by Jenny Koralek. Sandpoint, ID: Morning Light Press, 2009.

———. *The Taste for Things That Are True: Essays and Talks by a Pupil of G. I. Gurdjieff.* Shaftesbury, Dorset, UK: Element Books Ltd., 1994.

Walker, Kenneth. *Venture with Ideas: Meetings with Gurdjieff and Ouspensky.* New York: Pellegrini & Cudahy, 1952.

Webb, James. *The Harmonious Circle: The Lives and Work of G. I. Gurdjieff, P. D. Ouspensky, and Their Followers.* New York: G. P. Putnam's Sons, 1980.

Welch, Louise. *Orage with Gurdjieff in America.* Boston: Routledge & Kegan Paul, 1982.

Welch, William J. *What Happened in Between: A Doctor's Story.* New York: George Braziller, 1972.

Wertenbaker, Christian. *The Enneagram of G. I. Gurdjieff: Mathematics, Metaphysics, Music, and Meaning.* New Paltz, NY: Codhill Press, 2017.

———. *Man in the Cosmos: G. I. Gurdjieff and Modern Science.* New Paltz, NY: Codhill Press, 2012.

Wilson, Colin. *The Strange Life of P. D. Ouspensky.* London: Aeon Books, 2005.

Wolfe, Edwin. *Episodes with Gurdjieff.* San Francisco: Far West Press, 1974.

Zuber, René, *Who Are You, Monsieur Gurdjieff?* Translated by Jenny Koralek. London: Routledge & Kegan Paul, 1980.

Works by Louis Pauwels

Pauwels, Louis. *Ce que je crois.* Paris: Grasset, 1974.

———. *Comment devient-on ce que l'on est?* Paris: Stock, 1978.

———. *L'Apprentissage de la sérénité.* Paris: Retz - C.E.P.L, 1978.

——. *Les Voies de petite communication*, with drawings by Robert Lapoujade. Paris: Editions du Seuil, 1949.

——. *Monsieur Gurdjieff: Documents, témoignages, textes et commentaires sur une société initiatique contemporaine.* Paris: Editions du Seuil, 1954, with subsequent editions. All citations from the English-language edition: *Gurdjieff.* New York: Samuel Weiser, 1972.

——. *Les dernières chaînes.* Paris: Editions du Rocher, 1997.

Pauwels, Louis, and Bergier, Jacques. *Le Matin de magiciens: introduction au réalisme fantastique.* Paris: Gallimard, 1960 (see also idem, *The Morning of the Magicians.* New York: Stein and Day, 1963).

Veraldi, Gabriel. *Pauwels ou le malentendu.* Paris: Grasset, 1989 (biography).

OTHER MATERIAL

Amin, Kamal. *Reflections from the Shining Brow: My Years with Frank Lloyd Wright and Olgivanna Lazovich.* Santa Barbara, CA: Fithian Press, 2004.

Bennett, John Godolphin. *Approaching Subud: Ten Talks.* New York: Dharma Publishing, 1962.

——. *Christian Mysticism and Subud.* London: Institute for the Comparative Study of History, Philosophy and the Sciences, 1961.

——. *Our Experiences in Subud.* New York: Dharma Book Co., 1959.

Bennett, John Godolphin and Thakur Lal Manandhar. *Long Pilgrimage: The Life and Teaching of Sri Govindanda Bharati, Known as the Shivapuri Baba.* London: Hodder & Stoughton, 1965.

Daumal, René. *L'Évidence absurde: Essais et notes I (1926–1934)* Paris: Gallimard, 1972.

Diogenes Laertius. *The Lives of Eminent Philosophers.* Vol. 2. Translated by Robert Drew Hicks. Loeb Classical Library, 185. Cambridge, MA: Harvard University Press, 1925.

Donato, Carla Di. *L'invisibile reso visibile: Alexandre de Salzmann (1874–1934). Vita, opera e ricerca tra teatro, luce e movimento.* Rome: Aracne editrice, 2013.

Fawcett-Yeske, Maxine, and Bruce Brooks Pfeiffer, eds. *The Life of Olgivanna Lloyd Wright: From Crna Gora to Taliesin, Black Mountain to Shining Brow.* Novato, CA: ORO Editions, 2017.

Friedland, Roger, and Harold Zellman. *The Fellowship: The Untold Story of Frank Lloyd Wright and the Taliesin Fellowship.* New York: HarperCollins, 2009.

Lipsey, Roger. "Signore: Parabola Visits the Monastero di Bose in the Foothills of the Italian Alps." *Parabola Magazine* (October 2015). Available online at https://parabola.org.

Martin, Frank, Tibor Dénes et al. *Émile Jaques-Dalcroze: L'homme, le compositeur, le créateur de la rythmique.* Neuchâtel, Switzerland: Editions de la Baconnière, 1965.

Nicoll, Maurice. *The New Man: An Interpretation of Some Parables and Miracles of Christ.* London: Watkins Books, 1981.

Pascal, Blaise. *Pensées and Other Writings*. Translated by Honor Levi. Oxford: Oxford University Press, 1995.

Stock, Noel. *The Life of Ezra Pound*. London: Routledge, Kegan Paul, 1970.

Washington, Peter. *Madame Blavatsky's Baboon: A History of the Mystics, Mediums, and Misfits Who Brought Spiritualism to America*. New York: Schocken Books, 1996.

Credits

Every effort has been made to contact rightsholders. Grateful acknowledgment is made to the following institutions and publishers for citations included in this book:

Beinecke Rare Book and Manuscript Library, Yale University.
The Library of Congress, Washington, DC.
Institut G. I. Gurdjieff, Paris.
Archive of the Gurdjieff Foundation of New York.

Anderson, Margaret. *The Unknowable Gurdjieff*. New York, Samuel Weiser, 1962.
Grunwald, François. *Un chemin hors de l'exil: De Freud à Gurdjieff*. Paris: L'Originel, 2017.
Hands, Rina. *Diary of Madame Egout pour Sweet: With Mr. Gurdjieff in Paris 1948–1949*. Aurora, OR: Two Rivers Press, 1991.
Nott, Charles Stanley. *Teachings of Gurdjieff*. New York, Samuel Weiser, 1961.
Ouspensky, Peter Demianovich. *In Search of the Miraculous: Fragments of an Unknown Teaching*. New York: Harcourt, Brace and Company, 1949.
Perry, Whitall. *Gurdjieff in the Light of Tradition*. Perennial Books, 1978.
Phillpotts, Dorothy. *Discovering Gurdjieff*. Author House. 2008.
Staveley, Annie Lou. *Memories of Gurdjieff*. Aurora, Oregon: Two Rivers Press, 1978.
Taylor, Paul Beekman. *Gurdjieff in the Public Eye: Newspaper Articles, Magazines and Books 1914–1949*. Utrecht: Eureka Editions, 2011.
Tchekhovitch, Tcheslaw. *Gurdjieff, A Master in Life—Recollections of Tcheslaw Tchekhovitch*. Toronto: Dolmen Meadow Editions, 2006.

The Estate of J.G. Bennett and Elizabeth Bennett:
Bennett, Elizabeth. *My Life: J.G. Bennett and G. I. Gurdjieff—A Memoir*. Create Space, 2016.
Bennett, John Godolphin and Elizabeth Bennett. *Idiots in Paris: Diaries of J.G. Bennett and Elizabeth Bennett, 1949*. Daglingworth Manor, Gloucestershire, UK: Coombe Springs Press, 1980.
Bennett, John Godolphin. *Gurdjieff: Making a New World*. London: Turnstone Books, 1973
———. *Witness: The Autobiography of John G. Bennett*. London: Turnstone Books, 1973.

The Estate of Jenny Koralek:
Zuber, René. *Who Are You, Monsieur Gurdjieff?* London: Routledge & Kegan Paul, 1980.

Index

Page numbers in *italics* refer to images.

About the Author

ROGER LIPSEY is the author most recently of a widely acclaimed biography of Dag Hammarskjöld and (with Shambhala Publications) of two books on the monk and author Thomas Merton. His *An Art of Our Own: The Spiritual in Twentieth-Century Art* (Shambhala, 1988, now available under the subtitle) has proved to be a classic, particularly among working artists. A participant in the Gurdjieff teaching for more than fifty years, he brings to *Gurdjieff Reconsidered* the scope and objectivity of a veteran scholar-author and the warmth of long familiarity with the life, teachings, and legacy of G. I. Gurdjieff.